NATIVE TREES AND SHRUBS OF THE HAWAIIAN ISLANDS

NATIVE TREES & SHRUBS OF THE HAWAIIAN ISLANDS

BY SAMUEL H. LAMB

Sunstone Press
Santa Fe, New Mexico

ON THE COVER:

OHIA LEHUA
*Metrosideros
Collina Variety
Polymorpha*

MAMANI
*Sophora
Chrysophylla*

PUKEAWE
*Styphelia
Tameiameiae*

COPYRIGHT © 1981 BY SAMUEL H. LAMB

ALL RIGHTS RESERVED.
NO PART OF THIS BOOK MAY BE REPRODUCED IN ANY FORM
OR BY ANY ELECTRONIC OR MECHANICAL MEANS
INCLUDING INFORMATION STORAGE AND RETRIEVAL SYSTEMS
WITHOUT PERMISSION IN WRITING FROM THE PUBLISHER, EXCEPT
BY A REVIEWER WHO MAY QUOTE BRIEF PASSAGES IN A REVIEW.

BOOK DESIGN: MINA YAMASHITA

LIBRARY OF CONGRESS CATALOGING IN PUBLICATION DATA:

LAMB, SAMUEL H.
NATIVE TREES AND SHRUBS OF THE HAWAIIAN ISLANDS

BIBLIOGRAPHY: P. 158
INCLUDES INDEX.
1. TREES - HAWAII - IDENTIFICATION.
2. SHRUBS - HAWAII - IDENTIFICATION.   I. TITLE.
QK493.H4L35   582.1609969   80-19715
ISBN: 0-913270-91-1

PUBLISHED IN 1987 BY SUNSTONE PRESS
POST OFFICE BOX 2321
SANTA FE, NM 87504-2321 / USA

TABLE OF CONTENTS

Acknowledgements & Introduction	9
KEY TO THE FAMILIES	15
DICKSONIACEAE / FERN / TREE FERN	19
Cibotium	
PALMAE / PALM / COCONUT	21
Cocos,	
Pritchardia	
LILIACEAE / LILY / YUCCA	25
Cordyline, Syn. Taetsia	
Pleomele, Syn. Dracaena	
MUSACEAE / BANANA	27
Musa	
ULMACEAE / ELM	28
Trema	
MORACEAE / MULBERRY	28
Artocarpus	
Broussonetia	
Pseudomorus	
URTICACEAE / NETTLE / STINGING NETTLE	30
Pipturus	
Touchardia	
Urera	
SANTALACEAE / SANDALWOOD	33
Exocarpus	
Santalum	
CHENOPODACEAE / GOOSEFOOT / RAGWEED	36
Chenopodium	
AMARANTHACEAE / AMARANTH / COCKSCOMB	38
Charpentiera	
Nototrichum	
NYCTAGINACEAE / FOUR-O-CLOCK	40
Pisonia	
LAURACEAE / LAUREL / AVOCADO	40
Cryptocarpa	
SAXIFRAGACEAE / SAXIFRAGE / HYDRANGEA	41
Broussaisia	
PITTOSPORACEAE / PITTOSPORUM	42
Pittosporum	
ROSACEAE / ROSE / WILD ROSE	45
Ostomeles	
LEGUMINOSAE / LEGUME, PEA / SWEET PEA	46
Acacia	
Cassia	
Erythrina	
Mesoneuron	
Sophora	
PANDANACEAE / SCREWPINE	51
Freycinetia	
Pandanus	
RUTACEAE / RUE, CITRUS / ORANGE	53
Pelea	
Platydesma	
Zanthoxylum	
EUPHORBIACEAE / SPURGE / CASTORBEAN	64
Aleurites	
Antidesma	
Claoxylon	
Drypetes	
Euphorbia	
ANACARDIACEAE / CASHEW, MANGO	74
Rhus	
AQUIFOLIACEAE / HOLLY	75
Ilex	
CELASTRACEAE / BITTERSWEET	75
Perrottetia	

SAPINDACEAE / SOAPBERRY / HOPSEED 76
    Alectron
    Dodonea
    Sapindus
RHAMNACEAE / BUCKTHORN 80
    Alphitonia
    Colubrina
TILIACEAE / LINDEN / BASSWOOD 82
    Elaeocarpus
MALVACEAE / MALLOW / HIBISCUS, COTTON 82
    Hibiscadelphus
    Hibiscus
    Kokia
    Sida
    Thespesia
THEACEAE / TEA 88
    Eurya
GUTTIFERAE / MANGOSTEEN / ST. JOHNSWORT 88
    Calophyllum
FLACOURTIACEAE / FLACOURT 89
    Xylosma
THYMELIACEAE / AKIA 90
    Wikstroemia
MYRTACEAE / MYRTLE / EUCALYPTUS 92
    Eugenia
    Metrosideros
ARALIACEAE / GINSENG / ENGLISH IVY 96
    Cheirodendron
    Reynoldsia
    Tetraplasandra
ERICACEAE / HEATH / CRANBERRY 103
    Vaccinium
EPACRIDACEAE / EPACRIS 104
    Styphelia, Syn. Cyathoides
MYRSINACEAE / MYRSINE 105
    Myrsine, Syn. Suttonia, Syn. Rapanea
SAPOTACEAE / SAPODILLA / BROMELIA 109
    Nesoluma
    Planchonella, Syn. Sideroxylon, Syn. Pouteria
EBENACEAE / EBONY / PERSIMMON 111
    Diospyros, Syn. Maba
OLEACEAE / OLIVE / PRIVET HEDGE 113
    Osthmanthus
LOGANACEAE / STRICHNINE, LOGAN 114
    Labordia
APOCYNACEAE / PERIWINKLE 117
    Ochrosia
    Pteralyxia
    Rauvolfia
    Alyxia
BORAGINACEAE / BORAGE / HELIOTROPE 119
    Cordia
SOLANACEAE / NIGHTSHADE / ANGEL'S TRUMPET 120
    Nothocestrum
GESNERACEAE / GESNERIA / AFRICAN VIOLET, GLOXINIA 122
    Cyrtandra
MYOPORACEAE / NAIO 126
    Myoporum
RUBIACEAE / COFFEE / GARDENIA 127
    Bobea
    Canthium
    Coprosma
    Gardenia
    Gouldia
    Morinda
    Psychotria

LOBELIACEAE / LOBELIA 142
    Brighamia
    Clermontia
    Cyanea
    Delissia
    Lobelia
    Rollandia
    Trematolobelia
GOODENACEAE / NAUPAKA 147
    Scaevola
COMPOSITAE / SUNFLOWER / ASTER 150
    Bidens
    Dubautia
    Hesperomannia
    Railliardia
    Wilkesia
Glossary of Botanical Terms 155
Bibliography & Suggested Reading 159
INDICES
Generic Names, Alphabetical Index 157
Scientific Family Names, Alphabetical Index 155
Common Family Names, Alphabetical Index 156
Hawaiian Names, Alphabetical Index 158
Mainland Equivalent, Common Family Names, Alphabetical Index 159

ACKNOWLEDGEMENTS & INTRODUCTION

My interest in the native trees and shrubs of the Hawaiian Islands dates back to 1934 when I first landed in Hawaii. I was reporting for duty with Hawaii National Park as it was then called. Since I was a forester by training, my inclination was to study the trees around me whenever I could. My interest was heightened by Charles S. Judd, Territorial Forester and more especially by Col. L.W. Bryan, District Forester for the island of Hawaii.

In the preparation of this book, I have continued to lean heavily on L.W. Bryan and have used the information he has gathered in several publications as well as his list of the big trees of each species as given in the *American Forestry* Magazine. He has also provided me with information on locations on several rare trees.

Don Reeser and Chris Zimmer of Hawaii Volcanoes National Park staff have helped in locating rare trees and in making information in the Park files available.

On the island of Kauai the Pacific Tropical Botanical Garden staff made every effort to help me find many rare trees found only on Kauai. Steven Perlman, Garden nurseryman, was especially helpful in taking me on field trips to find rare trees.

Drs. Otto and Ilsa Degener have been consulted from time to time and their 6-volumes of *Flora Hawaiiensis* and his *Plants of Hawaii National Park* have been carefully studied. Norman K. Carlson, then with the Bishop Estate, took me on a drive through Honaunau Forest Reserve to point out rare plants in that area. Stanislaw Modzelewski of Captain Cook, Hawaii, showed me rare plants in Ocean View Estates of South Kona. George Schattauer, Honomolino, Hawaii gave me a tour of Hoomau Ranch and Adolph Johansen, manager of Manuka State Park, was helpful in pointing out native trees that had been planted there.

Upon the advent of publication of *List of Flowering Plants of Hawaii* by Dr. Harold St. John, long time professor of Botany, University of Hawaii, I decided to follow his nomenclature of the Hawaiian Plants. In many cases, synonyms have been given so that the followers of Hillebrand, Rock and Degener can more readily identify with the plant names as given by St. John.

Hawaiian names of the trees are confusing and often vary from island to island. I have chosen to follow Bryan and Walker for the preferred name, falling back on St. John where necessary.

Many of the Hawaiian uses of trees are from a sheet prepared long ago by Charles S. Judd. Degener and Rock also frequently mention uses.

Between the wood collections of L.W. Bryan and my own extensive collection I was able to give descriptions of the wood of a large number of Hawaiian species. This is new material not previously published, to my knowledge.

Placing of species in the forest types follows closely the work of Rock with further observations of the writer. The place of various plants in ecological succession is based on observations of the writer, as is much of the material on what species previously occupied the vast areas now supporting sugar cane plantations.

Carlquist discusses at length how plants arrived and subsequently evolved in Hawaii, a subject only lightly touched upon by me.

The plant descriptions are purposely very simple so that they may be readily understood by people not trained in botany. This will seem to be an over simplification to botanists but standard botanical descriptions can be found in Hillebrand, Rock and Degener for those in need of more scientific descriptions. Both Hillebrand and Rock have been reprinted recently and are readily available.

The island or islands upon which plants occur is given, but no attempt has been made to map the occurrence on individual islands. The notation that the plant occurs in wet or dry forest, in low-lying areas or middle or upper elevations will give the reader the best clues as to where the plant may be found. In addition the writer has noted the presence of plants in Hawaii Volcanoes National Park or Haleakala National Park by placing the Park initials at the beginning of the description of each applicable plant. Also many readily located place or locality names have been used to tell where specific trees are located.

Hawaiian forests have been subjected to human use for 500 to 1000 years but it is doubtful if they were seriously altered until after the islands were discovered by Captain Cook in 1778. Following that event things happened in rapid sequence causing vast and often irreversible changes. The first of these was introduction of cattle to the islands by Capt. Vancouver in 1793. Goats and sheep soon followed, all introduced so that mariners could replenish their meat supply when they visited the islands.

The native forest had never been subjected to grazing or browsing animals of any kind. Many of the plants were soft and without spines or thorns. Thus cattle, sheep and goats found feed plentiful and easy to get. Since there were no predatory animals to feed on the domestic stock, the herds grew rapidly and soon large areas were devastated. As early as 1833 William Ellis saw large herds of cattle. This devastation has continued in certain forest areas to this day until only minor remnants of the original forest are left in some places.

Soon after the arrival of domestic stock the picture was further complicated when areas with the best soil were cleared so that sugar cane, and later pineapples, could be raised. This resulted in total destruction of the original plant cover on vast acreages of lowland to about 2500 feet elevation.

Perhaps the next serious threat was the introduction of a multitude of plant species. Some of these, such as many species of *Eucalyptus*, silky oak *Grevillea robusta*, keawe *Prosopis pallida*, African tulip *Spathodea campanulata*, guava *Psidium guajava* and trumpet tree *Cecropia peltata*, to name a few of the more common, have invaded the native forest and taken over large areas.

Still another assault on the native forest came about when it was found that the poor quality and low yielding native forest could be cleared away and replaced by introduced trees. The purpose was to produce a local supply of lumber and forest products. There have been many successes in this program, but it does displace native tree species.

Many other assaults have been made on the native forest for a variety of reasons. In the process many species of trees and other plants have become endangered or extinct.

However, due to the large areas of virtually inaccessible forest on ancient lava flows and other rough areas, a surprising amount of native forest remains. To be sure there has been modification by reason of invasion of non-native species in much of the area but it is still possible to find a very large percent of the originally known species.

Various agencies such as the National Park Service, State Forest Service, Pacific Tropical Botanical Garden, Manuka State Park and other parks, private arboreta and gardens, and other groups are now working hard to perpetuate many of the threatened and endangered species. Areas have been set aside where protection is assured and much progress has been made. Thus, baring catastrophies of one kind or another, the future looks bright for the preservation of at least remnants of the native forest and perpetuation of most of the native tree species.

The basic purpose of this book is to alert people to the large variety of native species, their present state of abundance or scarcity, the place of the various species in the environment, as well as describing and locating the species.

Through knowledge of the Hawaiian forest and the tree species that compose it will come an awareness of the need to protect it.

That the native forest is the home of many species of native birds is well-known. The dependence of these birds on their specialized habitat is also well-known. The writer has not commented on these relationships as he did not feel that it was within the scope of this book to do so.

However, this is a very important subject, for as parts of the forest have been destroyed, certain species of birds have become extinct. Since this is also an irreversible process, it is hoped that destruction of the remaining forest can be prevented so that no more species of birds need be lost.

SAMUEL H. LAMB
Santa Fe, New Mexico

NATIVE TREES AND SHRUBS OF THE HAWAIIAN ISLANDS

KEY TO THE FAMILIES
Adapted from Rock and Hillebrand

MONOCOTYLEDONOUS OR ENDOGENOUS PLANTS

Ovary superior, naked flowers unisexual, on spathaceous spadices.
    Flowers dioecious, in heads or spikes, leaves elongate, prickly at the edges.
                                                        Pandanaceae
Ovary superior, syncarpous, 3-celled, perianth of 6 segments in 2 series.
    Perianth regular, wholly corolla-like, cells of ovary 2 to many ovulate.
                                                        Liliaceae
    Perianth small, calyx-like, fruit drupaceous or baccate, 1-seeded, leaves
        palmate or pinnate, flowers on a branching spadix . . . . **Palmae**
Ovary inferior, 3-celled; perianth segments free or connate and often inflated
    and surrounding anthers and style; stamens free; fruit fleshy . . . . **Musaceae**

DICOTYLEDONOUS OR EXOGENOUS PLANTS

I. Perianth simple or none.
    Ovary of 3 or rarely 2 or more than 3 united carpels, with 1 or 2
    pendulous ovules in each
        Fruit either capsular separating into as many 2 valved cocci as
        carpels, or succulent and indehiscent . . . . **Euphorbiaceae**
    Ovary free with one ovule, styles 2 or rarely 1.
        Ovule anatropous or amphitropous.
            Fruit indehiscent nut or drupe-like, one seeded . . . . **Ulmaceae**
            Fruit small, drupe-like, milksap present, leaves with 2 axillary
                stipules . . . . **Moraceae**
        Ovule orthotropous.
            Polycarpium or drupe often enclosed by and united with the
                perianth; usually without milksap . . . . **Urticaceae**
    Ovary 1-celled with few ovules, seed single.
        Perianth partly adnate to maturing ovary, ovules 1-3 . . . . . **Santalaceae**
    Ovary 1-celled with a single ovule; embryo curved.
        Perianth dry, supported by 3 bractlets, stamens connate at the base,
        as many as perianth segments . . . . **Amarantaceae**
        Perianth tube persistent around the fruit, stamens not of the same
        number as lobes of perianth, hypogynous . . . . **Nyctaginaceae**
        Perianth lobes herbaceous or membranous; stamens free; 1-celled
        ovary with several stigmas or a 2-3 cleft style; fruit an
        indehiscent utricle . . . . **Chenopodiaceae**
    Ovary 1-celled, free, with a single ovule, embryo not curved.
        Perianth segments 6 in 2 circles, persistent; fruit a one-seeded
        berry or drupe . . . . **Lauraceae**
        Perianth segments 4, stamens twice as many, sessile in 2 alternate
        rows, fruit a drupe-like reddish berry . . . . **Thymelaeaceae**

II. Petals united, at least at the base.
    Corolla epigynous, regular.
        Ovary 3-10-celled, stamens free from the corolla, generally twice
        as many as lobes of the corolla; anthers opening by terminal
        pores; leaves alternate without stipules . . . . **Ericaceae**
        Ovary 2- or more celled, stamens adnate to the corolla, as many as
        corolla lobes; leaves opposite . . . . **Rubiaceae**
        Ovary 1-celled, 1-ovulate; stamens adnate, as many as corolla lobes.
                                                               Compositae

    Corolla epigynous, irregular.
        Stamens 5, filaments and anthers connate, the latter bearded at the
        top; milksap present . . . . **Campanulaceae**
                                                                        Lobelioideae
        Stamens free, stigma surrounded by a hairy indusium . . . . **Goodeniaceae**

Corolla hypogynous or perigynous bearing the stamens, regular
  Ovary 3 or more celled; 1 or 2 ovules in each cell.
    Stamens 5, alternate with corolla lobes; a single ovule in each
      cell .... **Epacridaceae**
    Stamens indefinite; flowers unisexual .... **Ebenaceae**
    Stamens 5-6, opposite the corolla lobes when of same number
      often alternating with staminiodia; milky sap present .... **Sapotaceae**
  Ovary 1-celled, with a free central placenta
    Stamens opposite the corolla lobes; drupe with a single basilar
      seed .... **Myrsinaceae**
  Ovary 2 or incompletely 4-celled.
    Corolla contorted in the bud; leaves opposite
      Capsule 2 or 3-celled, with axile placentas, leaves stipulate.
                                                                        Loganiaceae
      Carpels 2, more or less distinct, milky sap present .... **Apocynaceae**
    Corolla not contorted, leaves generally alternate.
      Ovary 2-celled with 1-3 ovules in each cell; corolla colored,
        4-lobed, imbricate .... **Oleaceae**
      Ovary 2-celled, with many ovules in each cell; corolla plaited
        or imbricate, 5-4 lobed.......................... **Solanaceae**
      Ovary 4-celled, with 1 ovule in each cell; corolla 5-lobed
        imbricate.. **Borraginaceae**
Corolla perigynous, bearing the stamens, irregular
  Ovary 1-celled, with 2 bilamellate parietal placentas and many
    ovules to each; leaves opposite..................... **Gesneriaceae**
  Ovary 2-10 celled, one ovule in each cell; corolla 5-7 lobed,
    as many as stamens .... **Myoporaceae**

III. Petals free. Stamens perigynous or epigynous.
  Disc conspicuous, perigynous or hypogynous; flowers small, regular.
    Stamens alternate with petals; ovary 2-5 celled, with 2 or rarely
      1 ovule in each cell .... **Celastraceae**
    Stamens opposite the small petals; ovary free 2-4 celled, with a
      single erect ovule in each cell .... **Rhamnaceae**
    Stamens alternate with the petals, or twice as many, ovary superior
      1-5 celled, fruit usually a 1-celled drupe; leaves pinnate .. **Anacardiaceae**
  Carpels free, or connate only at the base.
    Flowers irregular and imbricate or regular and valvate; fruit a
      2-valved pod .... **Leguminosae**
    Flowers regular; petals imbricate when present; stamens mostly
      indefinite, very perigynous .... **Rosaceae**
  Ovary syncarpous, superior, with axile placentas, ovules 1 or few in each cell.
    Corolla monopetalous, ovary many-celled .... **Aquifoliaceae**
  Ovary syncarpous with axile placentas and many seeds on each placenta.
    Ovary inferior, stamens indefinite; calyx-lobes imbricate..... **Myrtaceae**
  Ovary syncarpous with parietal placentas and many ovules on each of the latter.
    Ovary partly adnate to calyx, 2-5-celled; leaves opposite.... **Saxifragaceae**
  Ovary inferior with an epigynous disc, 2- to several celled, with a
    single ovule in each cell.
    Calyx adnate to ovary, the latter 2 to many celled, with one ovule
      in each cell; leaves compound....................... **Araliaceae**

IV. Petals free from the calyx and from each other, wanting in *Xylosma*.
  Ovary syncarpous, placentas parietal.
    Petals as many as sepals or none, stamens indefinite....... **Flacourtiaceae**
    Sepals, petals and stamens isomerous, 5 each; fruit a 2- to
      4-valved woody capsule .... **Pittosporaceae**
  Ovary syncarpous, placentas axile.
    Disc wanting, sepals imbricate.
      Sepals and petals tetramerous, stamens indefinite; ovary 1-celled;
        leaves opposite .... **Guttiferae**
      Sepals and petals pentamerous, the latter often cohering at the
        base; stamens indefinite, leaves alternate .... **Theaceae**
    Disc wanting, sepals valvate.
      Stamens indefinite, monadelphous; fruit capsular; seed usually
        reniform, flowers often showy .... **Malvaceae**
      Stamens indefinite, polyadelphous .... **Elaeocarpaceae**

Disc annular, inside the stamens.
    Leaves entire and opposte or imparipinnate and alternate;
      stamens as many or twice as many as petals; ovary 4-celled and
      in fruit 4-lobed, or of a single carpel . . . . **Rutaceae**
Disc annular, outside the stamens.
    Leaves entire, impari-pinnate or dissected, alternate; petals
      sometimes wanting; ovary 3-celled . . . . **Sapindaceae**

DICKSONIA FAMILY
Tree Ferns

Dicksoniaceae
Cibotium Kaulf

1. Tree ferns as understory in Ohia forest.

There are three species of tree ferns growing in the Hawaiian Islands. All are endemic and occur on all the islands. The genus has undergone revision so that it is difficult to compare the nomenclature in the older books with that of the newer publications. It appears that the present accepted nomenclature is as follows:

New Name	Old Name
Cibotium splendens (Gaud) Kraj.	*Cibotium chamissoi* Kaulf
Cibotium chamissoi Kaulf	*Cibotium menziesii* Hook
Cibotium hawaiiensis	*Cibotium glaucum* (Smith) H&A

Key to the Species

Frond stem covered full length with PULU, a hair-like growth, short bristly and red to nearly black . . . . **C. chamissoi**

Frond stem covered with matted PULU only at the base.
- Frond dull green or whitish and covered with cobweb-like hairs on under side . . . . **C. splendens**
- Frond bright green on underside, naked . . . . **C. hawaiiensis**

All three tree ferns are truly tree-like in growth form. They have a single straight trunk crowned by several huge fronds. The trunk is rough from the scars left by mature fronds that have fallen off. The trunks are not woody. The outer portion is a stiff, hard mass of fibers and the center is a starchy matrix with fibers.

Hawaiians ate the young fronds while still coiled and they are still being eaten and said to be delicious boiled. PULU was used for a wound dressing to staunch the flow of blood and also in embalming bodies. During the mid-1800s PULU was gathered extensively, dried and sold for pillow and mattress stuffing. The trade was so good that vast areas of ferns were cut down so that PULU could be gathered easily. Fortunately the felled trunks took root and continued to grow so that little permanent harm came to the forest. Recently an industry has grown up wherein the trunks are gathered and cut up into poles for use in green houses to support orchids and other house plants or are made into bowls in which house plants may be potted. These uses are much more destructive as the whole trunk is moved out of the forest and utilized. Many other tree ferns have been taken out of the forest intact and planted in gardens to furnish shade needed in anthurium culture.

The starchy interior of the trunk is said to have been utilized by early Hawaiians as a famine food. It also is relished by hogs that roam the forest.

Tree ferns are called "Mother of the Ohia." Ferns commonly grow as an upper layer of the understory in the OHIA forest. Seeds of the OHIA fall on fern trunks, germinate and seedlings then send roots down to the soil. In time the OHIA chokes out the fern and many large OHIA trees are seen standing as if on stilts. Other trees such as OLAPA have this same growth habit.

Tree ferns occur in wide spread areas of the islands in the wetter habitats. *C. hawaiiensis* has been considered rare but careful study of the fern forest indicates it is much more plentiful than had been supposed. The other two species are very common. Very fine examples of tree fern stands can be seen in Hawaii Volcanoes National Park along the Crater Rim Road in the vicinity of Thurston Lava Tube and along the Stainback Highway near Hilo.

Degener's *Plants of Hawaii National Park* gives a good account of the PULU industry and the attempt to start a starch industry.

Other species of tree fern are found in tropical Mexico and other tropical countries.

[1] HVNP: This symbol indicates that the plant described below may be found in Hawaii Volcanoes National Park.

[2] Kilauea: This further indicates that the plant may be seen in the Kilauea region of the Park.

[3] HAP'U: Hawaiian names are capitalized.

[4] See:
Degener, Plants HNP, pp. 27-32.
Neal, pp. 10-11.
Rock, pp. 89-95.
Hillebrand, pp. 545-548.

[5] HNP: This symbol indicates the plant is found in Haleakala National Park.

HVNP[1] Kilauea[2]

| HAP'U or HAPU'U[3] | **C. hawaiiensis** |
| Tree fern | Syn.: **C. glaucum** |

This HAP'U is not readily distinguished from *C. splendens* on the basis of size of trunk or frond. However, the undersurface of the frond tends to be bright green and naked rather than dull green or whitish and hairy as in the latter. It is much less common than either of the other two tree ferns.

HVNP Kilauea

| HAP'U I'I'I | **C. chamissoi** |
| Tree fern | Syn.: **C. menziesii** |

HAP'U I'I'I or HAP'U I'I as it is sometimes written, is readily distinguished from the other two tree ferns by the PULU on the stipe or frond stem. The whole length of the stipe is covered with hairs, or PULU, rather than just the base as in the HAP'Us. Also this PULU is stiff and dark red to blackish on the upper portion of the stipe. Although all three ferns may be the same size in any given stand, HAP'U I'I'I becomes the largest upon maturity. Trunks of 25 ' (7.6m) with fronds reaching 12' (3.8m) beyond the tops are not uncommon. In fact the champion tree fern measured by L.W. Bryan in Honaunau Forest Reserve, Kailua, Kona was 15' 10" (4.8m) in circumference, 35' (10.6m) high and had a crown spread of 24' (7.3m).[4]

4. Detail of Hapau stems showing long, matted pulu.

1. Frond of Hapu i'i'i, *C. chamissoi*.
2. Hapuu, *C. splendens*, along Maunaloa road.
3. Detail of bristly red pulu on stem of Hapu i'i'i, not long and matted as on Hapuu.

HVNP Kilauea
HNP[5]

| HAP'U or HAPU'U | **C. splendens** |
| Tree Fern | Syn.: **C. chamissoi** |

This tree fern has a trunk up to 8' (2.5m) high, crowned by great fronds 5' (1.5m) wide and with stipes up to 12' (3.6m) long. The single trunk may be one (.3m) to two feet (.6m) in diameter.

The fronds are compound, with many branches to the stipe or frond stem, with many pinnae attached to each branch and many pinnules on each pinnae. The stipe is covered at the base with long matted PULU but the upper portion of the stipe is bare. The underside of the frond is dull green to whitish and often coated with fine cobweb-like hairs.

PALM FAMILY / COCONUT — Palmae or Palmaceae (Arecaceae)

Two genera of palms are considered native to the Hawaiian Islands: *Cocos* and *Pritchardia*.

Key to the Genera

Leaves pinnate, long and slender .... **Cocos** L.
Leaves palmate, fan shaped .... **Pritchardia** Seem & H. Wendl

Cocos is represented in Hawaii by one species, *C. nucifera*, known by the Hawaiians as NIU and around the world as coconut palm. *Pritchardia* may be found on all the islands where it is called LOULU.

Whether the coconut arrived on Hawaiian shores by itself thus being indigenous, or was brought here by early Hawaiians and thus being introduced, is a question that may never be resolved. However, it occupies too prominent a place in the Hawaiian landscape to be omitted here.

LOULU is an endemic palm, meaning that it migrated to Hawaii long ago and has undergone such changes that all the kinds found here are species found nowhere else. How its progenators may have arrived in Hawaii, and from where, is not known. Many of the same arguments used against the coconut arriving naturally work as well against LOULU's. St. John lists 33 species and six varieties for the Hawaiian Islands and Neal lists 5 others occurring in Fiji and the Tuamotos. These palms occur scattered widely throughout the Hawaiian forests but generally as individual trees or in small clumps.

1. *Healthy young coconut palm, Kamoamoa, HVNP.*

HVNP

NIU   **Cocos nucifera** L.
Coconut Palm

Coconut palms occur on all the islands along the coast and inland for some distance locally. They are very abundant and are also widely spread throughout the tropical regions of the world.

Coconut palms grow as tall slender trees with a single trunk and a crown of leaves at the top. It is said to reach 100' (30m) in height. The

2. *Detail of coconuts and fronds, cocos nucifera.*

3. *Grove of coconut palms, City of Refuge, Hawaii.*

¹ See'
Hillebrand, p. 451.
Neal, p. 119.
Carlquist, p. 105.
St. John, p. 53.
Degener, PHNP, pp. 68-78, full account of uses.

² In this list and all subsequent lists, a notation is made in the left hand margin as to the relative abundance of the various species. The status as 'threatened' is represented by '*'; 'endangered' by '**'; and 'extinct' is represented by '***'. The status is quoted from the Federal Register, Tuesday, July 1, 1975, Washington, D.C., Volume 40, Number 127. If there is no notation, the plant is considered to be sufficiently abundant to survive in the foreseeable future. In the right hand margin is a notation showing whether the plant is endemic and if so on what island or islands it is found. If found on all the islands the initials H.I. are used. Where the word 'indigenous' is used, it indicates the same species is found elsewhere, but arrived in the Hawaiian Islands without the assistance of man. A few species are marked 'introduced' when the evidence seems clear that the plant was brought to the islands by the Hawaiians before the arrival of Captain Cook.

1. Loulu, P. afinis, Kona, Hawaii.

slender fronds, 10' (3m) long or longer, have as many as 100 pairs of long slender leaflets per frond. These leaflets may be as much as 1" (2.5cm) wide by 30" (75cm) long attached to a greenish yellow midrib. The flowers occur in large clusters among the leaves, with the male flowers toward the outer end of the cluster and the female flowers closer to the trunk. The fruits occur in clusters close to the trunk. The large ripe fruit is somewhat the size and shape of a football that has been flattened on one end. It consists of an outer fibrous husk about 2" (5cm) thick and an inner nut. This nut has a very hard brown shell, slightly tipped at one end and blunted at the other. Near the blunt end are 3 spots that give the nut a monkey faced appearance. The radicle grows out of the soft center spot. Inside the hard shell, in a mature nut, is a layer of pure white coconut meat about .5" (1cm) thick. The hollow center is partly filled with a clear palatable liquid called coconut water.

The trunks of old, mature trees are rough with the marks of old leaf scars. The outer part of the trunk consists of a layer of tan to brown wood-like material consisting of very numerous fibers in a matrix. Thus the texture of the wood is very coarse, the grain is coarse, the wood is soft and light weight, and stability and workability are both poor. Inside this outer layer the core is a soft matrix with no strength or workability. Thus when coconut logs are used in construction they are left whole and not sawed into lumber.

NIU is very valuable where ever it occurs. The nut supplies very nourishing food and a palatable drink. Shells are used for cups and other utensils. Fibers of the husks are braided into cordage known as sennit. Leaves are used, or have been, for fans, brooms, thatch, weaving, symbols of rank, and the midrib for various purposes such as a stem upon which to string KUKUI nuts for use as a candle. Logs are used in making drums, inferior canoes, building logs, etc. In modern times the trees are used in ornamental planting, nuts are the source of commercial coconut and coconut syrup.

The largest known Hawaiian coconut is found in the State Forestry Arboretum, Hilo and is 4'8" (1.43m) in circumference, 94' (29.6m) tall and has a crown spread of 28' (8.8m).¹

List of Species of **Pritchardia**²

Pritchardia Seem. & H. Wendl., 1862, nom conserv. (*Eupritchardia*).
All species called lo'ulu, hawane.

	affnis Becc., 1921, var. **affinis**. N:98	end. Hawaii
	var. **gracilis** Becc., 1921.	end. Hawaii
	var. **halophila** Becc., 1921. (by error *holaphila*).	end. Hawaii
	var. **rhopalocarpa** Becc., 1921.	end. Hawaii
	arecina Becc., 1913, R:107	end. e. Maui
**	**Aylmer-Robinsonii** St. John, 1959. Wahane, hawane.	end. Hiihau
	Beccariana Rock, 1916, var. **Beccariana.**	end. Hawaii
	var. **Giffardiana** Becc., 1921	end. Hawaii
	brevicalyx Becc. & Rock, 1921	end. Molokai
	donata Caum, 1930	end. Molokai
**	**elliptica** Rock and Caum, 1930	end. Lania
**	**eriophora** Becc., 1913. R:105	end. Kauai
	eriostachya Becc, 1913. R:107	end. Hawaii
	Forbesiana Rock, 1021	end. w. Maui
**	**Gaudichaudii** (Mart.) H. Wendl, 1862. H:450; R:100; N:98	end. Molokai
	Livistona? Gaudichaudii Mart., 1845.	
	glabrata Becc. & Rock, 1921. N:99	end. w. Maui
	Hardyi Rock, 1921	end. Kauai
	Hillebrandi Becc., 1890. R:103; N:98. Lo'ulu-lelo	end. Molokai
	insignis Becc., 1913. N:99	H.I.?
**	**kaalae** Rock, 1921, var. **kaalae**	end. Oahu
**	var. **minima** Caum, 1930	end. Oahu
**	**kahanae** Rock & Caum, 1921	end. Oahu

	kamapuaana Caum, 1930	end. Oahu
**	**lanaiensis** Becc & Rock, 1921. N:98	end. Lanai
	lanigera Becc., 1890. R:103	end. Hawaii
	Lowreyana Rock, 1921, var. **Lowreyana**	end. Molokai
	var. **turbinata** Rock, 1921	end. Molokai
	Macdanielsi Caum, 1930	end. Oahu
	Martii (Gaud.? H.Wendl., 1862. H:451; R:101; N:98. Lo'ulu-hiwa	end. Oahu
	Livistona? Martii Gaud., 1842	
	martioides Rock & Caum, 1921	end. Oahu
	minor Becc., 1910. R:104	end. Kauai
***	**montis-kea** Rock, 1921[3]	end. Hawaii
**	**Munroii** Rock, 1921	end. Molokai
	pacifica Seem. & H.Wendl., 1862. N:98. Vin, Fiji fan palm.	
		cult Fiji, Tonga, Samoa
**	**remota** Becc., 1890. R:104	end. Nihoa I.
	Rockiana Becc., 1913. R:105	end. Oahu
	Thurstoni F. Muell. & Drude, 1887. N:98	cult. Fiji
	viscosa Rock, 1921	end. Kauai
	Weissichiana Rock.	end. Kauai

[3] *Correspondence of Colonel Bryan states it is extinct.*

[4] *See:*
Neal, p. 98.
St. John, p. 57.

LOULU   **Pritchardia affinis** Becc

This species and all its varieties are endemic to the island of Hawaii. It occurs in South Kona and one may be seen near the junction of highways 18 and 19. Although it does not appear to be common, it is not listed as endangered. The leaf stems are about 3' (90cm) long with blades about the same width. The upper surface is green, the under surface has yellowish scales. Flowers occur in large clusters just below and among the crown of leaves. Seeds are .5 to .75" (1 to 2cm) in diameter, brown, and born in clusters at the end of 2' (60cm) stalks. The trunk is smooth and grey like a concrete column, with circular leaf scars. The trunk consists of a thick outer shell of hard, fibrous wood and a soft inner core. In all species of LOULU the hard wood was used in making spears, if the trunk was long enough, seeds were eaten, leaves were used for thatching and more recently, for making hats and fans.

The largest LOULU of this species is located in Keaau, Hawaii and measures 3'8" (1.1m) in circumference, 42' (14m) high and with a crown spread of 13' (4m), measured by L.W. Bryan.[4]

HVNP Kipuka Puaulu

LOULU   **Pritchardia beccariana** Rock

This LOULU occurs as a well-developed tree generally about 30' (9m) or more tall with a trunk about 8" (20cm) in diameter, or more. This

2. Two tall Loulu, P. beccariana, with tree ferns at base and amid decadent Ohia trees.

1. Fronds of young Loulu, P. beccariana, HVNP.

3. Trunk detail, Loulu, P. beccariana, Stainback Hwy, Hawaii.

[5] See:
Carlquist, p. 303.
St. John, p. 57.

[6] See:
Neal, p. 98.
St. John, p. 57.

[7] See:
Neal, p. 98

[8] See:
Neal, p. 98.
Hillebrand, p. 450.

[9] See:
Neal, p. 98.
Carlquist, p. 302.
Hillebrand, p. 451.

[10] See:
Carlquist, p. 302.

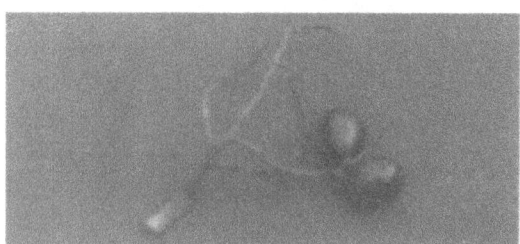

1. Nuts of Loulu, P. eriostachia.

2. Young Loulu, P. eristachia. Manuka State Park, Hawaii.

endemic species and its variety are endemic to the island of Hawaii and are quite abundant in the wet forest along the Stainback Highway back of Hilo.

The fan shaped leaves are up to 3.5' (1m) in diameter with stems 2.5 to 3' (.7 to .9m) long. The trunk gives the appearance of a concrete column with short vertical cracks. The seeds are edible. This might account for the distribution of this heavy seeded plant back from the shore. Since there were no rodents or other animals in the primitive forest to carry the seeds some other method of distribution was necessary. The early Hawaiians penetrated the forest deeply in search of the various products they used. Thus they may have actually planted trees that bore edible fruit or may have planted them accidentally as they carried edible seeds about with them.

The wood is very dark brown, texture is coarse, grain coarse, outside 1.5" (4cm) ring of wood on a 7" (18cm) trunk is very dense and hard; the center is soft and pithy, making it a hard wood to work with primitive tools.

The largest known tree is located in Waiakea Forest Reserve back of Hilo and measures 4'6" (1.4m) in circumference, 55' (16.7m) tall, with a crown spread of 19' (6m), measured by L.W. Bryan.[5]

LOULU   Pritchardia eriostachia Becc

P. eriostachia is also endemic to Hawaii. There is a good immature specimen growing in Manuka State Park in the Kau District of Hawaii. The tree is similar to P. beccariana except that the nuts are larger, 1" (2cm) in diameter and 1.75" (4cm) long, black and shining. The short stemmed fruits, or drupes, are quite smooth with a fibrous cover that erodes away in time, exposing a woody shell. When this shell is cracked the edible nutlike fruit is exposed. The seeds occur in large clusters on long stems that are attached to the trunk in the axils of the leaves. LOULU seeds are readily taken by roaming hogs and rats. Neal sites several early legends concerning LOULU in the life of the Hawaiians.[6]

LOULU   Pritchardia hillebrandi Becc

This LOULU, endemic to Molokai is listed as endangered. Neal states that it reaches a height of 21' (6.4m) with leaves 4' (1.2m) long. The downy leaf stem is also 4' long. The round fuits, bluish-black when ripe, are about .8" (2cm) in diameter.[7]

LOULU   Pritchardia gaudichaudi (Mart.) H.Wendl

Another LOULU endemic to Molokai and endangered grows, according to Neal, as a dwarf, 1' to 6' (.6 to 1.8m) high with a small leaf 2.5' (.75m) long, somewhat silvery below, stem shorter and silvery downy. The fruits are round, brown and 1.5" (4cm) in diameter.[8]

LOULU   Pritchardia martini H.Wendl

P. martini is endemic to Oahu where it occurs on the leeward side or dry side of the crest of the Koolau Mountains. It grows 10' to 15' (3 to 4.4m) tall with thick trunk. It is distinguished by masses of yellow flowers. Neal states the ovoid fruits, brown or greenish when ripe, are 1.5" (4cm) long. Leaves are 3' (.92m) long with tawny felt underside and leaf stems about as long and tawny felted.[9]

LOULU   Pritchardia macdonaldsii Caum

Carlquist relates that this LOULU occurs near the location of P. martini on Oahu but on the windward or wet side of the crest of the Koolau Range. It is also endemic to Oahu. This makes an interesting case of adaption with one species on the wet side and one on the dry side of the same range.[10]

LOULU   **Pritchardia minor** Becc

P. minor is endemic to Kauai where several nice trees were found growing in the Kokee area, 15 to 20' (4.5 to 6m) tall with very slender trunks. The fan shaped leaves are 2 to 3' (.6 to .9m) long and light green. The seeds are slender, ovoid, black 1" (2.5cm) long, borne in large clusters. Although several trees were seen, as well as several seedlings, the tree is not abundant. Pigs rooting for seeds destroy many seedlings. Efforts are being made by the Pacific Tropical Botanical Garden to increase the numbers of this species. One step taken is to place galvanized metal bands around the trunks of key trees to keep rats from climbing trees and destroying the ripening seeds. In a clump of trees all individuals must be banded to keep rats from jumping from tree to tree. Good seeds thus brought to maturity are taken to the nursery where seedlings are raised and later transplanted into likely habitats.

LILY FAMILY / YUCCA   **Liliaceae**

There are two native genera of the Lily family in the Hawaiian Islands that are tree-like in stature, *Cordyline* (Syn. *Taetsia*), and *Pleomele* (Syn. *Dracaena*). The former is represented by one species introduced by early Hawaiians and the latter by three endemic species. Botanically the two genera may be distinguished by a difference in the flowers.

Neal outlines this in a key to the genera as follows:

Flower stems usually single, each with three bracts at base
                                     Cordyline Commers, ex Juss

Flower stems usually in 2s with none to 2 bracts at base . . . . **Pleomele** Salisb

1. Mature Loulu tree, P. minor, Kokee, Kauai.

In the field the observer will see that the leaves of *Cordyline* are broader and more upright, while those of *Pleomele* are narrower and generally reflexed. Also the inflorescence or flowering head of *Cordyline* appears to be much finer and smaller than the large, coarse inflorescence of *Pleomele*. Both have been spread widely by people using them in landscape planting. In general *Cordyline* grows in wetter situations while *Pleomele* is more often found in drier habitat. However, on Kauai *Pleomele* is found in the quite wet habitat of Kokee. *Pleomele* generally is larger at maturity than *Cordyline*.

HVNP Kipuka Puaulu and others
HNP

TI or KI   **Cordyline terminalis** (L) kunth
                                       Syn.: **Cordyline fruticosa**
                                     Syn.: **Taetsia fruticosa** (L) Merrill

TI or KI is generally seen growing as a short, single stemmed, shrub-like plant but if protected long enough may make a tree-like plant 20' (6m) or more tall with a trunk 4 to 6" (10 to 15cm) in diameter. The stems are generally branchless with a cluster of leaves at the top. It occurs on all the islands but reaches its best development where well watered. It is very abundant in the lower forest edges and in areas associated with landscaping. It is presumed to have been introduced by the early Hawaiians because it was a very useful plant.

The leaves are spirally arranged in terminal clusters, the lower ones dropping off at maturity, leaving spirally arranged leaf scars on the trunk. Leaves are about 4" (10cm) wide and up to 2' (.6m) long in a well developed, vigorous plant. They are normally deep green but horticultural varieties with red or green and white varigated leaves are common. The flowers occur in drooping, branched, terminal panicles about 1' (30cm) long. Buds normally white tinged with purple, flowers have six white lobes with six

2. Young trees, Loulu, P. minor, with Steve Perlman, PTBG. Kokee, Kauai.

[1] See:
Neal, p. 202-204.
Hillebrand, P. 442.
Degener, PHNP, pp. 95-98.
St. John, p. 82.

[2] See:
Neal, p. 205.
Hillebrand, p. 442.
Rock, pp. 109-112.
St. John, p. 84.

1. A clump of Ti, T. fruticosa, in Kipuka Puaulu, HVNP.

2. Closeup of flower cluster of Ti.

3. Halapepe, P. aurea, in dry forest, South Kohala, Hawaii.

yellow stamens and a white pistil. Horticultural varieties may have red flowers.

The bright red fruit is .25" (.75cm) in diameter when ripe, born in a large showy cluster. Mature trunks are quite smooth when the leaf scars are outgrown. The wood is very light, soft and coarse and shrinks very badly. The trunk exudes sap freely when cut.

The leaves were and still are used for wrapping items of food, etc., cooked for greens, waved in battle as a flag of truce, made into grass skirts, and plucked, stem and all, and used like a sled in sliding down steep slopes. The root can be baked and eaten or fermented. From the fermented root an alcoholic beverage is prepared. In modern times TI has been widely used as an ornamental and vast quantities of cuttings are prepared for sale to tourists to take home for house plants. The author's 16-year-old house plant is now 5' (1.5m) tall and has bloomed twice.

In some areas TI plants form a conspicuous component of the understory of the forest. One such place is the lower slopes of Waipio valley on Hawaii where dense stands may be seen.[1]

| HALAPEPE | **Pleomele** Salisb. |
| | Syn.: **Dracaena** |

The species of *Pleomele* are as follows:
- ****Pleomele aurea** (H.Mann) N.E. Br. — end. H.I.
- **Pleomele fernaldii** St. John — end. Lanai
- ****Pleomele forbesii** Deg. — end. W. Oahu

HALEPEPE **Pleomele aurea**
Golden dracaena Syn.: **Dracaena aurea** H. Mann

HALAPEPE develops at maturity into a tree up to 30' (9m) tall or more, generally branched part way up the trunk. The leaves occur as spirally arranged terminal clusters. The tree is quite common in the dry forest in the vicinity of Puuwaawaa in the Kona District of Hawaii and in the moderately wet forest in the Kokee region of Kauai. Although it is listed as endangered it appears to be much more abundant than many species of Hawaiian trees.

The leaves are about 1.25" (3cm) wide and up to 18" (45cm) long. They bend down under their own weight giving the tree a droopy appearance. The flowers, each about 1.5" (4cm) long and golden yellow or greenish, are arranged in long drooping terminal panicles. The oval fruits are .25 to .5" (.5 to 1cm) long, orange colored and very numerous.

The stiff, erect branches are ridged by the numerous leaf scars. They taper to about 1" (2cm) in diameter at the ends. On 6" (15cm) trunks the bark is quite smooth and grey.

The wood is white with reddish or yellow streaks, largely composed of pithy material filled with fibers, figure plain, grain straight, very soft and light weight. It is very unstable with poor workability.

The Hawaiians used the soft wood to carve into idols. Branches were used to decorate the altars of the Goddess Laka.

The largest measured tree is located in Kaupulehu reserve of the Pacific Tropical Botanical Garden between Puuwaawaa and Kaiula, Kona, Hawaii and is 3'6" (1m) in circumference, 20' (6m) high and has a crown spread of 14' (4.25m), measured by L.W. Bryan.

Neal states that *P. forbesii* can be recognized by its smaller leaves, .33" (1cm) by up to 18" (45 cm) and *P. fernaldii* by very small leaves, .5" (1.5cm) wide by 8" (21cm) long. In both species the trees also tend to be smaller than those of *P. aurea*.[2]

1.

2.

3.

HVNP Puna coast
HNP

1. *Halapepe in wet forest of Kokee, Kauai.*
2. *Flowering branch of Halapepe. Joseph E. Rock, photo.*
3. *Closeup of Halapepe leaf cluster.*

BANANA FAMILY — **Musaceae**

MAIA
Banana

Musa paradisiaca L.
Syn.: **Musa sapientum** L.
Musa troglodytarum L.
plus varieties and subspecies

It has been said that at the time of discovery of the islands by Captain Cook the Hawaiians had developed 60 or more varieties of bananas, likely most all of which were related to one or the other of the two above species.

A banana tree grows fruits once and dies back to the ground. Trees may become 30' (9m) tall and 6" (15cm) in diameter. The trunk is made up of leaf sheaths and contains no wood. The leaves are 8 to 10' (2.4 to 3m) long on a 2' (.6m) long stem that clasps the trunk. These leaves are 1' to 1.5' (.3 to .45m) wide with a heavy midrib and veins at right angles to the stem. The wind soon tears new leaves along these veins giving them a tattered appearance.

An oblong flower cluster arises from within the column of leaf sheaths and protrudes out the top of the tree. In most varieties the heavy flower and newly forming bunch of large bananas may bend the plant until the bananas touch the ground. The bananas sit along the fruit stem in clusters of up to 20, called hands. Ten hands constitute a good bunch. The outer tip of the stalk ends in a red, bulbous structure containing the staminate flower organs.

The fruits need no description except to say that they come in many sizes and may be the common yellow color or red. Some are best eaten raw and some are best cooked.

4. *Clump of banana.*

Banana trees are common on all the Hawaiian islands. Wild bananas grow where Hawaiians planted them and many more have been planted either for commerical production or as a feature of landscaping.

Bananas were used for food in the old Hawaiian economy but the use was associated with many ancient taboos, or KAPUs in Hawaiian. One special KAPU denied women the right to eat bananas. Leaves are used for wrapping, dry leaves for thatching; green leaves and stems can be cooked for food.

The State Forest Service and the Pacific Tropical Botanical Garden are cooperating to propagate and plant old native strains in suitable habitat.[1]

[1] See:
Neal, p. 248.
St. John, p. 91.
Degener, PHNP, pp. 105-111, for a detailed account of Hawaiian use.

[1] See:
Hillebrand, p. 405.
Neal, p. 298.
Rock, p. 113.
St. John, p. 139.

ELM FAMILY
No known Hawaiian name

Ulmaceae
Trema cannabina Lour
Syn.: **Trema amboinesis** (Willb) Bl

This shrub or small tree with long limbs, reaches heights of 20 to 30' (6 to 9m). No Hawaiian name has been recorded but since it was used as a source of fiber for making fish nets it surely had a local name, at least. The tree is indigenous to Hawaii and can be found in many of the other island groups in the Pacific. It may have disappeared completely from the island of Hawaii. Hillebrand found it on Oahu and Molokai.

The alternate leaves, rough above, are 3 to 6" (8 to 15cm) long, heart shaped, with long slender tips, and three prominent veins. The numerous, tiny 5-parted, white flowers are borne in inch long clusters in the leaf axils. Fruit is an ovoid drupe, one seeded, slightly fleshy, sometimes with a wing. Young branches are covered with soft grey pubescence. Wood is golden brown, flecked with brown pores, coarse textured, straight grained, of low density and soft. It is rather ring porous with scattered pores between the faint rings. Faint rays are visible. Stability and workability are rated fair.

A purgative was produced from some part of the plant and as stated, fibers from the bark were used in making fish nets.[1]

MULBERRY FAMILY

Moraceae

This family is represented by two genera introduced by early Hawaiians, *Broussonetia* and *Artocarpus,* and by one endemic genus, *Pseudomorus.* Each genus is represented by a single species. The introductions were doubtless made due to the valuable products derived from the plants.

Key to the Genera

Female flowers in spikes . . . . **Pseudomorus** Bureau
Female flowers on a globose receptacle.
    Leaves entire, up to 6" (15cm) long, fruit small
                                            Broussonitia L. 'Herr. ex Vent
    Leaves large, up to 18" (46cm) long, and deeply incised,
        fruit large . . . . **Artocarpus** JR&G. Forst

ULU
Breadfruit

Artocarpus atilis Parkins. ex (z) Fosb.
Syn.: **A. incisus** (Thumb) L
Syn.: **A. communis** Forst

ULU develops into a large, wide spreading tree 40 to 60' (12 to 18m) tall, with heavy, angular branches. It is generally believed to have been brought to the Hawaiian Islands by early Hawaiians where it was raised for the food it supplies. It now occurs on all the islands, but is not abundant, even though frequently seen in and near houseyards.

The large, leathery, alternate leaves are up to 18" (46cm) long, cut deeply into eight or more lobes. They are yellowish green with prominent red or green veins. The female flowers are borne on a large round green globe that develops into the fruit. The fruit is a large ball 5 to 8" (13 to 20cm) in diameter, brownish green when ripe, somewhat flattened at the stem end. The rind is warty and rough, pulp is sweet and mealy. The male flowers occur on 6 to 12" (15 to 30cm) yellow spikes. Both flowers occur on the same tree. No fertile seeds are produced so all trees must be started from suckers or cuttings. The twigs are very stout and rough with large leaf scars. The bark is smooth on small trees but later becomes rough, gradually breaking into plates with deep furrows between. The sap is milky.

Wood is brownish tan, occasionally with a greenish tint, coarse texture, straight grain, low in density and soft. Vessels are large and scattered, rays fine. Shrinkage is low and workability good.

1. Breadfruit tree, *A. incisus*, South Kona, Hawaii.

Wood was used in house construction and for doors, for POI boards, calabashes, canoe bodies and a small thin surfboard called ALAIA. The male flower was mixed with the fiber of WAUKE in the manufacture of a rare TAPA. The sap was used for gum and for bird lime, the rough leaves for sandpaper for polishing wood.

Since no viable seeds are produced the tree did not spread widely into the forest. L.W. Bryan's big tree is 10'4" (3m) in circumference, 54' (16m) tall and with 59' (18m) crown spread.[1]

[1] See:
Neal, p. 302.
Hillebrand, p. 407.
Rock, p. 115.
St. John, p. 139.

[2] See:
Neal, p. 301.
Hillebrand, p. 407.
St. John, p. 140.

1. Fruit and leaves of breadfruit.

2. Large Wauke shrub, Manuka State Park, Hawaii.

WAUKE
Paper Mulberry

Broussonetia papyrifera (L) Vent

WAUKE grows as a large shrub or small tree to 20' (6m) with a stout trunk up to 12" (31.5cm) in diameter. It was formerly quite plentiful but when Hawaiians ceased to cultivate it the plants became scarce. It can now be seen in gardens or arboreta such as the State Forest Nursery at Hilo, Manuka State Park, Hawaii, Pacific Tropical Botanical Garden, Lawai, Kauai, and in Mahanaloa valley, Kauai.

The heart shaped or 1-3 lobed leaves are 4 to 6" (10 to 15cm) long and 3 to 5" (7 to 13cm) wide with petiole 1 to 6" (2 to 15cm) long with a large stipule at the base. Leaves are rough on the upper surface and wooly underneath. Pinnately branched veins are very prominent on the under side. The male and female flowers are borne on separate plants. The female flowers from a round head 1" (.25cm) in diameter on a peduncle, fuzzy with long stigmas and hairy bracts. These flowers are seldom seen in Hawaii. The male flowers form a long catkin 3 to 4" (7 to 10cm) long. The small fruits, when they can be found, are orange colored. The twigs are light brown and hairy, aging to medium brown with a conspicuous pattern of white lines. These lines become more prominent on large smooth trunks. Wood is white, soft and of low density.

Bark was used in making better grades of TAPA cloth. This cloth was said to be warmer, softer, more flexible and more water resistant than that made from MAMAKE. The bast was also used for twine and rope and for making netting bags and sandals. The plant was cultivated near habitations and did not spread into the forest.[2]

3. Leaves of Wauke, B. papyrifera.

3. See:
Neal, p. 299.
Rock, p. 114.
St. John, p. 142.

1. Aiaa tree. Puuwaawaa, Hawaii.

2. Leaf detail of Aiaa, P. sandwicensis.

A'IA'A, False Mulberry, **Pseudomorus sandwicensis** Deg
literal translation of *Pseudomorus* Syn.: **P. brunoniana** bureau

A'IA'A is generally a small slender tree with few branches but may become a tree 40' (12m) tall and 1.5' (45cm) in diameter. It is endemic and occurs on Kauai, Oahu, Lanai, Maui and Hawaii. In the early 1900s Rock found the tree common in various dry forest areas of several of the islands but it does not appear to be abundant at the present time. One cultivated plant was seen at Puuwaawaa, Hawaii and one at Kokee, Kauai.

The alternate oblong leaves resemble mulberry leaves somewhat. They are generally entire, narrow ovate, shiny and thin, often rounded at the base on very short petioles. The midrib is prominent and there are 10 to 12 pairs of light pinnate veins united at the outer edge of the leaf by a marginal vein. The flowers are borne in spikes, the male white turning purple on wilting, and the female, green. Fruit, four or less per spike, brownish purple, shiny, fleshy, smooth, juicy and sweet with whitish juice.

The twigs are brown and smooth except for small whitish dots. Bark is whitish grey and exudes a milky sap. Wood is light brown, somewhat resembling oak. It has medium texture, close grain, density of 56 pounds per cubic foot cured, hard and tough. Vessels are fine and clustered in annular bands. Rays are numerous with cross banding between rays. Stability appears poor and workability only fair.

This tree is not sufficiently abundant to be an important component of the dry to moderately moist forest. The largest known tree, measured by L.W. Bryan, is 4' (12.2m) in circumference, 38' (5.5m) tall and with a 20' (6m) crown spread located at Kaupulehu, Kona.[3]

NETTLE FAMILY / STINGING NETTLE Urticaceae

Three endemic genera of tree-like plants of the nettle family are found in Hawaii, *Pipturus*, *Touchardia* and *Urera*. All were important to the Hawaiian people because of the valuable products harvested from them.

Key to the Genera

Flowers in cymes, broad, more or less flat topped clusters . . . . **Urera** Guad.
Flowers in axillary clusters . . . . **Pipturus** Wedd
Flowers on globose receptacles . . . . **Touchardia** Guad.

The genus *Urera* is represented by the following taxa:

Urera glabra, H&A, Wedd.	end. H.I.
** **kaalae** Wawra	end. Oahu
sandwicensis Wedd.	end. Hawaii
var. **kauaiensis** Rock	end. Kauai
var. **mollis** Wedd.	end. Hawaii

The genus *Touchardia* is represented by only one species, *T. latifolia* Gaud., endemic to H.I.

The genus *Pipturus* was considered to be represented by only one species, *P. albidus*, by Neal, Rock and Hillebrand. As other botanists studied it more closely, a total of 13 species, 5 varieties and one form emerged. One of the keys to the 13 species is based on leaf characteristics, frequently overlapping between pairs of species.

Dr. St. John lists the taxa of *Pipturus* as follows:

Pipturus Wedd., 1854.
  albidus (H&A) Gray in Mann, 1867. H:413; N:318; R:123. Mamaki end. Oahu
    Boehmeria albida H0A, 1832.
  Brighamii Skottsb., 1932, F. **Brighamii** end. Hawaii
    f. **kohalae** Skottsb., 1944 end. Hawaii
  Forbesii Krajina, 1930 end. e. Maui
  Gaudichaudianus Wedd., 1854, var. **Gaudichaudianus** end. Lanai, Hawaii

var. **asperrimus** Skottsb., 1934	end. Hawaii
var. **hualalaiensis** Skottsb., 1934	end. Hawaii
hawaiensis Lévl., 1911, var. **hawaiensis**	end. Maui, Hawaii
var. **eriocarpus** (Skottsb.) Skottsb., 1944	end. Maui
eriocarpus Skottsb., 1932.	
var. **integrifolius** Deg. & Deg., 1968	end. Hawaii
var. **molokaiensis** (Skottsb.) Deg. & Deg., 1968	end. Molokai
subsp. *molokaiensis* Skottsb., 1934	
Helleri Skottsb., 1932	end. Kauai
kauaiensis Heller, 1897	end. Kauai
albidus (H&A) Gray in Mann, var. *grosseserrata* Skottsb., 1926.	
albidus, var. *kauaiensis* Hochr., 1925.	
oahuensis Skottsb., 1932	end. Oahu
pachyphyllus Skottsb., 1932	end. Hawaii
pterocarpus Skottsb., 1944	end. Molokai
Rockii Skottsb., 1932	end. Molokai, Lanai, Maui
ruber Heller, 1897	end. Kauai
Skottsbergii Krajina, 1930	end. Oahu

HVNP Kilauea
HNP

MAMAKI or MAMAKE   **Pipturus hawaiiensis** Levl

This species was chosen to describe since the writer is best acquainted with it and perhaps it is relatively characteristic of the genus.

All specimens of *Pipturus* gathered for and stored in Hawaii Volcanoes National Park herbarium have been labeled *P. hawaiiensis*. This MAMAKE is a large shrub or small tree often forming a border around the edges of forest openings, rights-of-way and other open spaces. The number of clumps of plants in Kipuka Puaulu in HVNP has increased remarkably with the protection the area has had from cattle, pigs and goats in the last 45 years.

The leaves are dark green, alternate and extremely variable in size from about 3" (7.5cm) long on a suppressed plant to 6 or 8" (15 to 20cm) long on vigorous plants. The leaves have prominent palmate veins, often quite red in color, are finely toothed and rough to the touch. Tiny green flowers are borne in tight, axillary clusters attached closely to the branches. The fruit is waxy white, insipid, somewhat fleshy, growing as a small irregular ball tightly attached to the limbs. Twigs are long and drooping, brown and rather rough, with wooly grey hairs. The bark of larger stems is light brown, smooth and fibrous. Wood is pinkish brown, turning brown with age. Texture is very coarse, grain straight, density low, very soft, with plain figure. Vessels are few and scattered and the rays are very fine. Stability and workability are very poor. Thus the wood is virtually worthless. The value of the plant lay in use of its bark in making TAPA cloth. It was second only to WAUKE in popularity. The fruits were said to have been given to children as a laxative.[1]

HNP

OLONA   **Touchardia latifolia** Guad.

OLONA is a shrub or small tree 4 to 8' (1.25 to 2.5m) tall, slender and branched. It occurs in the wet forest in gulches and depressions. It is endemic and occurs on all the islands sparingly. Hillebrand found it "by no means common."

Large alternate leaves are pointed at both ends, 8 to 10" (20 to 25cm) long and 3 to 5" (8 to 12cm) wide, making it the largest leaved member of the Nettle family in Hawaii. They are light green on both sides with heavy red midrib and many prominent pinnate veins. The leaf petiole is short. Flowers are borne on globular receptacles attached to axils of leaves on pedicles as long as or longer than the globe. Fruits are orange colored when

[1] See:
Degener, PHNP, pp. 130-143, gives a very good account of TAPA making.
Neal, p. 318.
Hillebrand, p. 413.
Carlquist, p. 316.
Rock, p. 123.
St. John, p. 144.

1. Mamake shrubs border an opening in Ohia forest. Kipuka, Puaulu, HVNP.

2. Mamake tree, Kipuka Puaulu, HVNP.

3. Leaf and fruit of Mamake, P. hawaiiensis.

[2] See:
Neal, p. 319.
Hillebrand, p. 415.
St. John, p. 144.

[3] See:
Hillebrand, p. 410.
Rock, p. 119.
Carlquist, p. 317.
Neal, p. 144.

ripe. Long slender twigs are roughened by leaf scars. Bark on older stems is thin and smooth. No wood was seen to describe. The plants are too scarce to make it an important component of the forest.

Hawaiians used the fibers in making fish nets and carrying nets. These fibers are said to be the toughest in the world for their weight and were also prized for making fish lines, mesh for feather capes or helmets, strangling cords, waist bands for chiefs and for sewing TAPA cloth. Early whalers sought it for harpoon lines.[2]

1. Olona shrub in forest near Hilo, Hawaii.
2. Olona, T. latifolia, showing leaf detail.
3. Small Opuhe suppressed by Ti on left, Pilo on right, Ohia behind. Kipuka Puaulu, HVNP.
4. Bark detail of Opuhe.
5. Leaves of Opuhe, U. sandwicensis.

HVNP Kipuka Puaulu
HNP

OPUHE   **Urera sandwicensis** Wedd.

This species of OPUHE, and *U. mollis* are both endemic to the island of Hawaii. *U. kauaiensis* Rock is endemic to Kauai. The varieties were not seen. OPUHE on Hawaii occurs as a tree but is generally considered to be a shrub on the other islands. The species *U. glabra* is endemic to all the islands and *U. kaalae* wawra is endemic on Oahu.

This description applies to *U. sandwicensis*. OPUHE may be a tree 35' (11m) tall and with trunk 12" (31.5cm) in diameter. The opposite leaves, 3 to 6" (7.5 to 15cm) long, are short stemmed, pointed at both ends, and light green, smooth above, rough below with heavy pinnate veins impressed on the upper surface and conspicuous below. Flowers are borne in thick clusters in the leaf axils and along the stem, male on one tree, female on another. The small fruits are orange in color. New twigs are moderately heavy, green and smooth, quite long, aging to medium brown with prominent leaf scars. Sap is milky, bark on older trunks is smooth and fibrous. The fibers were used in much the same way as OLONA but were not considered as good.

Wood is light straw colored, coarse, straight grained, very light weight and soft. Figure is plain. Very large vessels are scattered, no rays are visible. The wood shrinks badly and workability is very poor.[3]

SANDALWOOD FAMILY Santalaceae

The Sandalwood family is represented by two genera and all the native species are endemic with the possible exception of *Santalum salicifolium*. The genus *Exocarpus* is represented by three species and the genus *Santalum* by seven species, five varieties and two forms.

Key to the Genera

Leaves mostly rudimentary .... **Exocarpus** Labill.
Leaves all perfect .... **Santalum** L.

The species of *Exocarpus* are as follows:

E. gaudichaudii A.DC.	end. H.I.
E. luteolus Forbes	end. Kauai
E. menziesii Stauffer	end. Lanai, Hawaii

The species of *Santalum* as listed by St. John are as follows:

Santalum L., 1753. 'Iliahi
  album L., 1753. N:326. White sandalwood. cult. Indonesia. 1932
  ellipticum Gaud., 1829, var. **ellipticum**, f. **ellipticum**. R:131. 'Ili-ahi-a-lo'e, coast sandalwood. end. H.I.
    Freycinetianum Gaud., var. *ellipticum* (Gaud.) Gray, 1860. H:390.
    Freycinetianum Gaud., var. *xunwRUM* Hbd., 1888. H:389.
    cuneatum (Hbd.) Rock, 1916.
    cuneatum (Hbd.) Rock, var. *gracilius* (Skottsb.) Deg., 1937 D:fam.100, 10/4/37.
    cuneatum (Hbd.) Rock, F. *gracilius* Skottsb., 1927.
    ellipticum Gaud., var. *gracilius* (Skottsb.) Deg., 1937 D:fam.100, 10/4/37.
      f. **annectens** Deg., 1937. D:fam. 100, 10/4/37 end. Hawaii
      f. **physophora** Deg., 1937. D:fam 100, 10/4/37 end. Oahu
    var. **latifolium** (Gray) Fosb., 1962 end. Hawaii
      Freycinetianum Gaud. var. *latifolium* Gray, 1860. H:389; R:129.
    var. **littorale** (Hbd.) Skottsb., 1927. end. Laysan, Oahu
      Freycinetianum Gaud. var. *littorale* Hbd., 1888. H:390; R:129.
      littorale (Hbd.) Rock, 1916.
      cuneatum (Hbd.) Rock, var. *laysanicum* Rock, 1916.
    var. **luteum** (Rock) Deg., 1937. D:fam. 100, 10/4/37 end. Hawaii
      Pilgeri Rock, var. *luteum* Rock, 1916.
      Pilgeri Rock, 1916.
  Freycinetianum Gaud., 1829, var. **Freycinetianum**. H:389; R:127; D:fam. 100,8/6/37. 'Ili-ahi, la'au'ala, Freycinet sandalwood. end. Oahu
    var. **longifolium** (Meurisse) Deg., 1937. D:fam. 100, 8/6/37. end. Oahu
      longifolium Meurisse, 1892.
  haleakalae Hbd., 1888. H:390; R:133; D:fam. 100, 2/10/40. 'Ili-ahi, Haleakala sandalwood end. e. Maui
  lanaiense (Rock) Rock 1916 end. Lanai
    Freycinetianum Gaud., var. *lanaiense* Rock, 1913. R:129.
  paniculatum H&A, 1832 end. Hawaii
  pyrularium Gray, 1860, var. **pyrularium**. H:390; R:133; D:fam. 100, 10/26/56. Kauai sandalwood end. Kauai
    var. **sphaerolithos** Skottsb., 1944 end. Kauai
  salicifolium Meurisse, 1892 dubious end.?

All the scented sandalwoods were used to give a pleasant scent to TAPA cloth. The stands of trees were largely decimated during the time of the sandalwood trade with China in the years 1778 to 1822 or later. Degener in *Plants of Hawaii National Park* gives a good account of exploitation.

HVNP Mauna Loa Strip 7200'

HEAU Exocarpus menziesii Stauffer

HEAU occurs as a shrub or small tree 10 to 12' (3 to 3.75m) tall with upright branches. It has been found as a small shrub in Hawaii Volcanoes National Park high on the slopes of Mauna Loa at 7200' (2268m) and in Kau

[1] See:
Hillebrand, p. 391.
St. John, P. 148.
Carlquist, p. 295.

[2] See:
St. John, p. 148.

1. *Heau, E. menziesii*, showing leafy and leafless growth form on one twig and one fruit in upper left twig. South Kona, Hawaii.

2. Large sandalwood, *S. ellipticum v. luteum*, North Kona, Hawaii. Rock photo.

in the dry OHIA forest at about 1500' (470m). It is not common but Carlquist found it to be frequent on Hualalai Mountain on Hawaii. However, he determined the ones he saw to be *E. gaudichaudii*.

HEAU is easily recognized because most of its foliage is rudimentary and resembles mistletoe. The terminal green, scale-like leaves look like the ends of twigs that have lost their leaves. Lower down on the branch are a few leaves .5 x 2" (1 x 5cm) that look like widened twigs or the phyllodes of some acacias. These leaves are light yellowish-green, alternate, with numerous palmately arranged veins. The very small greenish flowers are borne on spikelets. Small, colorful fruits look somewhat like acorns, with a white or greenish nut immersed part way into the bulbous, fleshy red cup or perigone which is about .375" (1cm) in diameter. The twigs are yellowish-green in the new growth, aging to yellowish-brown and smooth. The bark on 3" (7.5cm) stems is very rough and warty, dark grey to black.

Wood is light pinkish tan streaked with light brown. It is fine textured, with close grain, dense and quite hard. Figure is mild, the vessels are small, numerous, and the rays are numerous but barely visible with a land lens. Since I had only a limb to examine I could not determine the stability or workability except that the grain tears under a plane.

Since this plant has a native name it is evident that it was recognized by the Hawaiians but no use for it has been recorded. The straight, slender growth form, together with the hardness and strength of the wood suggests that it would make good spears.

HEAU is generally found on high dry ridges or in other parts of the dry forest where it is scarce.[1]

ILIAHI **Santalum ellipticum** var. **luteum** (Rock) Deg.
Syn.: **S. pilgeri**

From the study of the literature it is obvious that it is difficult to give a specific sandalwood tree the proper scientific name. However, this variety is generally accepted to be the one growing in the Kau and Kona districts of Hawaii. In the vicinity of Honomolino, Kau it forms a large tree and is an important component of the mature OHIA forest. However, Degener pointed out to the author that there is gradation between the different sandalwoods on Hawaii through the varieties of *S. ellipticum* to *S. paniculatum*.

Leaves are yellowish-green and shiny above, pale green below, thick and pinnately veined. They are 2 to 3.5" (5 to 9cm) long by 1 to 2" (2.5 to 5cm) wide on a .5" (1.2cm) petiole. Flowers are greenish or yellowish, borne in panicles terminally or in the axils of leaves. Fruit is drupe-like with a subapical ring, ovary half superior, .25" (.6cm) in diameter and .375" (1cm) long. A single seed is found inside a shell, purplish-black when ripe. Twigs stout, grey or reddish, prominent scars make the branch rough. The bark is rough, broken into plates, with large white patches showing on larger trunks. Wood is golden tan to light brown with nearly white sapwood, texture fine, figure streaked, grain close, density high and hard. The numerous medium sized open vessels are scattered uniformly throughout the wood, rays are faint and closely spaced. The wood has good stability with little shrinkage and moderately good workability. It takes a high polish readily.

The largest tree was found on Honomolino Ranch and measured 7'8" (2.4m) in circumference, 65' (20m) tall and had a crown spread of 48' (15m). Sandalwood constitutes a conspicuous part of the forest in this moderately dry area of old, mature OHIA forest that has developed on ancient lava flows. Prize trees of many other species have been found in this same environment as contrasted with the almost pure stand of OHIA on the more recent lava flows nearby.[2]

HVNP Kilauea

ILI'AHI **Santalum paniculatum** H&A

This ILI'AHI occurs in the OHIA forest in the vicinity of Kilauea Volcano on Hawaii. It is generally a rather small tree up to 20' (6m) tall and wide spreading with trunk to 12" (31cm) in diameter. It is fairly abundant in the dryer phase of the forest and is much more noticeable now than it was 40 years ago, due probably to its protection from domestic stock grazing.

The opposite leaves are yellowish-green and dull above, pale beneath and glaucous, not as wide as long, with tip pointed or round, pinnate veins show faintly on the underside, midrib moderately depressed. The small, 4-parted greenish flowers are numerous in terminal and axillary panicles. Drupe-like fruit has a subapical ring very near the apex. Twigs are red to reddish brown, rough and rather stout. Bark is rough on larger trunks. Wood is probably similar to other island sandalwood but no piece could be cut for comparison in HVNP where the species grows.[3]

[3] See:
St. John, p. 149.
Carlquist, p. 278-285.
Degener, PHNP, p. 142-148. *Good description of sandalwood parasiteism and early harvest.*

[4] See:
Hillebrand, p. 390.
Rock, p. 133.
St. John, 149.

3.

1.

2.

4.

1. Bark detail, Iliahi, Central Hawaii.
2. Leaves and terminal fruits, Iliahi, S. pyrulum, Kokee, Kauai.
3. Leaves, flowers and fruit, Iliahi, S. paniculatum, HVNP.
4. Small Iliahi tree suppressed in Ohia forest, HVNP.
5. Large Iliahi, Central Hawaii.

ILI'AHI **Santalum pyrularium** Gray
Kauai Sandalwood

This ILI'AHI is endemic to the island of Kauai where trees 15 to 20' (4.7 to 6.3m) tall may be found along the moderately dry Milolii ridge in the vicinity of Kokee. It is not common here.

Leaves are larger and more slender than other species, about 1" (2.5cm) wide and 3" (7.5cm) long, dull green, glossy above, glaucous below with thin reddish petioles on new growth. Flowers are borne in terminal or axillary clusters, a few dull red to purplish flowers in each cluster. Rough drupe-like fruits are the largest of the sandalwoods, about 1" (2.5cm) long, obovoid with annulus near apex, reddish-purple to purplish-black when ripe. Twigs brown and smooth, bark smooth with reddish lines. No wood was examined.[4]

5.

[5] See:
Carlquist, p. 362-63.
Rock, p. 133.
Hillebrand, p. 390.
St. John, p. 149.

[6] See:
Rock, p. 129.
St. John, p. 149.

HNP Along road to summit

ILI'AHI   **Santalum haleakalae** Hbd.
Haleakala sandalwood

Haleakala sandalwood grows high on the slopes of Haleakala on the island of Maui in Haleakala National Park. It is a shrub or small tree to 25' (8m) tall, and it grows among the PUKIAWE, AALII and Raillardia bushes.

The leaves are thick, dull green, 1 to 2" (3 to 5cm) long by 1 to 1.25" (2.5 to 3 cm) broad on petioles about .25 to .375" (.4 to .6cm) long, with blunt or rounded tips. The bright scarlet flowers are borne in densely crowded clusters at or near the ends of the twigs. The outer coating of the drupe-like fruit is bright red and the seed is purplish-black, glaucous and juicy. Twigs are stiff and reddish. Rock found the wood of trees grown at high altitude to be exceedingly fragrant and dark yellowish-brown in color. I did not have access to a; piece for more complete description.

This ILI'AHI is not common, at least along the park entrance road, but it is very conspicuous because of the bright red flowers and fruits.[5]

1. Flowers and leaves of Iliahi, S. haleakalae. Rock photo.

2. Iliahi; Haleakala Sandalwood tree in background. Haleakala NP, Maui.

ILI'AHI   **Santalum lanaiense** (Rock) Rock
Lanai Sandalwood

This sandalwood, endemic to Lanai, is said by Rock to be a medium sized tree with stiff, gnarled branches. It has the largest leaves of the genus, dark green above, bright glaucous below with red veins. Flowers are borne in very small axillary panicles, one or two on a minute pedicle. Individual flowers are large and bright red. Fruits not seen.[6]

GOOSEFOOT FAMILY   Chenopodiaceae

The goosefoot family is represented in Hawaii by only one genus of native woody shrubs, *Chenopodium*. St. John lists the species as follows:

Chenopodium oahuense var. **oahuense** f. **oahuense**	end. H.I.
f. **macrospermum**	end. H.I.
f. **microspermum**	end. H.I.
var. **discosperma** Fosb.	end. e. Molokai
pekeloi Deg.	end. e. Molokai

AHEAHEA

Chenopodium oahuense (Meyer) Aellen.
Syn.: **C. sandwicheum** Moq.

All of the woody AHEAHEAs are endemic to the Hawaiian islands. The species *C. oahuense* occurs as a shrub generally, but trees 12 to 15' (3.8 to 4.7m) tall have been found on Mauna Kea by Colonel Bryan. The shrub covers vast areas of the high plateau in the triangle between Mauna Loa, Mauna Kea and Hualalai on the island of Hawaii. It is found less extensively on all the other islands except possibly Molokai which has a separate variety. It is a low shrub in coastal areas.

Leaves are small, somewhat triangular, broad as long, with notches on the broad top, covered generally with a whitish, mealy pubescence that gives the whole plant a light green or whitish appearance; strong smelling when crushed. The petiole is shorter than the leaf blade, which is about 1" (2.3cm) long. Tiny flowers are borne along the branches of terminal panicles, 2 to 3" (5 to 7.5cm) long and slender. The fine seeds are light brown, not shiny, thickly clustered. Twigs are light greenish-brown, striate and slender. The newest growth is green. As the bark ages, it becomes whitish-grey in color.

Wood is light straw colored, generally badly infested with worms. Texture coarse, grain straight, figure plain, density medium and soft. Wood is strongly ring porous, rays are very fine. Stability is poor and one is not likely to find pieces large enough to work. This wood is really not a wood in the true sense but more like a woody vegetable with bands of wood alternating with rings of soft tissue like a garden beet.

This plant seems to have found an optimum environment on the island of Hawaii where it shares such a large area with NAIO and MAMANI trees. It is not quick to establish itself on the newer lava flows of the area but covers the older flows quite thickly.

2. *Leaves and terminal seed heads of Aheahea.*

3. *Dr. Harold L. Lyon by Aheahea tree, Pohakaloa, 1924. Bryan photo.*

1. *Lillian Lamb by large Aheahea, C. sandwichum. Central Hawaii.*

[1] See:
Hillebrand, p. 374.
Neal, p. 332.
Rock, p. 135.
St. John, pp. 152-53.

AMARANTH FAMILY

Amaranthaceae

Two genera of woody amaranths that may reach tree size are found, both endemic to the Hawaiian Islands. *Charpentiera* is represented by three species and *Nototrichum* by three species and 23 varieties according to St. John.

Key to the Genera

Flowers in long, thread-like paniculate spikes, leaves large and
    glossy.. **Charpentiera** Gaud.
Flowers in short terminal or axillary spikes, leaves small and covered
    with grey tomentum or not .... **Nototrichum** Hbd.

Key to the Species of *Charpentiera*

Short almost erect inflorescence
    Leaves long elliptical-lanceolate .... **C. elliptica** (Hbd.) Heller
        end. Kauai, Maui

Long drooping inflorescence
    Leaves ovate, broad at base .... **C. ovata** Gaud.
        end. H.I.
    Leaves obovate, contracted at the base .... **C. obovata** Gaud.
        end. H.I.

1. Bark of Papala.

2. Papala, *Charpentiera obovata*, leaves and long inflorescence.

HVNP Kipuka puaulu

PAPALA   **Charpentiera obovata** Guad.

PAPALA is plentiful in many areas of Hawaii and is found on the other islands also. It becomes a moderate sized tree 15 to 35' (4.75 to 11m) tall and up to 2.5' (.8m) in diameter. Such a large tree was seen at Puuwaawaa, Hawaii.

The large alternate leaves are obovate, wider above the middle, acutely pointed at base but rounded at apex, smooth and glossy green. Petiole is 1 to 2" (2.5 to 5cm) long and red, midrib prominent and veins pinnate. Very tiny red flowers occur along the branches of fine string-like, red, drooping panicles 8 to 20" (20 to 50cm) long or longer. The panicles are borne in axils of leaves near ends of branches. Fruit is tiny, enclosed or partly excerted. Twigs are dark green aging soon to scaly brown, slender. Bark is thin, smooth and light brown. Wood is extremely light, soft and fibrous. In fact it was so light that it was used in a fireworks display wherein a person standing on top of a cliff could ignite the sticks and hurl them over. The upcoming breeze would keep the burning brands in mid-air.

PAPALA appears in the OHIA forest rather late in succession and does not become a conspicuous component.[1]

KULUI	**Nototrichum** Hbd.

Since so many of the KULUIs are listed as extinct or endangered they are listed here just as they are listed by St. John with the addition of status.

[2] See:
Hillbrand, p. 372.
Rock, p. 141.
St. John, p. 153.
Degener, p. 112 FF.: *Many sheets under family.*

Nototrichum
**	**humile** var. **humile**	end. Oahu
**	var. **parvifolium**	end. Oahu
**	var. **subrhomboideum**	end. Oahu
	sandwicense var. **sandwicense**	end. Hawaii
**	var. **decipiens**	end. Kauai
***	var. **dubium**	end. e. Maui
***	var. **forbesi**	end. Molokai
**	var. **helleri**	end. Kauai
	var. **kavaiense**	end. Kauai
**	var. **kolekolense**	end. Molokai
***	var. **lanaiense**	end. Lanai, e. Maui
**	var. **lanceolatum**	end. Hawaii
***	var. **latifolium**	end. Lanai
**	var. **leptopodum**	end. e. Maui
**	var. **longispicatum**	end. Molokai, w. Maui
**	var. **macrophyllum**	end. Hawaii
**	var. **mauiense**	end. w. Maui
	var. **niihauense**	end. Niihau
**	var. **olokeleanum**	end. Kauai
***	var. **pulchelloides**	end. Molokai
***	var. **pulchellum**	end. Molokai
***	var. **subcordatum**	end. Molokai, Maui, Hawaii
***	var. **syringifolium**	end. H.I. indefinite locality
**	**viride** var. **viride**	end. Kauai
**	var. **oblongifolium**	end. Kauai
**	var. **subtruncatum**	end. Oahu

1. *Kului, N. sandwicense, with light silvery leaves. North Kona, Hawaii.*

HVNP Poliokeawe Pali area

KULUI	**Nototrichum sandwicense** (Gray in Mann) Hbd.

The KULUI described here is probably *N. sandwicense* var. *sanwicense* as it is the only one on the island of Hawaii not listed as endangered and is plentiful in the Kona district. It is a shrub or small tree 15 to 20' (4.7 to 6.3m) tall. It is very noticeable along the upper belt highway near Huehue due to its silvery grey color.

The opposite leaves are 2 to 3" (5 to 7.5cm) long and .75 to 1.5" (.8 to 4.6cm) wide, covered with a silvery grey tomentum. The flowers are borne in small spikes that droop from the ends of branchlets 1.5 to 2" (3.6 to 5cm) long. Seeds are small. Twigs are somewhat angular, covered with silvery tomentum to pale brown. Bark on 2" (5cm) trunks is light grey mottled in a rough diamond pattern. Wood is light tan in color, very coarse texture, coarse grain, very soft and light weight. Vessels are large and numerous in festooned clusters in annular arrangement. Rays are not visible with 10 power hand lens. Stability and workability are both poor.

Although this plant is conspicuous locally, it does not occur over large enough areas to be an important component of the Hawaiian forest.[2]

2. *Leaves and terminal flowers of Kului.*

[1] See:
Hillebrand, p. 369.
Rock, p. 147.
St. John, p. 154.

1. *Papala Kepau, P. brunoniana,* large glossy leaves and very sticky fruit. HVNP.

2. *Papala Kepau bark detail.*

3. *Lillian Lamb by Papala Kepau tree in small Kipuka.* HVNP.

FOUR-O-CLOCK FAMILY — Nyctaginaceae

The four-o-clock family is represented in Hawaii by one genus of trees, *Pisonia*, with three species which St. John lists as follows:

Pisonia
   brunoniana Endl.   end. Oahu, Lanai, Maui, Hawaii
   sandwicensis Hbd.   end. H.I.
   umbellifera (JR&G Forst)   seem end. Kauai, Oahu, Maui

Key to the Species of *Pisonia* from Rock

Leaves wedge shaped, narrow at base
   Inflorescence a terminal, loose umbel or contracted panicle **P. umbellifera**
Leaves broad at base, inflorescence a globose head . . . . **P. sandwicensis**
Leaves elliptical oblong, inflorescence a loose open panicle . . . . **P. brunoniana**

HVNP Kipuka Puaulu
HNP

PAPALA KEPAU   **Pisonia brunoniana** Endl.
                                                    Syn.: **P. inermis** Forst

PAPALA KEPAU is generally a small tree 15 to 18' (4.7 to 5.6m) tall but under prime environmental conditions may reach a height of 50' (15.75m). It is fairly abundant and reaches its greatest size in the Kau District of Hawaii on the Hoomau Ranch near Honomolino. Elsewhere it is only an occasional tree.

Leaves are opposite to whorled, 2" (5cm) wide by 6" (15cm) or more long, elliptical-oblong, pointed at the base and tip, glossy green. Flowers are borne in large, open, terminal clusters of 20 or more. Corolla tube is about .25" (.6cm) long, the five greenish-white petals are united. Each flower is only about .25" (.6cm) in diameter. Fruit grows in large open loosely branched panicles, each fruit about 1 to 1.5" (2.5 to 4cm) long, slender and covered with a sticky substance called KEPAU, thus this word in the tree name. The stout, smooth limbs are green, turning greenish brown with age. Bark is light brown and smooth even on trunks 12' (31cm) in diameter.

Wood is very light tan to light yellow in color, texture very coarse, figure striated, grain open and straight. The vessels are few, large and scattered, rays are very fine and closely spaced, visible under 10x lens. Stability is very poor as is workability. This is another case of a vegetable having become woody rather than true wood.

PAPALA KEPAU appears late in succession in openings in mature OHIA forest and is not a conspicuous component of the forest.

Hawaiians used the fruits to produce bird lime, sticky substance spread on tree limbs to catch birds from which to pluck feathers for use in making feather capes.

L.W. Bryan's big tree, measured on Hoomau Ranch, is 6'3" (2m) in circumference, 50' (16m) tall, with crown spread of 31' (10m).[1]

LAUREL FAMILY — Lauraceae

HOLIA or HOLIO   **Cryptocarya manni** Hbd.
                                                    C. oahuensis (Deg) Fosb.
                                         Syn.: **C manni** var. **oahunsis** Deg.

The species *C. manni* is endemic to Kauai and *C. oahuensis* to Oahu. *C. manni* is fairly common in the dryer forests of Kauai at elevations from 2000 to 4000' (630 to 1200m) where it may be seen at Kokee. *C. oahuensis* is rare in the forests of the Waianae Range of Oahu.

HOLIO is generally 20 to 30' (6 to 9m) tall and may reach 12" (31.5cm) in diameter. The leaves are alternate, thick, oblong, about 4" (10cm) long by 2" (5cm) wide, blunt at both ends, attached by a short petiole. Small flowers are borne in small axillary panicles of a few flowers each. Fruit is a drupe, ovoid, globose, bluish-black, 12-ribbed, about .5" (1.1cm) in diameter, crowned by the remains of the perianth. Twigs are somewhat angular. Bark is dark brown and slightly pebbly on a 3" (7.5cm) stem.

Wood is light tan in color, texture fine, figure plain, grain close, density moderately high and soft. Vessels and rays are so fine as to be only barely visible with a 10x lens. The rays are crossed at right angles by very faint lines that divide the end grain into small squares. Stability is good but workability is low due to the long fibers that make sawing difficult. Wood has a soft pith about .125" (.2cm) in diameter.

HOLIO is found in mature mixed forest indicating that it belongs with plants that represent near climax stage of succession. Rock did not find any Hawaiian use of the tree and even the name was not widely known.[1]

[1] See:
Hillebrand, p. 382.
Rock, p. 149.
St. John, p. 163.

SAXIFRAGE FAMILY — **Saxifragaceae**

In the Hawaiian Islands this family is represented by one endemic genus, *Broussaisia*, whose species are shrubs or small trees. St. John has combined the two species *B. arguta* and *B. pellucida* into *B. arguta* with var. *pellucida* and three forms. Rock had considered that there were two species and divided them on the basis that the leaves of *B. arguta* are opposite and the petals bluish-green while in *B. pellucida* the leaves are ternate and the petals reddish. These plants are a conspicuous part of older OHIA forests growing in the wetter districts.

Nomenclature of Broussaisia as given by St. John:

Broussaisia Arguta Gaud. var. **arguta**, f. **arguta** — end. Kauai to Maui
    f. **glabra** Fosb. — end. Kauai
    f. **ternatea** St. John — end. H.I.
  var. **pellucida** (Gaud) Fosb.
    f. **pellucida** — end. Kauai, Molokai, Maui, Hawaii
    f. **oppositifolia** — end. Kauai, Lanai, Maui

[1] See:
Hillebrand, p. 120.
Rock, p. 151.
Carlquist, p. 120.
St. John, p. 169.

HVNP Kilauea
HNP

KANAWAO or PUAHANUI — **Broussaisia arguta** Gaud.

KANAWAO, the preferred name, generally occurs as a low shrub whose resemblance to garden hydrangeas is striking. It may be a tree under the best environmental conditions.

Leaves may be ternate or opposite, depending on the variety in question, long and broad, 2.5" x 6" (4 x 15cm), rough to the touch, dark green, with very prominent midrib and prominent pinnate veins. The leaf edges are finely toothed. The petiole is 1" (2.5cm) long, fleshy and whitish. Flowers occur in dense rounded heads, but the individual florets are small. Dark red to black berries are borne in clusters up to 5" (13cm) in diameter, near the ends of the branches. Berries, attached by a short, red, fleshy stem, are .25" (.6cm) in diameter and filled with a dryish pulp. They are said to have been freely eaten by native birds. Twigs are stout, up to .5" (1.2cm) in diameter, new growth rusty green, older growth brown, showing parallel lines. Bark is smooth and light brown. Wood as a large pulp-filled pith and does not ordinarily occur in sizes large enough to be useful.[1]

1. *Puahanui or Kanawao, B. arguta, leaves and seed head. Hawaii.*

1. Hoawa flower detail.

PITTOSPORUM FAMILY — Pittosporaceae

This family has only one genus in Hawaii, *Pittosporum*. It is represented by 23 endemic species, 35 varieties and four forms for a total of 62 taxa. This is a very confusing array and it makes it difficult to determine with which taxa one may be dealing. It helps to know which species one may expect to find on any one island. For this reason the species are listed with the island or islands on which found.

Nomenclature for the genus *Pittosporum* as given by St. John:

	P. acuminatum Mann var. **acuminatum**	end. Kauai
	var. **degeneri**	end. Kauai
**	var. **leptopodum**	end. Kauai
**	var. **magnifolium**	end. Kauai
**	var. **waimeanum**	end. Kauai
	acutisepalum (Hbd.) Sherff	end. Oahu, Kauai
*	**amplectans** Sherff	end. Hawaii
*	**argentifolium** Sherff var. **argentifolium**	end. e. Maui
	var. **rockii**	end. e. & w. Maui
**	var. **sessile**	end. e. Maui
***	**cauliflorum** Mann var. **cauliflorum**	end. Oahu
**	var. **cladanthoides**	end. Oahu
	var. **fulvum**	end. Oahu
**	var. **pedicellatum**	end. Oahu
	cladanthum Sherff var. **cladanthum**	end. Oahu
**	var. **gracilipes**	end. Lanai
	var. **reticulatum**	end. Oahu
	confertifolium Gray var. **confertifolium**	end. e. & w. Maui, Hawaii
**	var. **longipes**	end. w. Maui
	var. **mannii**	end. Oahu, Lanai, Maui, Hawaii
**	var. **microphyllum**	end. Lanai
	dolosum Sherff var. **dolosum**	end. Oahu
	var. **aquilonium**	end. Oahu
	flocculosum Sherff var.	end. Oahu, Kauai?
	forbesii Sherff	end. Molokai
	gayanum Rock var. **gayanum**	end. Kauai
	var. **skottsbergii**	end. Kauai
	var. **waialealae**	end. Kauai
	glabrum H&A var. **glabrum**	end. Oahu
***	var. **glomeratum**	end. Oahu
***	var. **glomeratum**	end. Oahu
**	var. **entermedium**	**end. Oahu**
	var. **spathulatum**	
	forma **spathulatum**	end. Oahu, Molokai
	forma **hypoleium**	end. Oahu
	forma **subcondidum**	end. Molokai
*	**halophiloides** Sherff	end. Lanai
*	**halophilum** Rock	end. Molokai
	hawaiiensis Hbd.	end. Hawaii
**	**helleri** Sherff	end. Kauai
**	**hosmeri** Rock var. **hosmeri**	end. Hawaii
	var. **longifolium**	end. Hawaii
***	var. **saint-johnii**	end. Hawaii
	insigne Hbd. var. **insigne**	e. & w. Maui
	var. **fosbergii**	
	forma **fosbergii**	end. Molokai
	forma **pentinax**	end. Molokai
	var. **hillerbrandii**	end. Molokai
	var. **hydgatei**	end. e. & w. Maui
**	var. **micranthum**	end. e. Maui
	var. **pelekunuanum**	end. Molokai
*	**kahananum** Sherff	end. Oahu
	kauaiensis Hbd. var. **kauaiensis**	end. Kauai

2. Hoawa tree. HVNP.

	var. **phaeocarpum**	end. Kauai
***	var. **repens**	end. Kauai
	napaliense Sherff	end. Kauai
	sulcatum Sherff var. **sulcatum**	end. Oahu, Molokai
	var. **remyi**	end. Oahu
	var. **rumicifolium**	
	forma **rumicifolium**	end. Oahu
	forma **tomentellum**	end. Oahu
	terminalioides Planch var. **terminalioides**	end. Oahu, Lanai, Maui, Hawaii
**	var. **lanaiense**	end. Lanai
	var. **macrocarpum**	end. Hawaii
*	var. **macropus**	end. Hawaii
**	var. **mauiense**	end. e. & w. Maui

[1] See:
Hillebrand, p. 26.
Rock, p. 171.
St. John, p. 170.

Degener, in *Flora Hawaiiensis*, Family 156 has published a key to the species and varieties, by the island upon which found. Keys depend largely on leaf size, presence or absence of tomentum and size of the fruit capsule. Keys also contain valuable information concerning the part of each island where the species or variety is found.

1. Hoawa, P. confertifolium, leaf and fruit. Hawaii.

HVNP Dry forest
HNP Dry area – Haleakala Crater

HOAWA   **Pittosporum confertifolium** Gray

HOAWA is a small tree 20 to 30' (6.3 to 9.5m) tall with stiff, ascending branches. It is generally found in dryer forest areas and occurs in one variety or another on all the islands except Kauai and Molokai. It is a minor component of the forest.

The alternate or whorled leaves are crowded toward the ends of the branches, the margins are rolled under. They are shiny and wrinkled above, undersides with light brown tomentum. Flowers in terminal, densely packed racemes, cream colored or white. Fruit is globose-ovoid, somewhat flattened, generally wrinkled or rough, seeds purple, closely packed in each cell. Wood is light yellow but cannot be further described as it was not collected.

Rock found the var. *mannii* common on Lanai. The Haleakala National Park var. is believed to be *mycrophyllum*.[1]

2. Hoawa, leaf and fruit detail. HVNP.

HVNP Kipuka Puaulu

HOAWA   **Pittosporum hosmeri** Rock

In addition to the specific variety of *P. hosmeri* varieties *P.h. longifolium* and *P.h. saint johnii* are listed as endemic to Hawaii. However, the latter is listed as extinct. Even so there is a herbarium specimen in the Hawaii Volcanoes National Park herbarium identified as *P. hosmeri* var. *saint johnii* and there is a tree growing in a small kipuka near Kipuka Puaulu that has leaves that appear to be the same as those of the herbarium specimen, the distinction being that the leaves of var. *saint johnii* are glabrous beneath in contrast to var. *longifolium* which has leaves rusty red with tomentum beneath. Thus it is considered that both varieties occur in Hawaii Volcanoes National Park.

The varieties of *P. hosmeri* occur as small trees 18 to 25' (5.7 to 7.9m) tall with long, slender, stiff and ascending branches. The leaves are long and slender, 2 to 6" (5 to 15cm), with margins slightly curled under. They are pointed at both ends, have a short petiole, are covered with tomentum on the underside or smooth as above stated. Flowers are creamy white, in small clusters along the branches, mostly below the leaves on short spurs. Corolla is cream colored, tube about .25" (.8 to 1cm) long, lobes are about .5" (1.25cm) in diameter, stamens as long as the tube. Seeds are arranged in two rows in the capsule which distinguishes it from other species in which the capsules are full

3. Hoawa, P. hosmeri, v. longifolia, bark detail. HVNP.

[2] See:
Rock, p. 163.
St. John, p. 171.

[3] See:
Hillebrand, p. 22.
Rock, p. 155.
St. John, p. 169.

[4] See:
Hillebrand, p. 24.
Rock, p. 159.
Degener, Flora Hawaiiensis, p. 156.

1. *Hoawa, P. terminaloides, leaf and flower detail. HVNP.*

2. *Hoawa, P. acuminatum, leaf detail. Kokee, Kauai.*

3. *Hoawa, P. terminaloides, tree. HVNP.*

of seeds. Capsules are about 1.5" (4cm) in diameter, globose and quite smooth. Inner lining is bright orange color. Pea-sized seeds are black. Slender new twigs are dark brownish-green, aging to light brown and smooth except for leaf scars. The bark on older trunks is mottled light grey and light brown, smooth. Wood of var. *longifolium* gathered by L.W. Bryan is light straw colored with fine black lines, texture very fine, figure plain, grain straight, density high and medium hard. Vessels are very fine and scattered and rays very fine. The unstable wood warps and would not be very workable. The author measured a vigorously growing *P.h. longifolium* to be 1'6" in circumference, 14' crown spread and 26' tall, and another tree believed to be *P.h. saint johnii* to be 1'8" in circumference, 12' crown spread and 24' tall, both in HVNP.

HOAWA is a tree of the mature OHIA forest. The trees are not numerous but are conspicuous where they appear.[2]

HOAWA   **Pittosporum acuminatum** Mann

There are four additional varieties of *P. acuminatum*, all endemic to Kauai. Since the key is based in part on flowers, which were not seen, it was not possible to identify the variety.

The trees seen were 18 to 20' (5.7 to 6.3m) tall, leaves long, slender and glabrous, dark green, tipped at the outer end and acute at the base with a short green petiole. Midrib prominent as are the pinnate veins. Flowers are said to be cream colored and quite beautiful, borne in axillary clusters. The capsules are deeply wrinkled, seeds black. Twigs light brown, smooth, except for large leaf scars. A 5" (13cm) trunk is very light greenish grey with thin, smooth bark, except for very small raised brown spots.

Wood is very light yellow, texture fine, grain straight and close, density quite high but wood quite soft. Vessels very numerous and very fine and fine rays closely spaced. There is very fine cross banding between the rays spaced about 10 times as far apart as the inter-ray distance. Wood warps and checks badly in curing but works fairly well.

Again HOAWA is seen to be a minor component of the mature mixed forest. Parts of the plant were used medicinally but no other use is recorded.[3]

HVNP Ainahou

HOAWA   **Pittosporum terminaloides** Planch ex Gray

There are three varieties of this species listed for the island of Hawaii but the specific one in Hawaii Volcanoes National Park has not been determined. The tree is staging a nice comeback in the Ainahou area since grazing has been eliminated. Many small trees and seedlings are seen. The varieties of *P. terminaloides* are found on all the islands except Kauai and Molokai.

Leaves are culstered near the ends of the branches, are relatively flat, long and slender, pointed at the base and blunt at apex, except for slight point at the tip, 1.5 to 4" (4 to 10 cm) long, midrib prominent. White flowers are borne in axillary clusters and along the trunk below the leaves. Fruits are .5 to .75" (1 to 2 cm) in diameter. Twigs light grey and somewhat rough, light grey bark covered with lenticles.

No wood was gathered. These trees are found growing in openings of the OHIA forest in an early successional stage.[4]

HOAWA   **Pittosporum gayanum** Rock

This HOAWA is found along Pihea trail in the Kokee area and on the slopes of Mt. Waialeale, Kauai, not abundant. Leaves are relatively small for HOAWA, clustered at branch ends, not so distinctly rolled under at the margins, narrow at the base, ending in a point at the tip, midrib, prominent, pinnate veins distinct. Green petiole is about 1" (2cm) long. Flowers are borne in clusters along the stem below the leaves. Fruits are dark green or brown, small for HOAWA, rough and borne tightly clasped to the stem, which is slender, nearly white and roughened by leaf scars.[5]

ROSE FAMILY **Rosaceae**

The only native genus of the rose family to become tree-like is *Osteomeles*, though generally it is a sprawling shrub.

HVNP Kilauea

ULEI or UULEI **Ostomeles anthyllidifolia** Lindl

ULEI is generally a freely branching shrub that may spread over an area of 100 square feet (10 square meters) or more. C.S. Judd noted that it grew as high as 14' (4.4m) in the Kona district of Hawaii and Col. Bryan found it as a tree in Kona and Kau. Hillebrand found it common on all islands to 3,000' (945m) elevation and it may now be seen, at least in Hawaii Volcanoes National Park, at an elevation of almost 4,000' (1260m) at Kipuka Puaulu picnic area.

Leaves are dark green above, silvery below because of silky hairs. The compound leaves have 9 to 19 .5" (1cm) long leaflets per leaf, 1.5" (3cm) long, leaflets pointed at apex. White flowers are small, single, wild rose-like, about .5" (1cm) in diameter, clustered at branch ends of new growth and have sweet aroma. Inedible fruits are whitish, .33" (1cm) in diameter with five small seeds. The pulp is sweetish. Twigs are long and slender, dark brown and smooth. Bark on 1" (2.5cm) stems is light brown and slightly roughened.

Wood is reddish brown with very fine texture, close straight grain, high density, very hard, strong and flexible. Very fine vessels and rays are barely visible with 14x lens. Wood warps but is workable in the round.

Hawaiians used ULEI in the round to form hoops for fish nets. Small bows were also made for shooting mice. Also the wood was good for OO, a tool for digging, TAPA mallets, UKEKE boards, back scratchers, bearing sticks and short tapered sticks or javelins used for playing the game of PAHEE. ULEI occurs quite early in the OHIA forest in dryer areas.[1]

[5] See:
St. John, p. 170.

[1] See:
Hillebrand, p. 119.
Neal, p. 387.
Carlquist, p. 296.
St. John, p. 173.

2. *Hoawa, P. gayanum*, leaves and small fruit. Kokee, Kauai.

1. *Ulei, O. anthyllidifolia*, leaf, flower and fruit. HVNP.

3. Ulei - notice bow-shaped branching growth habit.

[1] Hillebrand describes A. kauaiensis from Kauai, saying that the flowers occur in terminal racemes. Rock did not concur and merely mentioned it, page 177. St. John, however, concurred with Hillebrand. One problem for the field worker on Kauai is that a single tree often has both axillary and terminal racemes. Thus, I describe only A. koa.

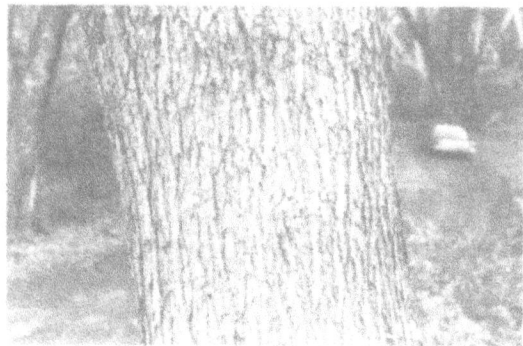

1. Koa bark.

2. Koa, A. koa, leaves and flower clusters.

3. Acacia Koa tree about 80 feet tall, with diameter of trunk about 4 feet; growing in Kipuka Puaulu near Volcano Kilauea, Hawaii; elevation 4000 feet. Rock photo.

PEA or LEGUME FAMILY — Leguminosae

The pea family is well represented in Hawaii by five native woody genera, all of which are trees. All the native species are endemic to the Hawaiian Islands except *Cassia gaudachaudii* which is endemic to Tahiti and Hawaii. The legume family is a very large one, spread worldwide with many species producing trees in tropical regions. Since it is so well represented in the tropics it is surprising that there are not more genera in Hawaii, but in general, the seeds are large and heavy and this may have limited their distribution.

Key to the Genera from Rock

Suborder **Papilionaceae**
  Corolla very irregular, the upper petal (standard) outside in the bud
    Stamens all united except the upper one free
      Leaves with three leaflets, standard much longer than
        keel wings, flowers red .... **Erythrina** L.
    Stamens all free, leaves compound, with many leaflets,
      flowers yellow .... **Sophora** L.
Suborder **Caesalpinicae**
  Corolla regular or nearly so, imbricate, the upper petal inside the bud
    Leaves twice pinnate, flowers red .... **Mesoneuron** Desf.
    Leaves once pinnate, flowers yellow .... **Cassia** (Tourn) L.
Suborder **Mimoseae**
  Corolla regular, petals small, valvate, leaves twice pinnate, flowers
    in heads or spikes .... **Acacia** Mill.

Key to the Species of *Acacia*

Flower heads in axillary racemes
  Pod flat, broad and straight .... **A. koa** Gray
  Pod narrow and curved .... **A. koaia Hbd.
Flower heads in terminal racemes .... **A. kauaiensis** Hbd.[1]

HVNP Kilauea and Mauna Loa strip
HNP

KOA — Acacia koa Gray

St. John lists *A. koa* var. *koa* as being endemic to the Hawaiian islands. He then lists *A. koa* var. *hawaiiensis* as endemic to Hawaii, *A koa* var. *lanaiensis* endemic to Lanai and *A koa* var. *waimeae* endemic to Kauai.

KOA is the second most abundant tree of the Hawaiian forests, second only to OHIA. KOA occurs in a broad band around the wetter sides of Mauna Loa, Mauna Kea, Hualalai and Kohala on the island of Hawaii, above the OHIA forest. It holds a similar position on the other islands. It appears to invade the OHIA forest in later stages of succession.

Leaves are of two kinds. On seedlings, and some new growth, may be found compound leaves, finely divided, twice pinnate. Later the petioles undergo a thickening growth process that produces sickle shaped phyllodia. In an intermediate stage, compound leaves may be found growing at the apex of phyllodia. Sickle shaped leaves may be up to 6" (15cm) long and 1" (2cm) wide, grey-green in color. Flowers are borne in dense round heads about .5 (1cm) in diameter, florets greenish-yellow. Heads may be borne axillary to the leaves or terminally. Fruit is a pod or 'legume' nearly straight, up to 7" (18cm) long by .75" (2cm) broad, flat, with up to 12 flat, black seeds per pod. Twigs are smooth, light brown, lightly zig-zag, and fine. Bark is moderately rough and somewhat scaly on large trees, light tan in color.

Wood is beautiful reddish brown, texture medium coarse, figure beautiful, varied from plain to striate, to banded, to fiddleback. Grain is fine and generally straight, density medium, hardness medium with harder streaks. Vessels are few, fine and scattered, rays very fine; very good stability, low shrinkage, fine workability. Fine large bowls can be turned from green wood and cured without cracking.

KOA grows to huge size in old growth stands. The largest one found by L.W. Bryan was 37'4" (11.7m) in circumference, 115' (36.25m) tall, with a crown spread of 148' (46.6m), on the land of Keauhou, Kau, Hawaii. Other very large ones can be seen in Kipuka Puaulu. In a dense forest the trees develop long, clear boles. These large boles were ideal for construction of the great Hawaiian war canoes. Degener, *PHNP*, pages 174-179 has a good account of canoe construction. KOA was also used for house timbers, bearing sticks, spears, paddles and KAHILI handles. When modern lumbering was introduced to the islands KOA became the wood of choice for furniture and many of the best museum pieces are made of KOA. Modern use includes paneling, cabinetry, plywood, furniture, and turning. Large bowls are popular now but KOA was not used for calabashes as it imparted a bad flavor to foods.

KOA forest is very sensitive to grazing by sheep, cattle, hogs and goats. KOA evolved in a land complete devoid of grazing animals. Thus it is not thorny as are so many of the legumes that evolved in continental areas subject to grazing and browsing. When grazing animals invade a KOA forest trampling kills out the older trees and young ones cannot survive the grazing. A classic example of a forest killed may be seen on the slope of Mauna Loa on the south side of the Mauna Loa Strip of Hawaii Volcanoes National Park. Forty years ago the forest within the Park was in equally bad condition but when livestock was excluded, KOAs sprouted resulting in beautiful stands of pole sized trees where before nothing but dead trees were to be found. At the present time the contrast between the live forest inside the park strip and the total lack of forest just across the fence on the outside can easily be seen as one stands at Uwekahuna in the Park and faces toward Mauna Loa. To the left is a large area of bright green grassland. To the right is the grey-green of the revitalized KOA forest. Thus the KOA forest can be regenerated if strict conservation measures are taken.

Another example of a different kind can be seen in the Honaunau Forest Reserve in the Kona district of the island of Hawaii. Here some rather large areas were bulldozed to clear away remnents of an old forest to make way for the planting of introduced tree species in hopes of growing valuable forest products. In some areas the best growth has been made by KOA that has come back naturally. It appears that KOA is not very shade tolerant and reproduces best in fairly open sunlight.[2]

Endangered

KOAIA or KOA OHA   **Acacia koaia** Hbd.

KOAIA is endemic to Molokai, Maui and Hawaii but is listed as endangered. There is a small grove on the slope of Kohala, north of the junction of the Kohala Road and the belt highway on Hawaii. The trees are small, gnarled and stunted looking, 20 to 25' (6.3 to 7.8m) tall with trunks 1' (31cm) in diameter.

The leaves and flowers are much the same as KOA. Pods are narrow and linear, about .33" (1cm) wide by 4 to 6" (10 to 15cm) long and curved. Twigs are slender, light brown and smooth. Bark is rough and corrugated.

Heart wood is medium reddish brown streaked with brown, sapwood is straw colored, texture medium fine, grain open and straight, density high and hardness greater than KOA. It has many small scattered vessels and very fine, numerous rays. It warps in curing but workability is good. The wood was used for fancy paddles, house timbers, TAPA beaters, spears,

[2] See:
Hillebrand, p. 112.
Rock, p. 173.
Neal, p. 409.
St. John, p. 176.
Degener, PHNP, p. 174-79.

1. Clump of Koaia trees, Kohala, Hawaii.

2. Koaia, A. koaia, leaf detail.

3. Trunk of Koaia.

[3] See:
Hillebrand, p. 113.
Rock, p. 177.
St. John, p. 176.

[4] See:
Hillebrand, p. 110.
Neal, p. 435.
Rock, p. 181.
Carlquist, p. 280.
St. John, p. 188.

calabashes and shark hooks, the latter made by tying knots in young shoots. The wood is now too scarce to use.[3]

Endangered

UHIUHI or KEA   **Mesoneuron kavaiensis** (Mann) Hbd.

UHIUHI is endemic to Kauai, Oahu, Maui and Hawaii. It is included on the endangered list as the whereabouts of only one or two trees are known on Kauai and Oahu but there are several on Hawaii near the Kaupulehu tract of the Pacific Tropical Botanical Garden. In this latter area it grows on such very rough old AA lava flows that there could be many more farther from the belt highway that have not been reported. The writer had known of two and found two more in the same area, one being a large, well developed specimen. The tree may grow to 25 or 30' (7.8 to 9.5m) tall and 1' (31cm) in diameter with a wide spreading crown but most of the known trees are old and deteriorating.

Leaves are 9 to 10" (23 to 25cm) long, twice compound or bipinnate, made up of 1 to 5 pairs of pinnae or branches, each with 4 to 8 pairs of leaflets. The common rachis is 4 to 6" (10 to 15cm) long, the pinnae 2 to 4" (5 to 10cm) long. Leaflets are .5 by 1.25" (1cm by 3cm) long, oblong, obtuse at both ends, attached closely to the pinnae, bright green upper side and lighter underneath. Flowers are arranged in loose, terminal and cone shaped racemes 4 to 7" (10 to 18cm) long, with numerous dark red flowers per raceme. Stamens extend .5 (1cm) or more beyond the petals. Pod or legume is 3 to 3.5" (7.5 to 8.5cm) long by 2" (5cm) wide, flattened, reddish and showy. The pods have a wing on one side and a circular disk on the stem above the pod. Pods have 2 to 4 flattened seeds, each about the size and shape of small lima beans. New growth of twigs is light reddish brown, aging to light brown and smooth. Bark is rough and scaly, dark grey to brown; wounds exude thick black sap.

Heart wood is almost black, sapwood is light straw colored, texture fine, grain fine and close, figure plain, very hard and so dense it sinks in water. Vessels are few, scattered, large, open. Rays are not visible at 10x. It is a very stable and durable wood with good workability and takes a high polish. Hawaiians used it for house timbers, sled runners, OO, TAPA beaters and spears.

The tree is a minor component of the complex mixed forest of the dry areas. It appears to have been driven nearly to extinction by grazing and repeated fires that burn through the area, so rough that effective fire control is exceedingly difficult. The tree is said to propogate readily from seed so it may be saved from extinction by planting it in protected places.[4]

1. Uhiuhi, M. kauaiense, North Kona, Hawaii. Rock photo.

2. Uhiuhi trunk.

3. Uhiuhi seed pod, leaves and inflorescence. North Kona, Hawaii.

HVNP Wahaulu

WILIWILI **Erythrina sandwicensis** Deg.
Hawaiian coral tree / Hawaiian erythrina Syn. **E. monosperma** Gaud.

[5] See:
Hillebrand, p. 99.
Neal, p. 458.
Rock, p. 189.
St. John, p. 185.

From the species St. John also recognizes the forms *alba* endemic to Oahu and *lutea* endemic to Molokai, Lanai and Maui, and the variety *luteosperma* endemic to Niihau. *Erythrina* is from a Greek word alluding to the color of the flowers. The species *E. americana* occurs in Mexico where it is called 'Colorín' for the colorful flowers. In New Mexico the species *E. flabelliformis* has scarlet beans that are very poisonous but no mention is made of poison in the Hawaiian species.

WILIWILI is a large three 20 to 30' (6.3 to 9.5m) tall and 3 to 4' (.9 to 1.1cm) in diameter, with stiff, gnarled branches and spreading crown. It inhabits dry lowland forest 1,500 to 2,000' (475 to 630m) elevation and is quite plentiful locally. There is a nice stand mixed with *Pleomele aurea* and *Reynoldsia sandwicensis* north of the Puuwaawaa Ranch gate on the belt highway, along the high fault scarp. On Maui a good number can be seen along the road between Ulapalakua and Kaupo, in an area called Auahi by Rock, associated with *Reynoldsia sandwicensis*, OHE OHE MAKAI.

Leaves are compound, with three ovate, leathery leaflets to a stem, similar to the leaves of the common string bean, but more angular. They are bright green and drop off in the later summer or late fall. Flowers appear in early spring before the leaves. Flowers are brick red to orange or white in clusters 3 to 8" (7.5 to 20 cm) long near the branch tips with several large flowers per cluster, very showy. Flowers are claw shaped so the tree or similar trees are sometimes called Tiger Claw. Seeds occur mostly one to the pod, thus the old name *monosperma* or one seed. They are bright red. Twigs are stout and rough with large leaf scars, green, aging to grey green, with strong, light colored lines. Bark is thin, smooth and yellow or yellowish-grey, sometimes with prickles.

Wood is white to light straw, texture coarse, grain straight, density said to be the lowest of any Hawaiian wood and very soft. Vessels are few, medium large and scattered. Rays are prominent with very fine cross banding. Stability poor and workability poor. The extreme light weight made this wood good for canoe outriggers and William Ellis found it being used for surf boards. In fact it is so light that according to legend the mighty KAPUNOHU hurled a spear through 800 WILIWILI trees with one thrust! Bryan's big tree is 3'6" (1m7cm) in circumference, 26' (8m) high, 31' (9.7m) crown spread.[5]

1. Wiliwili, *E. monosperma*, leaves, pod and flowers. HVNP.

KOLOMONA **Cassia gaudichaudi** H. & A.
HEUHIUHI
Solomon in all his Glory

The name KOLOMONA is the Hawaiianization of Solomon from the name 'Solomon in all his Glory,' sometimes given for this plant. KOLOMONA is usually a shrub or small tree up to 10' (3m) tall. It is endemic to all the islands and Tahiti. It occurs in the mixed forest on the Kona side of the island of Hawaii where one was found in the Pacific Tropical Botanical Garden tract known as Kaupulehu. Herbst reported to have found other plants on Oahu above Sea Life Park and on the north face of Mt. Haupu, Kauai. Perlman reported it in Wailau Valley, Kauai near cliffs by the beach

2. Wiliwili tree. HVNP.

The leaves are compound with three to five pairs of leaflets per 4" (10cm) rachis. Leaflets are 1. to 1.5" (2.5 to 4cm) long by .5 to .75" (1 to 1.8cm) wide, elliptical-oblong, broadly blunt at apex and narrowed at base. The small, mildly sweet smelling pea-like flowers are yellow to orange-yellow or greenish yellow or sometimes pinkish, borne in axillary racemes, 8 to 10 flowers per cluster. The pods are 3" (7.5cm) long by .5" (1.2cm)

[6] See:
Hillebrand, p. 111.
Neal, p. 432.
St. John, p. 181.

1. Kolomona, leaves, flowers and fruit.

2. Kolomona, C. gaudichaudi, small tree, South Kohala, Hawaii.

wide, brown and flattened, impressed between the seeds. Seeds are small and black. Twigs are very slender, light brown, somewhat zig-zag, with prominent leaf scars. Bark is smooth and light brown on trunks to 2" (5cm) in diameter. No wood was available and no Hawaiian uses are known. Bryan found a tree 10" (25cm) in circumference, 18' (5.6m) tall with 12' (3.8) crown spread at Kaupulehu.[6]

HVNP Kilauea and Mauna Loa Strip
HNP Haleakala

MAMANI or MAMANE   **Sophora chrysophylla** (Salisb) Seem
Syn. **Edwardsia chrysophylla** Salisb.

Although only one species of *Sophora* is recognized by St. John, he lists three subspecies, seven varieties, three subvarieties and nine forms for a total of 23 taxa. His list is given below to show the endemicy by island and the endangered status of several taxa.

List of taxa under the genus *Sophora*

Sophora L.
   chrysophlyya, subsp. **chrysophylla**, var. **chrysophylla**

	forma **chrysophylla**	end. Hawaii
	forma **haleakalensis**	end. e. Maui
	forma **obovata**	end. Hawaii
**	var. **makuaensis**	end. Oahu
**	subsp. **circularis**, var. **circularis**	end. Hawaii
**	var. **kauensis**	end. Hawaii
***	subsp. **glabrata**, var. **glabrata**	end. Hawaii
**	var. **grisea**, subvar. **grisea**	end. Oahu
	subvar. **obtusa**, f. **obtusa**	end. Hawaii
	forma **maunaloaensis**	end. Hawaii
	forma **parva**	end. Hawaii
	subvar. **ovatifoliolata**	end. Kauai
***	var. **lanaiensis**	end. Lanai
	var. **ovata**, subvar. **ovata**, f. **ovata**	end. Hawaii
	f. **puuwaawaaensis**	end. Hawaii
	f. **maunakeaensis**	end. Hawaii
	subvar. **mauiensis**. f. **mauiensis**	end. e. Maui
	f. **lualailuaensis**	end. e. Maui
	f. **olindaensis**	end. e. Maui
	subsp. **unifoliata**, var. **unifoliata**	end. e. Maui
**	var. **eliptica**	end. e. Maui
**	var. **kanaioensis**	end. e. Maui

MAMANI occurs as a small to medium sized tree 3' (.92m) in diameter and 40' (12m) tall in good sites. It occurs widely from just above sea level to 10,000' (3,125m) on Mauna Kea. It, along with NAIO, forms an extensive belt of pygmy forest on the higher slopes of the mountains of Kauai, Maui and Hawaii. Leaves are compound with 6 to 10 pairs of small leaflets .25 to .75" (.5 to 1.5cm) long per rachis, that in turn is 5 to 6" (12.5 to 15cm) long. Leaflets light green, obovate-oblong. Flowers are beautiful golden, pea-like flowers in drooping, terminal or lateral racemes, coloring the whole tree yellow in full flower. Seed pods or legumes are short, brown, 4-angled, deeply constricted between seeds. Seeds are small, yellow or orange and pea-like. Twigs are light brown and smooth, bark is light brown and deeply corrugated on 12" (31cm) trunks.

Heart wood is deep brown with blackish areas, sapwood is light brown to straw colored. Texture is uniformly fine, figure flame, grain crossed but close, very dense and very hard. Vessels are unusual in that they are very fine and in chains, rays are numerous and very fine. Wood warps badly and is very hard to work due to the cross grain and hardness. Hawaiians used the timbers in house construction, wood for OOs, spades and sled runners.

They made a type of long monorail sled for use in sliding down steep rocky paths, thus very hard wood was needed. MAMANI has been used extensively for fence posts in modern times and it is said that it was necessary to develop a hardened staple as ordinary staples could not be driven into the hard wood. L.W. Bryan's big tree is 12'2" (3.8m) in circumference, 39' (12.25m) tall with 42' (13.25m) crown spread located in Mauna Kea Forest Reserve, Hawaii.

MAMANI occurs as pure stands or mixed with NAIO and AHEAHEA in the very extensive parkland forest between Mauna Loa, Mauna Kea and Mt. Hualalai on Hawaii, also as a component of KOA forests and even as a minor component of the OHIA forest around Kilauea.[7]

[7] See:
Hillebrand, p. 108.
Neal, p. 442.
Rock, p. 185.
St. John, p. 193.
Carlquist, p. 365-69.

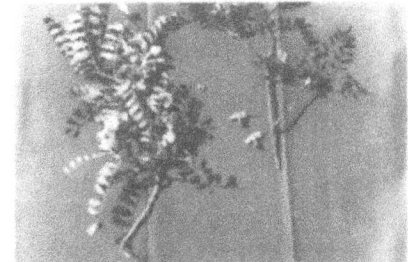

2. Mamani, leaves and flowers, bright yellow.

1. Mamani tree, S. chrysephylla, central Hawaii.

3. Trunk of Mamani.

SCREW PINE FAMILY — Pandanaceae

Two genera of this family occur in Hawaii, *Pandanus* and *Freycinetia*. The former is the common screwpine tree while the latter is a heavy woody climber that grows high into the OHIA trees of the wetter forests.

Key to the Genera

An erect tree .... **Pandanus** Stickm.
A woody climbing vine .... **Freycinetia** Gaud.

HVNP
HNP

IE'IE **Freycinetia arborea** Gaud.
Syn. **F. arnottii** Gaud.

Although IE'IE is neither a shrub nor a tree it is a woody plant and deserves a place in this book as it is a conspicuous part of the forest. The vine is generally about 1" (2.5cm) in diameter and as tall as the trees it grows in. Branches have terminal tufts of long, slender leaves. Beautiful red flowers are borne in the center of the leaf tuft. Fruit is a spike crowded with many-seeded, pulpy, orange berries. The stem is ringed with leaf scars. As the vine climbs an OHIA tree it often tends to spiral tightly around the trunk. As the OHIA tree grows the stem tightens causing a spiral groove to be formed in the trunk. These spirally grooved logs are much sought after for decorative poles. Neal recites an interesting legend concerning the IE'IE on page 54. Degener also gives an interesting story on pages 49-56 of PHNP.[1]

[1] See:
Hillebrand, p. 453.
Neal, p. 54.
Degener, PHNP, pp. 49-56.

[2] See:
Hillebrand, p. 453.
Neal, p. 51.
Degener, PHNP, p. 43.
Rock, p. 97.
St. John, p. 142.
Carlquist, p. 102.

1. Hala tree on the shore, Hilo, Hawaii.

2. Fruit of Hala with a crown of long, slender leaves. Hilo, Hawaii.

HVNP

HALA, LAUHALA, Screwpine or Pandanus   **Pandanus**

St. John gives the following list of species and varieties of *Pandanus* endemic or indigenous to the Hawaiian Islands.

Pandanus chamissonis Gaud.	end. H.I.
P. douglasii Gaud.	end. H.I.
P. menziesii Gaud.	end. H.I.
P. odoratissimus var. **odoratissimus** L.	indig. (?) Ceylon
var. **levigatus**	end. H.I.
var. **oahuensis**	**end. Oahu**
P. tectorius Warb. var. **sandwicensis**	end. H.I.

Most references agree that the commonly seen HALA in Hawaii is *Pandanus odoratissimus* L. This is a general description without attempting specific designation.

The plant occurs as a tree up to 12" (31.5cm) in diameter and 35' (11m) tall. It is found widely on all the islands along the sea shore and extending far up the cliffs facing the sea. It also occurs a considerable distance inland and may have covered extensive areas now devoted to cane culture. In the sea side habitat it shares space with coconut palms, HAU and KAMANI and in recent times with such introduced trees as Casurina, *Casurina equisetifolia*, false KAMANI, *Terminalia catappa*, guava, *Psidium guajava* and others. It occurs very abundantly in suitable habitat to 2,000' (630m) elevation.

HALA is the name of the tree and LAUHALA literally means leaf of the HALA. Leaves are long and slender, 2" (5cm) wide and 3 to 6' (.92 to 1.8m) long, arranged spirally around the trunk, giving rise to the name screwpine. Leaves have sharp prickles along the edges. Male flower spikes, HINANO, are about 1' (31cm) long, surrounded by narrow, pointed, fragrant, white, edible bracts. Fruit is about the size of a pinapple and quite conspicuous as it grows out from the center of the leaf clusters at the ends of branches. The fruit is made up of 50 or more wedge shaped yellow to red drupes about 1 to 2" (2.5 to 5cm) long, each with several one-seeded or empty cells. The inner, fleshy end of the drupe (PUA HALA) contains starch and sugar and the nut-like seeds in the outer end (IWI HALA) can be used as emergency food. Red fruit are strung into leis. The branches are thick and stocky, very rough with spiral leaf scars. Bark is whitish with prickly lenticles. The plants produce many stocky aerial roots that serve as props.

Wood of the male tree is said to be hard and beautiful but few males are found in Hawaii. Wood of female trees is very soft, coarse in texture, no figure, straight, open grain, low density, no visible vessels or rays, very poor stability and workability. Hawaiians used the wood for pipes to allow water to flow from one TARO patch to another as the soft core was easily dug out to form the pipe.

The more important use of HALA involved the use of leaves, PUAHALA. These were stripped of the prickly edges, then sliced to desired width and woven into mats, mattresses, sails and many useful articles. Degener, PHNP, pages 43 to 49 and Neal, pages 51 to 53 give interesting accounts of early uses. The harder wood was used for house timbers and canoe rollers. In modern times place mats, comic hats, rugs, etc., are made of LAUHALA and sold in curio stores.

L.W. Bryan's big tree is 4'6" (1.4m) in circumference, 35' (11m) tall and with crown spread of 40' (12.6m) located in Keaau, Hawaii.[2]

RUE or CITRUS FAMILY — Rutaceae

Native trees and large shrubs of the Rue family occur in Hawaii in the following genera: *Pelea, Platydesma* and *Zanthoxylum.*

Key to the Genera

Leaves simple, opposite or whorled
    Stamens free; petals valvate (petals whorled
        not overlapped) .... **Pelea** Gray
    Stamens united; petals imbricate (overlapped) .... **Platydesma** Mann
Leaves compound, alternate; flowers unisexual .... **Zanthosylum** Colden in L.

Trees of this family constitute a prominent part of the Hawaiian forest complex in the latter stages of succession but are a minor component of the early OHIA forest. *Platydesma* comes into the OHIA forest earlier than the other two. These latter two find better environment in the more open forest
The genus *Pelea* was dedicated to Pele, Hawaiian goddess of volcanoes.

ALANI, MANENA, MOKIHANA — Pelea Gray

The *Pelea*'s in Hawaii are extremely variable from plant to plant and have been the subject of intensive study. The ultimate in species fracturing seems to have been achieved with St. John's list of 80 species and 43 other taxa at the level of variety and form. As an illustration of how a genus may be divided, Hillebrand lists 20 species and one variety. Rock lists 24 species and several varieties. Neal states "about 50 species". And so the list grows. St. John's is reproduced here to give the latest complete picture as well as for convenience in listing both abundancy status and endemicy.

Taxa of the genus *Pelea*

Pelea Gray, 1854
    adscendens St. John & Hume in St. John, 1944. D:fam. 179, 6/10/70
        end. e. Maui
    anapanapaensis St. John, 1971   end. e. Maui
    anisata Mann, 1866, var. **anisata.** H:64; R:229; D:fam. 179, 7/16/62;
        N:478. Mokihana.   end. Kauai
        kavaiensis Mann, var. *glabra* Hbd., 1888. H:64
        Hillebrandii Lévl., 1917
        ? nodosa Lévl., 1917
        subpeltata Lévl., 1912
        Evodia anisata (Mann) Drake, 1890
**   var. **haupuana** Stone, 1966   end. Kauai
    apoda St. John, 1944   end. Hawaii
        parvifolia Hbd., var. *apoda* (St.John) Stone, 1969. D:fam. 179, 6/10/70.
**   **Balloui** Rock, 1913. R:228. (as *balouii,* in Stone, 1969.)
        D:fam. 179, 6/10/70   end. e. Maui
        ukuleleensis St. John, 1944
    barbigera (Grey) Hbd., 1888. N:70; R:235. Uahi-a-Pele   end. Kauai
        Melicope barbigera Gray, 1854
        M. cinerea Gray, F. *barbigera* (Gray) Wawra, 1873
        Evodia barbigera (Gray) Drake, 1890
**   **Christophersenii** St. John, 1944. D:fam. 179, 6/10/70   end. Oahu
**   **cinerea** (Gray) Hbd., 1888, var. **cinerea.** H:68; R:237
        D:fam. 179, 6/10/70. Manena   end. Oahu
        Melicope cinerea Gray, 1854
        Evodia cinerea (Gray) Drake, 1890.
***   var. **mauiana** Stone, 1966   end. Maui
**   var. **Skottsbergii** Stone, 1966   end. Maui
**   **cinereops** St. John & Hume in St. John, 1944. D:fam. 179, 6/10/70   end. Oahu
    clusiaefolia Gray, 1854. Alani, Clusia-leaved pelea.
        clusiifolia Gray altered by Skottsb., 1944.
        subsp. **clusiaefolia,** var. **clusiaefolia.** H:62;R:215;D;fam. 179,
        12/28/60   end. Oahu, Molokai, Maui
        f. *microcarpa* Wawra, 1873

1. *Alani: close-up of typical cream-colored flower.*

2. *Alani trunk.*

3. *Alani tree, Kokee, Kauai.*

1. *Queer branching in Pelea species.*

Evodia clusiaefolia (Gray) Drake, 1890.
  var. **crassiloba** Stone, 1966, f. **crassiloba.** D:fam. 179, 6/10/70   end. Oahu
     clusiaefolia, f. *macrocarpa* Wawra, 1873
    f. **Degeneri** Stone, 1966   end. e. Maui
  var. **cuneata** St. John & Hume in St. John, 1944, f. **cuneata.**
    D:fam. 179, 6/10/70   end. Hawaii
    f. **aurea** Stone, 1966. D:fam. 179, 6/10/70   end. Hawaii
  var. **Fauriei** (Lévl.)St. John & Hume in St. John, 1944   end. Molokai
     Fauriei Lévl. 1911
  var. **ecuneata** St. John, 1944. D:fam. 179, 6/10/70   end. Kauai
  var. **minor** St. John, 1971, f. **minor**   end. e. Maui
    f. **stenophylla** St. John, 1971   end. e. Maui
  subsp. **Cookeana** (Rock) Stone, 1966, var. **Cookeana,** f. **Cookeana.**
    D:fam. 179, 6/10/70   end. Molokai, Lanai, Maui, Hawaii
     Cookeana Rock, 1913
     clusiaefolia Gray, var.*Cookeana* (Rock) St.John & Hume in St. John, 1944
    f. **longipes** Stone, 1944   end. Molokai
  subsp. **dumosa** (Rock) Stone, 1966, var. **dumosa.** D:fam. 179, 6/10/70
       end. Kauai, Oahu
     sapotaefolia Mann, var. *dumosa* Rock, 1913. R:218
     microcarpa Heller, 1897
     Evodia sapotaefolia (Mann) Drake, 1890.
    f. **puberula** (St. John) Stone, 1966   end. Oahu, Molikai
     clusiaefolia Gray, var. *puberula* St. John, 1944
  cruciata Heller, 1897. D:fam. 179, 6/10/70   end. Kauai
**   **Degeneri** Stone, 1966. D:fam. 179, 6/10/70   end. Kauai
**   **descendens** St. John, 1944. D:fam. 179, 6/10/70   end. Oahu
  elliptica (Gray) Hbd., 1888, var. **elliptica,** f. **elliptica**
    H:69;R:237;D:fam. 179, 7/16/62. Alani, Awianae pelea   **end. Oahu**
     kaalae Wawra, 1873
     Melicope elliptica Gray, 1854
     Evodia elliptica (Gray) Drake, 1890.
    f. **coccinea** (St. John & Hume in St. John) Stone in Degeners & Stone,
      1962. D:fam. 179, 7/16/62   end. Oahu
     var. *coccinea* St. John & Hume in St. John, 1944
***   var. **mauiensis** St. John, 1944. D:fam. 179, 7/16/62   end. w. Maui
  elongata (Hbd.) St. John, 1944   end. Oahu
    elliptica (Gray) Hbd., var. *elongata* Hbd., 1888. H:69
    Saint-Johnii Hume, var. *elongata* (Hbd.) Stone in Deg. Deg. & Stone,
      1966. D:fam. 179, 6/10/70
  Feddei Lévl., 1912. Ka lei o Hiiaka   end. Kauai
    resiniflora Skottsb., 1936
    punctata St. John & Hume in St. John, 1944
  Gayana Rock, 1918. D:fam. 179, 6/10/70. Kaleiohiiaka   end Kauai
    sapotaefolia Mann, var. ?*procumbens* Hbd., 1888. H:63
  grandfolia (Hbd.) St. John & Hume in St. John, 1944, var. **grandfolia.**
    D:fam. 179, 6/10/70   end. Hawaii
    volcanica Gray, 1854, var. *grandifolia* Hbd., 1888. H:67
  var. **hualalaiensis** (St. John) Stone, 1966   end. Hawaii
    hualalaiensis St. John, 1944
**   var. **lianoides** (Rock) Stone, 1966   end. Lanai
    volcanica Gray, var. *lianoides* Rock, 1913
**   var. **montana** (Rock) Stone, 1966   end. Maui
    volcanica Gray, var. *montana* Rock, 1913
**   var. **ovalifolia** (Hbd.) St. John, 1944   end. Maui, Hawaii
    volcanica Gray, var. *ovalifolia* Hbd., 1888. H:67
    volcanica, var. *terminalis* Rock, 1913. H:223
    grandifolia, var. *terminalis* (Rock) Stone, 1969
  haleakalae Stone, 1966   end. e. Maui
    (as *haleakalana* Stone, changed by Deg.& Deg., 1970) D:fam, 179, 6/10/70
**   **haupuensis** St. John, 1944. D:fam. 179, 6/10/70   end. Kauai
**   **hawaiensis** Wawra, 1873, var. **hawaiensis.** D:fam. 179, 1/20/70. Manera

	cinera (Gray) Hbd., var. *hawaiensis* (Wawara) Roc, 1918	end. Maui, Hawaii
**	var. **Brighami** (St. John) Stone, 1963. D:fam. 179, 1/20/70	end. Hawaii
	Gaudichaudii St. John, 1944	
***	var. **molokaiana** Stone, 1963. D:fam. 179, 1/20/70	end. Molokai
***	var. **pilosa** St. John, 1944. D:fam. 179, 1/20/70	end. Lanai, Maui
***	var. **racemiflora** (Rock) St. John, 1944. D:fam. 179, 1/20/70	end. e. Maui
	cinera (Gray) Hbd., var. *racemiflora* Rock, 1913	
***	var. **Remyana** Stone, 1963. D:fam. 179, 1/20/70	end. Hawaii
***	var. **rubra** (Rock) Stone, 1963. D:fam. 179, 1/20/70	end. w. Maui, Hawaii
	cinera (Gray) Hbd., var. *sulfurea* Rock, 1918	
	sulfurea (Rock) St. John & Hume in St. John, 1944	
**	**Hiiakae** Stone, 1963. D:fam. 179, 6/10/70	end. Oahu
	honoluluensis St. John, 1944. D:fam. 179, 6/1/67	end. Oahu
**	**Hosakae** St. John, 1944. D:fam. 179, 6/10/70	end. Oahu
	kaalaensis St. John, 1944. D:fam. 179, 5/1/66. Alani, Kaala pelea	end. Oahu
	Sherffii Deg. & Deg., 1970	
**	**kauaensis** St. John, 1944	end. Oahu
	Stonei Deg. & Deg., 1970. D:fam. 179, 6/10/70	
**	**kavaiensis** Mann, 1866. H:64; R:225, (as *kauaiensis*) D:fam 179, 6/10/70	
		end. Kauai
	kipahuluensis St. John, 1971	end. e. Maui
***	**Knudsenii** Hbd., 1888. H:70;R:235;D:fam. 179, 6/19/70	end. Kauai
	Evodia Knudseni (Hbd.) Drake, 1890	
**	**lanceolata** St. John & Hume in St. John, 1944. D:fam. 179, 6/10/70	end Hawaii
**	**Lakae** Stone, 1963. D:fam. 179, 6/10/70	end. Oahu
**	**Leveillei** Faurie in Lévl., 1912. D:fam. 179, 6/10/70	end. Kauai
	Lohiauana Stone, 1963. D:fam. 179, 6/10/70	end. Kauai
	lucens (Hbd.) St. John, 1944	end. Oahu
	sandwicensis (H.&A.) Gray, var. *lucens* Hbd., 1888. H:67	
**	**Lydgatei** Hbd., 1888. H:65. D:fam. 179, 6/10/70	end. Oahu
***	**macropus** Hbd., 1888. H:65; R:227; D:fam. 179, 6/10/70	end. Kauai
	acutivalvata Lévl., 1911	
	Evodia macropus (Hbd.) Drake, 1890	
**	**makahae** Stone, 1963	end. Oahu
	makahaensis Stone, altered by Deg.& Deg., 1970. D:fam. 179, 6/10/70.	
	Mannii Hbd., 1888. H:66	end. e. Maui
	Stone (1969) considers this a species dubia	
	manukaensis St. John, 1944	end. Hawaii
	oblongifolia Gray, var. *manukaensis* (St. John) Stone, 1969	
	molokaiensis Hbd., 1888. H:65; R:227; D:fam. 179, 6/10/70	
		end. Molokai, w. Maui
	foetida Lévl., 1911	
	Evodia molokaiensis (Hbd.) Drake, 1890	
***	**mucronulata** St. John, 1944. D:fam. 179, 6/10/70	end. e. Maui
	multiflora Rock, 1911. R:233; D:fam. 179, 6/15/62. Alani, Auahi pelea	
		end. e. Maui
	Knudsenii Hbd., var. *multiflora* (Rock) Rock, 1916	
***	**Munroi** St. John, 1944. D:fam. 179, 6/10/70	end. Lanai
	(as *munroii* St. John, altered by Deg.&Deg., 1970)	
**	**Nealae** Stone in Degeners & Stone, 1960. D:fam. 179, 12/28/60	
	(as *nealiae* Stone, altered by Deg.&Deg., 1970), D:fam. 179, 6/10/70	
	niuensis St. John, 1944	end. Oahu
	peduncularis Lévl., var. *niuensis* (St. John) Stone, 1963. D:fam. 179, 6/1/67	
	oahuensis Lévl., 1912. D:fam. 179, 6/10/70	end. Oahu
	oahuensis var. *lucens* (Hbd.) Stone, 1966	
	sandwicensis (H.&A.) Gray, var. *lucens* Hbd., 1888. H:67	
**	**oblongifolio** Gray, 1854. H:64; D:fam. 179, 6/10/70	end. Hawaii
***	**obovata** St. John, 1944. D:fam. 179, 6/10/70	end. Maui or Lanai
**	**olowaluensis** St. John, 1944. D:fam. 179, 6/10/70	end. W. Maui
**	**orbicularis** Hbd., 1888, var. **orbicularis.** H:67; R:224; D:fam. 179, 6/10/70
		end. w. Maui

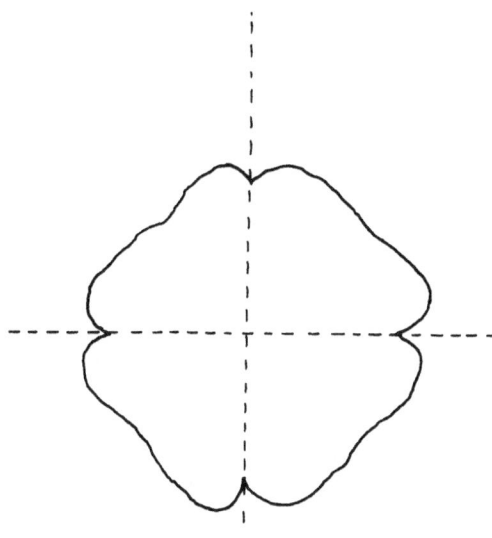

Cuboid capsule as in P. zalbruckneri.

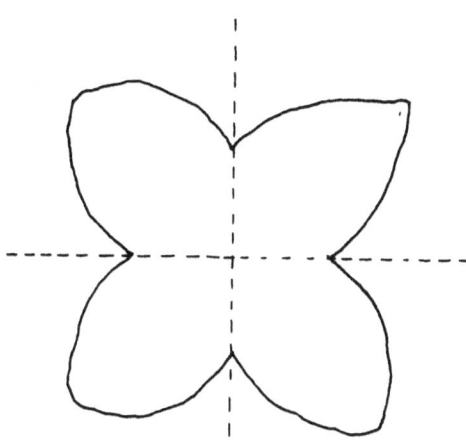

Shallowly divided capsule as in P. puauluensis.

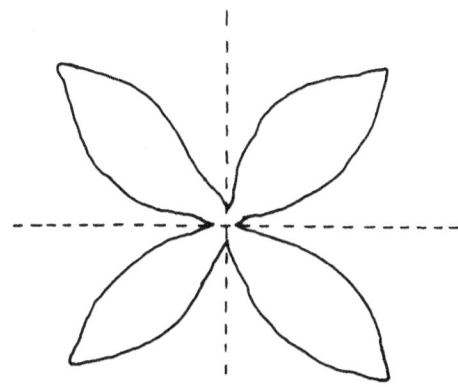

Capsule deeply parted as in P. hawaiiensis.

1. *Manena tree in HVNP.*

2. *Manena, P. hawaiiensis v. gaudachaudi. Leaf and flower detail.*

```
**           var. tonsa St. John & Huma in St. John, 1944. D:fam. 179, 6/10/70
                                                                    end. w. Maui
**        ovalis St. John, 1944. D:fam. 179, 6/10/70                end. e. Maui
**        ovata St. John & Hume in St. John, 1944. D:fam. 179, 6/10/70  end. Kauai
             Forbesii St. John & Hume in St. John, 1944
**        pallida Hbd., 1888. D:fam. 179, 12/28/60. Alani, pale pelea  end. Oahu
          paloloensis St. John, 1944                                   end. Oahu
             peduncularis Lévl., var. paloloensis (St. John) Stone, 1963. D:fam. 179, 6/1/67
**        paniculata St. John, 1944. D:fam. 179, 6/15/62. Alani, paniculate pelea
                                                                       end. Kauai
          parvifolia Hbd., 1888, var. parvifolia. H:65; D:fam. 179, 11/11/60
             Alani, pelea                                              end. Maui
**           var. sessilis (Lévl.) Stone, 1967. D:fam. 179, 6/10/70    end. Molokai
                sessilis Lévl., 1911
          peduncularis Lévl., 1912, var. peduncularis. D:fam. 179, 6/1/67.
             Boxfruit alani                                            end. Oahu
             grandipetala Lévl., 1912, in part
             somgi;of;pra Lévl., 1912
             penduliflora Lévl., 1911
             Rockii St. John, 1944
             sandwicensis (H.&A.) Gray, var. macrocarpa Hbd. ex Rock, 1918
**           var. cordata Stone, 1967. D:fam. 179, 6/1/67              end Oahu
**           var. nummularia Stone, 1967. D:fam. 179, 6/1/67           end. Oahu
             var. pauciflora (St. John) Stone, 1963. D:fam. 179, 6/1/67  end. Oahu
                Rockii St. John, var. pauciflora St. John, 1944
             var. quadrata Stone, 1963. D:fam. 179, 6/1/67             end. Oahu
                waianaiensis Lévl., 1911
          Pickeringii St. John, 1944                          end. H.I., indefinite
             clusiaefolia Gray subsp. slusiaefolia, var. Pickeringii (St. John) Stone, 1966.
             D:fam. 179, 6/10/70
**        pluvialis St. John, 1944. D:fam. 179, 6/10/70                end. Kauai
          pseudoanisata Rock, 1913, var. pseudoanisata. R:227, D:fam. 179, 6/10/70
                                                                       end. Hawaii
             var. oblanceolata (St. John) Stone, 1969. D:fam. 179, 6/10/70  end. Hawaii
                oblanceolata St. John, 1944
          puauluensis St. John, 1944. D:fam. 179, 6/10/70              end. Hawaii
          puberula St. John, 1944. D:fam. 179, 6/10/70                 end. Kauai
**        quadrangularis St. John & Hume in St. John, 1944. D:fam. 179, 6/10/70
                                                                       end. Kauai
          radiata St. John, 1944. D:fam 179, 6/15/62. Alani, radiate pelea  end. Hawaii
**        recurvata Rock, 1918. D:fam. 179, 6/15/62. Alani, recurved pelea  end. Kauai
**        reflexa St. John, 1944. D:fam. 179, 6/120/70                 end. Molokai
          rotundifolia Gray, 1854, f. rotundifolia. H:68; R:226; D:fam. 179
             6/10/70                                                   end. Oahu
             Evodia rotundifolia (Gray) Drake, 1890
             f. ternata Stone, 1966                                    end. Oahu
**        Saint-Johnii Hume in St. John, 1944. D:fam 179, 6/10/70. Alani,
             St. John pelea                                            end. Oahu
***       sandwicensis (H.&A.) Gray, 1854. D:fam. 179, 1/20/70   end. Oahu, Molokai
             Brunellia sandwicensis H.&A., 1832
          semiternata St. John, 1944. D:fam. 179, 6/10/70              end. Oahu
          stellata St. John, 1944                                      end. e. Maui
***       Storeyana St. John & Hume in St. John, 1944, D:fam. 179, 6/10/70  end. Oahu
***       tomentosa St. John & Hume in St. John, 1944. D:fam. 179, 6/10/70  end. e. Maui
          volcanica Gray, 1854, var. volcanica. H:67; R:221; D:fam. 179, 6/10/70
                                                              end. Lanai, Maui, Hawaii
**           var. kohalae Stone, 1966                                  end Hawaii
             var. kohalaensis Deg.&Deg., 1970., an invalid alteration
**        wahiawaensis St. John & Hume in St. John, 1944. D:fam. 179, 6/10/70
                                                                       end. Kauai
          waialealae Wawra, 1873, var. waialealae. H:63; R:218
             Anonia, alaniwai                                          end. Kauai
```

    waialaeana Deg.&Deg., 1970, an invalid alteration. D:fam. 179, 6/10/70
      var. **latior** St. John & Hume in St. John, 1944   end. Kauai
      var. **pubescens** Skottsb., 1944   end. Kauai
*** **waimeaensis** St. John, 1944. D:fam. 179, 6/10/70   end. Kauai
   waipioensis St. John, 1944   end. Oahu
   Wawraeana Rock, 1913, var. **Wawraeana**. R:231. D:fam. 179, 6/10/70
        end. Oahu
    sandwicensis sensu Hbd., 1888, non (H.&A.) Gray, 1854
      var. **pubens** St. John, 1944   end. Oahu
      var. **tenuifolia** St. John & Hume in St. John, 1944   end. Oahu
        var. *ternifolia* Stone, 1962
            peduncularis var. *ternifolia* Stone, 1966
** **Zahlbruckneri** Rock, 1913. R:231. D:fam. 179, 6/10/70   end. Hawaii

1. Manena leaf and fruit, deeply 4-parted.

HVNP Kipuka puaulu

MANENA   **Pelea hawaiiensis** var. **gaudichaudi**
                Syn. **P. cinerera** (Gray) Hbd.

According to the identifications now on the specimens in the herbarium of Hawaii Volcanoes National Park the MANENA that was considered to be *P. cinerea* in the era of 1935 is now identified as *P. hawaiiensis* var. *gaudichaudi*. St. John limits *P. cinerea* to Oahu and Maui. This species comes under the Rock grouping of *Apocarpa* with capsules apocarpus and with carpels discrete, the four parts of the fruit being separated to the base. The remainder of the *Peleas* that Rock included with *Apocarpa* are all endemic to other islands, thus this is the species found on Hawaii. It is a tree 20 to 24' (6.3 to 7.8m) tall and 1' (31.5cm) in diameter or larger in Kipuka Puaulu and in Kau in the Ocean View Estates.

Lemony-scented leaves are 2" (5cm) wide and 6" (15cm) long or smaller, dark green above, somewhat paler below, prominent midrib and pinnate veins, blunt at the apex and narrowed at the base with a 1" (2.5cm) petiole. Flowers cream colored and small, about .25" (.5cm) in diameter, somewhat like tiny tulip flowers. Fruits small, 4-parted capsules parted to the base, .75" (1.8cm) or less in diameter, yellowish tomentose. Twigs soft and flexible, hairy, slender, greenish. Bark smooth and pinkish to light brown.

Wood yellowish white with black streaks, texture fine and even, figure plain, grain straight, of medium density and soft. Vessels very fine and scattered, no rays visible with 10x lens. The tough wood warps and workability is only fair. Hawaiians used the bark and wood medicinally and used the wood for TAPA beaters and canoe trim and rigging. On the island of Hawaii this is one of the most readily distinguished of the *Peleas* because of the deeply parted fruit. It occurs late in succession in the OHIA forest.[1]

2. Manena bark detail.

HVNP Napau Crater
HNP

ALANI   **Pelea clusiaefolia** Gray

This ALANI includes 15 subspecies, varieties and forms and none of them is listed as endangered or extinct so it must either be a more viable species or was more abundant and widespread to begin with. There are endemic subspecies, varieties or forms on all the islands.

This species is treated without any attempt to differentiate between the subspecies, varieties and forms. However, the variety endemic to Kauai is *ecuneata* and to Hawaii it is *cuneata*. The writer has seen it in Hawaii Volcanoes National Park near Napau Crater and on Kauai in the Kokee area. It grows to be a tree 25 to 30' (7.8 to 9.5m) in height. It is distinguished by the leaves that generally grow in whorls of four. Rock put it in his group *Verticillifoliae* which refers to the whorled leaves. All of Rock's species in this group, except *P. waialealae*, have been reduced to subspecies or varieties of *P. clusiaefolia*.

[1] See:
Hillebrand, p. 68.
Neal, p. 477.
Rock, p. 239.
St. John, p. 200.

[2] See:
Hillebrand, p. 62.
Rock, p. 215.
St. John, p. 200.

[3] See:
Degener, FH, p. 179.

[4] See:
Rock, p. 231.

1. *Alani, P. clausifolia*, leaf detail. Kokee, Kauai.

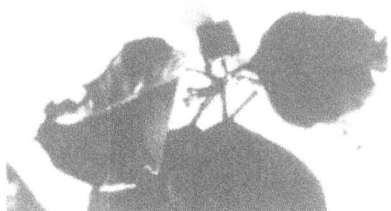

2. *Alani, P. zalbruckneri*, twig, leaves and very cuboid fruit.

3. *Alani, P. zalbruckneri*. Tree in HVNP.

As stated, leaves occur in whorls of four or sometimes five at the ends of branches. Leaves have prominent midrib, upper surface darker green and shinier than the underside, margin often revolute, narrowing at the base into a stout petiole about .5" (1.25cm) long. Small white flowers are borne in axillary clusters or in clusters along the stem below the leaves. Capsules are 4-lobed, woody and yellowish, the lobes united to the middle. Twigs are stout, green in current growth, aging to light brown, smooth, but with many minute light tan lenticles. Bark is rough on 2" (5cm) stems.

Wood is very light yellow color, texture moderately fine, figure plain, grain straight and open, denisty low, wood soft but tough and fibrous. Vessels few, medium sized and scattered, rays very fine and very closely spaced. Wood is quite stable and workable. This tree is a minor component of fairly wet forest in the late stages of succession.[2]

HVNP Makaopuhi to Kalapana trail

ALANI   **Pelea radiata** St. John

This ALANI has a very limited range and probably should be on the endangered list except that it is protected in the national park where it is found at about 1,500' (470m) elevation on the trail to Kalapana. Degener describes it as a shrub or small tree, the younger ones being wand-like, erect shrubs with a few wide spreading branches.

Leaves are opposite, short petioled, blades elliptic or ovate, 1.5 to 7" (3.5 to 15cm) long, 1.5 to 3" (3.5 to 7.5cm) broad, clear, light green above, duller beneath, lemony scented when crushed. Flowers in clusters of three are generally small and greenish. Fruit deeply 4-parted, .75 to 1" (1.8 to 2.5cm) across, sections 1 or more often 2 seeded, seeds black and shiny.[3]

HVNP Kipuka Puaulu

ALANI   **Pelea zalbruckneri** Rock

This ALANI falls in Rock's category of *Cubicarpae* and has cuboid fruits. Terminology on this species has not been changed. It is endemic to Hawaii.

It is a small tree to about 20' (6.3m) tall. Rock states it is "peculiarly branched" but does not say in what way. Opposite leaves are the largest of the *Peleas*, 6 to 9" (15 to 23cm) long on a 1" (2.5cm) petiole, eliptical-oblong, to obovate-oblong, thin, rounded at apex, wedge shaped toward the base. Flowers are very small. Fruits are up to 1.5" (3.7cm) across, cuboid, each section 2-seeded, seeds large, ovoid and black. Twigs are stout and smooth. No wood was available as the tree grows in the national park.

The largest *Pelea* measured by L.W. Bryan was identified by him as *P. volcanica* in Hawaii Volcanoes National Park and was 2'11" (89cm) in circumference, 40' (12.6m) tall and with a 36' (1.3m) crown spread.[4]

MOKIHANA   **Pelea anisata** Mann

MOKIHANA, the flower of Kauai, is endemic thereon. The tree is small and slender, 15 to 20' (4.7 to 6.3m) tall and somewhat viny in growth habit. It can be found in the Kokee area of Kauai.

The anise-smelling leaves are bright green, oblong, 3 to 4" (7.5 to 10cm) long by 1.5" (3.7cm) wide on short petioles. Midrib is green and prominent, veins inconspicuous and pinnate. Flowers borne on short stems along the twig and also axillary. Fruits are borne singly along the twig, cuboid and small, .375 to .5 (.9 to 1.25cm) across. Twigs are smooth and light brown. Bark is smooth and grey-green with red cambium layer. Wood contains the anise odor, is pale creamy white, texture fine, grain straight and close, figure very plain to lacking, density moderate and fairly hard. Vessels few and scattered, rays very faint and hard to see at 10x. Faint cross banding between the rays makes a very faint pattern of tiny squares.

Leaves of *Pelea* were put between layers of TAPA cloth to give the cured cloth a pleasant scent and its fruits were strung in LEIS and worn because of the nice scent. The tree is a minor component of the mixed forest.[5]

HVNP

ALANI   **Pelea puauluensis** St. John

This ALANI can be found near the Kipuka Puaulu picnic ground as a couple of poor, deteriorating trees. The sheet in the HVNP herbarium was originally labeled *P. volcanica* and is now labeled *P. puauluensis* var. *megacarpa* but St. John does not list such a variety.

The trees are 10 to 15' (3.2 to 4.7m) tall with long spreading limbs. The very faintly lemon-scented leaves are small, oblong, with very prominent veins. The small, tulip-like flowers are only about .25" (.6cm) in diameter, creamy white, borne on quite long axillary stalks. The fruits are shaped like 4-pointed stars, the divisions between the points extending about a quarter of the way to the center of the fruit which is about 1" (2.5cm) across. New growth of twigs is light green and smooth, aging to light brown and rough with leaf scars. Since the plant was growing in HVNP no wood was collected. The tree measured by the author was 11" (28cm) in circumference, 8'6" (2.6m) crownspread and 14' (4.25m) tall.[6]

HVNP

ALANI   **Pelea pseudoanisata** var. **oblanceolata** (St. John) Stone

Still another *Pelea*, formerly thought to be *P. volcanica*, is now labeled as above in the HVNP herbarium. It was gathered east of Makaopuhi Crater and had long stalked flowers. St. John lists it as endemic to Hawaii.

ALANI   **Pelea barbigera** (Gray) Hbd.
UAHE A PELE, Smoke of Pele

This ALANI also falls in Rock's category of *Apocarpae* because the four sections of the fruit are divided to the middle. It is a small tree 15 to 20' (4.7 to 6.3m) tall, slender and straight growing. It is found only on Kauai in the Kokee area at elevations of 3,600 to 4,000' (1.134 to 1,260m). It is called UAHE A PELE because of the peculiar smoky grey color of the leaves.

Leaves are 6" (15cm) long by 2" (5cm) wide, pointed apex, blunt base with 1.5" (3.7cm) petiole. Light green midrib is depressed, veins pinnate but indistinct. Terminal buds are whitish. Leaves are densely clothed along the midrib on the underside with cobweb-like wool that disappears as the leaf ages. Flowers are small and greenish, borne in clusters of three to five on a peduncle about 2" (5cm) long with short pedicels. Fruits are 4-parted, about 1.25" (3cm) across, cleft to the center. They open on ripening to show one to two black seeds per section. Twigs are smooth, green with whitish bloom on the new growth, aging to light tan. Bark on 3" (7.5cm) trunk is smooth, very thin, pale green with a brown layer just under the thin green layer. Wood is light creamy white, texture very fine, figure plain to lacking, grain close and straight, density medium high and wood fairly hard, vessels very small and numerous, rays very fine and closely spaced. Cross banding between the rays is very light. Wood warps but works fairly well. Small pith is filled.[7]

HNP

ALANI   **Pelea volcanica** Gray

Pelea volcanica has been listed as occuring in Haleakala National Park. No specimen was seen.

[5] See:
Hillebrand, p. 64.
Rock, p. 229.
Neal, p. 478.
St. John, p. 199.

[6] See:
St. John, p. 204.

[7] See:
Hillebrand, p. 70.
Rock, p. 235.
St. John, p. 200.

1. Mokehana, *P. anisata*, leaves and tiny buds.

2. Alani, *P. puauluensis*, flowers on long stalks and leaves.

3. Alani, *P. barbigera*, leaves and deeply parted fruit. Kokee, Kauai.

PILO KEA — **Platydesma** Mann

Platydesma is represented by the following in the Hawaiian Islands.

Platydesma Mann, 1866
    cornuta Hbd., 1888, var. **cornuta** H:72. D:fam. 179, 6/30/65   end. Oahu
        var. **decurrens** Stone, 1962. D:fam. 179, 6/30/65   end. Oahu
    Remyi (Sherff) Deg. Deg. Sherff & Stone, 1960. Pilokea, Remy platydesma
                                                                                                    end. Hawaii
        auriculaefolia sensu Hbd., 1888, non Gray, 1854
        campanulata Mann, var. *sessilifolium* Rock, 1913. R:243.
        Claoxylon Remyi Sherff, 1939.
    rostrata Hbd., 1888. H:72. Pilokea-lau-li'i   end. Kauai
    spathulata (Gray) Stone, 1962, var. **spathulata**, f. **spathulata**.
        (as *spathulatum* changed by Stone). D:fam. 179, 6/30/65. Kilokea,
            spatula-leaved platydesma   end. Kauai, Oahu, Hawaii
        campanulata Mann, 1866. H:71; R:211
        campanulata Mann, f. *coriaceum* Rock, 1913
        campanulata var. *macrophylla* Hbd., 1888. H:71; R:243
        oahuensis Lévl., 1911
        Melicope spathulata Gray, 1854
            f. **Stonei** Deg.&Deg., 1965. D:fam. 179, 6/30/65   end. Oahu
            f. **kalalauense** Deg.&Deg., 1965, D:fam. 179, 6/30/65   end. Kauai
    var. **pallida** (Hbd.) Stone, 1962. D:fam. 179, 6/30/65   end. Oahu, Maui
        campunalata Mann, var. *pallida* Hbd., 1888. H:71; R:242
    var. **pubescens** (Skottsb.) Stone, 1962. D:fam. 179, 6/30/65   end. Oahu
        campanulatum Mann, var. *pubescens* Skottsb., 1944

1. Pilo kea trunk showing fruits.
2. Close-up of Pilo kea fruit. Seekins photo.
3. Pilo kea, P. companulata, small tree in fern jungle, Stainback Highway, Hawaii.
4. Pilo kea leaf and flower.

PILO KEA   **Platydesma spathulata** (Grey) Stone
Syn. **P. companulata** Mann

[8] See:
Hillebrand, p. 71.
Rock, p. 241.
Carlquist, p. 132.
St. John, p. 205.

PILO KEA is a small tree 15 to 20′ (4.7 to 6.3m) tall and only about 3″ (7.5cm) in diameter in good habitat. The one I saw was a single slender stem 5′ (1.5m) tall and 1″ (2.5cm) in diameter with a crown of large leaves.

The leaves are 13 to 15″ (33 to 38cm) long by 6″ (15cm) wide with petioles 2 to 3″ (5 to 7.5cm) long, opposite and clustered at the end of the trunk. Leaf is smooth and shiny with a very large midrib and few prominent veins. Large creamy-white bud, about 1″ (2.5cm) in diameter, opens into a large white flower with four petals, borne on a short stem on the trunk just below the leaves. The 4- 5-part fruit is 1 to 1.5″ (2.5 to 3.5cm) in diameter. Each cell contains two black seeds, however some cells are empty. Twig is thick, brown and smooth. Bark is thin and smooth. No wood was gathered.

PILO KEA is a very minor component of the wet forest. A variety *P. spathulata* var. *pallida* is reported from Haleakala National Park.[8]

AE   **Zanthoxylum** Colden in L.
Syn. **Fagara**

Zanthoxylum includes 23 taxa as listed by St. John. The keys that were developed in Hillebrand and Rock do not cover all the species nor any of the varieties and depend on leaflet numbers. None is listed as threatened, endangered or extinct. St. John's list is as follows:

Zanthoxylum Colden in L., 1754
   Bluettianum Rock, 1913. R:201. A'e, hea'e   end. Hawaii
      Fagara Bluettianum (Rock) Engler, 1896
   dipetalum Mann, 1866, var. **dipetalum**.H:76; R:207. Kawa'u   end. Oahu
      Connarum kavaiensis Mann, 1867
     var. **Degeneri** (Skottsb.) St. John, comb. nov.   end. Oahu
      Fagara dipetala (Mann) Engler, 1896, var. *Degeneri* Skottsb.,
         Göteborgs Bot. Trädgård, Medd. 15:382, 1944.
      F. waianesis Deg.& Skotsb., 1937
     var. **geminicarpum** Rock, 1913. R:209   end. Hawaii
      F. dipetalum, var. *geminicarpum* (Rock) St. John, 1945
     var. **tomentosum** Rock, 1913. R:209   end. Hawaii
      F. dipetalum, var. *tomentosum* (Rock) Skottsb., 1936
   glandulosum Hbd., 1888. H:74; R:197   end. w. Maui
      F. glandulosa (Hbd.) Engler, 1896
   hawaiiense Hbd., 1888, var. **hawaiiense**.H:76; R:195   end. Hawaii
     var. **citriodorum** Rock, 1913. R:197   end. Lanai
     var. **velutinosum** Rock, 1913. R:197   end. Hawaii
   kauaense Gray, 1854, var. **kauaense**. H:73 (as **Kauaiense**); R:199
                                                 end. Kauai, Maui
      F. kauaiensis (Gray) Engler, 1896
     var. **kohuaha** (Skottsb) St. John, comb. nov.   end. Kauai
      Fagara kauaiensis (Gray) Engler, var. *kohuaha* Skottsb.,
         Göteborgs Bot. Trädgård, Medd. 15:381, 1944
   maviense Mann, 1866, var.**maviense**, f.**maviense**. H:74; R:203   end. w. Maui
      F. mauiensis (Mann) Engler, 1896
     f. **glabrum** Rock, 1913   end. Lanai
     var. **anceps** Rock, 1913, f. **anceps**. R:205   end. Hawaii
     f. **petiolulata** Rock, 1913   end Hawaii
      F. maviensis var. *anceps*, f. *petioluata* (Rock) St. John, 1945
     var. **Cranwelliae** (Skottsb) St. John, comb. nov.   end. Molokai
      F. mauiensis (Mann) Engler, var. *Cranwelliae* Skottsb.,
         Göteborgs Bot. Trädgård, Medd. 15:381, 1944
     var. **rigidum** Rock, 1913   end. e. Maui
   oahuense Hbd., 1888. H:75; R:193   end Oahu
      F. oahuensis (Hbd.) Engler, 1896
   Piperitum (L.) DC., 1824. H:478. Wu-chu-yu, san-sho   cult. e. Asia

1. A'e or Hea'e, *Z. kauaiense*. The three-foliolate form growing on the aa lava fields on the southern slopes of Mt. Haleakala, Auahi, Maui. Rock photo.

[9] See:
Hillebrand, p. 73.
Rock, p. 199.
St. John, p. 206.

1. Ae, Z. hawaiiensis, leaf detail. HVNP.

2. Ae, Z. kauaiense, leaf detail, Kokee, Kauai.

3. Ae, Z. hawaiiensis, slender tree against Ohia forest backdrop, HVNP.

F. *Piperita* L., 1759
semiarticulatum St. John & Hosaka in Deg., var. **semiarticulatum**, f. **semiarticulatum**. 1932. A'e, hea'e, semi-articulate prickly-ash   end. Oahu
    F. *semiarticulatum* (St. John & Hosaka in Deg.) Deg., 1936
       D:fam. 179, 1/15/36
       f. **laiense** (Deg.) Fosb., 1969   end. Oahu
          F. *semiarticulata* (St. John & Hosaka in Deg.) Deg.,
          f. *laiensis* Deg., 1936. D:fam. 179, 1/15/36
    var. **sessile** (Deg.) Fosb., 1969 (as *sessilis*)   end Oahu
       F. *semiarticulata*, var. *sessilis* Deg., 1936. D:fam. 179, 1/15/36
Skottsbergii (Deg.&Deg.) St. John, comb.nov. A'e, hea'e,
    Prickly-ash-with-many-leaflets   end. Oahu
       Fagara Skottsbergii Deg.&Deg., 1960. D:fam. 179, 5/20/60

AE   **Zanthoxylum kauaense** Gray
                       Syn. **Fagara kauaiensis** (Gray) Engler

This AE was collected at Kokee, Kauai under the impression that it was *Z. dipetalum* var. *geminacarpus*. St. John limits that species to Hawaii, and lists only *Z. kauaense* for Kauai. It is a small graceful tree about 35' (11m) tall.

Leaves are 3 to 5-foliate, the rachis about 3 to 4" (7.5 to 10cm) long, leaflet petioles very short and green. Leaflets are 1.75 to 2" (4.6 to 5cm) wide by 3 to 3.5" (7.5 to 9cm) long, pointed at the apex and blunt at the base, dark green and glossy upperside, light underside, midrib prominent and yellowish, veins pinnate and prominent. Flowers are in small panicles near the base of short branches. Fruit is a pointed capsule with one or two large black seeds .75" (1.8cm) long. Twigs are smooth, light brown, in current growth to quite rough in older growth. The under layer of bark is green. Wood is very light yellow to greyish, small filled pith, texture fine, grain close and straight, figure plain, density medium, quite soft. Vessels are very small and packed into annular rings that give the appearance of ring porous wood. Rays very fine and closely spaced. Wood fairly stable and workable, fibrous and tough.

This tree grows in moderately wet to dry mixed forest but does not become a conspicuous component of that forest.[9]

HVNP Kipuka Puaulu

AE   **Zanthoxylum hawaiiensis** Hbd.

One single, slender specimen of this AE has been found growing in Kipuka Puaulu. It is not otherwise known and the National Park Service is making efforts to reproduce the tree to preserve the species. A variety, *Z. hawaiiensis* var. *velutinosum*, is listed as endemic to Hawaii, growing on the lava fields near Puuwaawaa, Hawaii.

The tree is about 32' (9.75m) tall, 4" (10cm) in diameter, has a 6' (1.8m) crown spread, and is branchless for the first 20 feet. It appears to be a young tree so the parent tree, unless dead, must be nearby. This species was listed by Lamb as present in Kipuka Puaulu in 1936.

The tree is 5 to 7 foliate and the leaves are very faintly lemon scented in mature leaves found on the ground. The large leaflets are up to 5.5" (14cm) long by 3" (7.5cm) wide, on a rachis 1' (30.5cm) long, midrib very prominent, pinnate veins prominent, apex bluntly tipped, base blunt and fitted closely to the rachis. Neither flowers nor seeds were seen. This may be a male tree. Twigs are smooth and light brown. Bark is thin and smooth on this tree with parallel lines of whitish warts. L.W. Bryan's wood collection contains a specimen of this species. It is light golden brown, streaked with darker brown, medium fine texture, straight grain, plain figure, medium low denisty and soft. Vessels are few, medium sized and scattered, rays very indistinct. Wood showed good stability. This is another tree of the moderately dry forest far advanced in succession.[10]

AE or HEAE

Semiarticulate Prickly Ash

Zanthoxylum semiarticulatum
St. John & Hosaka in Deg.
Syn. **Fagara semiarticulatum**

[10] See:
Hillebrand, p. 76.
Rock, p. 195.
St. John, p. 206.
Lamb, p. 13.

[11] See:
Hillebrand, p. 76.
Rock, p. 209.
St. John, p. 206.

[12] See:
Rock, p. 205.
St. John, p. 207.

This AE is a small tree 6 to 18' (1.9 to 5.6m) tall. Leaves are clustered at the ends of ascending branches, smooth on both sides. The small flowers are green. Fruit is green to almost black; a rough capsule that splits to release the seeds at maturity. Bark is grey to greenish brown or nearly black at maturity. Wood is pale yellow.

HVNP Kipuka Puaulu

AE

Zanthoxylum dipetalum var. **geminicarpum** Rock

This may be the largest of the AEs, a tree 40' (12.6m) tall and 2.5' (76cm) in diameter with stout, ascending branches, located near the giant Koa in Kipuka Puaulu. It is endemic to Hawaii and perhaps should be listed as endangered.

Compound leaves have three leaflets, ovate-oblong or elliptical-oblong to round, about 2" (5cm) in diameter, glossy, margin slightly toothed, midrib prominent, pinnate veins indistinct. Flowers greenish-white or reddish-yellow, inconspicuous in loose panicles. Fruit follicles usually two with an ovoid, black seed in each. Bark smooth, covered with lenticles, dark on light grey. No wood available as only tree I found was in HVNP.

L.W. Bryan's big tree is 5'6" (1.7m) in circumference, 71' (22m) tall with 35' (11m) crown spread located in Kipuka Puaulu.[6]

2.

1.

1. Ae, Z. dipetalum v. geminicarpum, bark detail, HVNP.
2. Ae, Z. oahuense; male flowering branch and fruiting panicles in the upper corners. Rock photo.
3. Ae, Z. dipetalum v. geminicarpum; tree growing in the Kipuka Puaulu near Volcano Kilauea, Hawaii. Elevation 4,000 feet. Rock photo.

3.

HVNP Kipuka Puaulu

AE

Zanthoxylum maviense
v. **anceps** f. **petiolulata** Rock

This is another AE that has been collected from Kipuka Puaulu. It is a small tree up to 20' (6.3m) tall and pubescent throughout. Due to its very limited occurrence it might well be placed on the endangered list.

Leaves are trifoliate on petioles 4 to 6" (10 to 15cm) long, lanceolate to ovate-lanceolate, very uneven sided. Flowers are small and occur in large panicles up to 10" (25cm) long, many flowered, petals cream colored. Follicle only about .375 (.9cm) across and minutely pitted.[12]

SPURGE FAMILY — Euphorbiaceae

Spurge family is represented in Hawaii by five genera of native woody shrubs or trees. All are endemic except possibly *Aleurites* which is thought by some to be a Polynesian introduction from other Pacific islands. See *Aleurites moluccana* for further discussion.

Key to the Genera from Rock

Plants not milky:
    Phyllantheae. Flowers monoecious or dioecious; ovary cells two-ovulate:
        Leaves alternate entire, fruit a berry, three celled
            seeds arillate .... **Drypetes** Vahl.
            Syn. **Neowawraea**
        Leaves alternate, entire, fruits flat, one seeded .... **Antidesma** (Burm) L.
    Crotoneae. Flowers monoecious or dioecious; ovary cells one-ovulate:
        Leaves alternate, crenate or serrate; fruits capsular,
            two-three celled .... **Claoxylon** A. Juss.
        Leaves alternate, lobed; stone fruit one seeded, splitting
            into tow-four cocci .... **Aleurites** J.R.& G. Forst.
Plants milky:
    Euphorbieae. Flowers mostly monoecious, rarely dioecious; ovary
    three celled, one-ovulate:
        Leaves opposite, linear; fruit a three celled capsule .... **Euphorbia** L.

HVNP Wahaulu
HNP

KUKUI — Aleurites moluccana (L.) Hbd.

St. John lists *A. moluccana* as the only valid species of *Aleurites* in Hawaii but both Neal and Degener list *A. remyi* as a valid species. *A. remyi* is now popular as an ornamental and a nice specimen is found in Manuka State Park, Kau District, Hawaii. *A. remyi* is distinguished by its narrower lobed leaves.

KUKUI is a very common tree of the lowland forest in both moist and fairly dry regions to an elevation of 2,200' (671m). St. John and many other botanists consider it to have been introduced to the islands by early Hawaiians, in part at least, because one researcher did not find fossil pollen. When one considers that the Hawaiians may not have arrived before the year 1000AD, the tree has made wonderful inroads into the Hawaiian forest in that short time. One wonders how the heavy round seeds reached the tops of very steep sea-side cliffs without the help of any animals to carry them. The seeds are known to be a violent purgative when eaten raw so it is not reasonable to suppose that people carried them with them for food as they went about their tasks in the forest. Plant geographers postulate that plants with such heavy seeds had to be brought in by early settlers but if one accepts this theory then one has to consider Pritchardia palms, MAHOEs and many other heavy seeded species listed as endemic or indigenous. The whole subject of how specific plants reached the Hawaiian islands is a fascinating one.

KUKUI forms large stands of trees easily spotted on the hillsides by the light greygreen color of the leaves. The trees may be as large as 3' (92cm) or more in diameter and 60' (19m) tall or more.

Alternate leaves are angularly three pointed, lobed or heart shaped, up to 8" (20cm) long, with stems longer than the leaves; leaves covered with silvery-grey powder. Flowers occur in large terminal clusters, 6" (15cm) or more long. Each floret is about .5" (1cm) in diameter, white, 5-petaled, with yellow pistils. Large or round fruits up to 2" (5cm) in diameter have a fleshy outer husk that covers one or two hard nuts. The nut shell is shiny black when cleaned, meat is white, oily, and must not be eaten raw but can be cooked and eaten. Twigs are green, covered with grey to brownish powder. Bark of mature trees is spotted, whitish-grey to dark grey, smooth on trunks

1. *Kukui leaves and flowers.*

2. *Kukui, A. moluceana, leaves and fruit.*

3. *Kukui, A. remyi, flower and leaf detail. Manuka State Park, Hawaii.*

1. *Silvery colored groves of Kukui on cliffs, windward, Maui.*

[1] See:
Hillebrand, p. 399.
Rock, p. 257.
Neal, pp. 503-07.
Carlquist, pp. 303 & 433.
St. John, p. 210.

to 12" (31.5cm) in diameter. Large trunks are marked with vertical lines .5 to 1" (1.2 to 2.5cm) apart.

Wood is light straw color streaked with grey, texture fine, figure streaked, grain straight to curly, density low and it is soft. Vessels are medium sized, few and scattered, rays are not visible at 10x. Wood decays readily but is quite easily worked. Hawaiians used the wood for easily made but short lived canoes and fish floats. Nuts were strung on a palm leaf midrib and burned as candles, thus the name 'candlenut'. The oil was sometimes pressed out of the nuts and burned with a TAPA wick for light. In modern times much KUKUI nut oil has been used in paints but it is said to be slow drying.

The trees occupy a very conspicuous place in the lower forest and on hillsides where the dense shade inhibits reproduction of other trees. This tree may have covered large lowland areas now covered with cane fields.

L.W. Bryan's big tree is 10'7" (3.3m) in circumference, 67' (21m) tall with a crown spread of 59' (18.6m) and is located at Kapapala, Pahoa, Hawaii.[1]

HAME or HAA   **Antidesma** (Burm) L.

Antidesma is represented by *A. platyphyllum* with three varieties and one form, all endemic, and *P. pulvinatum* with two varieties, all endemic.

Key to the Species

Leaves ovate or obovate, glabrous .... **A. platyphyllum**
Leaves cordate with a patch of hairs in the angles of
   the midrib and veins .... **A pulvinatum**

List of the taxa from St. John

Antidesma
   x **kapuae** Rock (cross between the two species)   end. Hawaii
   platyphyllum Mann, var. **platyphyllum**, f. **platyphyllum**   end. H.I.
      f. **rubrum** Deg. & Shreff in Sherff   end. Oahu
      var. **hamakuaense** Fosb.   end Hawaii
      var. **hillebrandii** Pax and Hoffm   end Hauai
      var. **subamplexicaule** Sherff   end Hawaii
   pulvinatum var. **pulvinatum** Hbd.   end. H.I. except Lanai
      var. **contractum** Deg. & Sherff in Sherff   end. Hawaii
      var. **leiogonum** Sherff   end. Oahu, Lanai, Maui

[2] See:
Hillebrand, p. 420.
Rock, p. 249.
St. John, p. 211.

1. Haa or Mehame tree. Bryan photo.

2. Hame or Haa, A. platyphyllum, leaf, bud and fruit. Kokee, Kauai.

3. Haa or Mehame, A. pulvinatum, leaves and small stem of fruit.

HNP

HAME   **Antidesma platyphyllum** Mann

HAME is generally a small tree of the dry as well as wet forest, but may become 2' (63cm) in diameter and 50' (15.75m) tall under favorable conditions. It is found on all the islands, but not abundantly.

Leaves are large, bright green and glossy with prominent green midrib and few large pinnate veins interlaced with fine veins. Leaves are oblong, pointed at the apex and blunt at base with very short, reddish-brown petiole. Flowers occur along the simple branches of a rachis about 4" (10cm) long, small, with rudimentary petals. Fruits are dark red, fleshy, compressed berries .5" (1cm) in diameter, occurring along the branches of the rachis on short stems. Fruits resemble cherries. Twigs are reddish, rough and slender. Bark is fibrous, deeply corrugated and whitish.

4. Haa or Mehame bark detail.

Wood varies. The piece from Hawaii is reddish brown and streaked while my piece from Kauai is much lighter in color. In both pieces the wood is straight grained, dense and rather hard. It has numerous fine vessels in rows between the many very fine rays. Wood warps but is fairly workable. Bryan's big tree is 6'8" (2m) in circumference, 52' (16.3m) tall and with crown spread of 23' (7m), located at Kaupulehu, Hawaii. HAME is an inconspicuous component of the mixed forest.[2]

HVNP Dry areas

HAA, HAME or MEHAME   **Antidesma pulvinatum** Hbd.

This species is found on all the islands as one of three varieties, all endemic. The variety I saw in South Kona, Hawaii was not determined. Rock found it to be most common on the lava fields of South Kona. It may grow to 1' (31.5cm) in diameter and 20' (6.3m) in height.

Leaves are alternate, variable in size, from 1.5 by 2" to 3 by 6" (3.7cm by 5cm to 7.5cm by 15cm), heart shaped with 1" (2.5cm) petiole, dull green with brown spots of tomentum on the back at the angles of the veins with the midrib. Midribs are somewhat depressed, giving the leaf a slightly folded appearance. Veins are few and prominent. Flowers occur in short panicles branching only at the base, without petals. Male flowers on projecting, axillary spurs. Fruits are red to blackish, small, numerous, about .5" (1 cm) or less in diameter, juicy. Twigs are slender, light brown, covered with small lighter colored lenticles. Bark is deeply corrugated longitudinally, fibrous and whitish.

Wood is streaked light and medium brown, sapwood yellow, texture very fine, figure curly and banded due to darker annular layers. Grain is straight, density high, and wood hard. Vessels are very fine and scattered; rays extremely fine and closely spaced, slightly wavy. Wood warps but works well.

The pulp surrounding the seeds was mixed with oil of KAMANI nut to produce a red dye used on bathing malos. The tree is a minor component of the forest of the dry areas of South Kona and Kau and very rare in HVNP.[3]

[3] *Hillebrand, p. 403.*
Rock, p. 253.
Neal, p. 500
St. John, p. 211.

[4] *See:*
Hillebrand, p. 398.
Rock, p. 253.
Carlquist, p. 311.
Degener, FH, p. 190.
St. John, p. 211.

POOLA **Claoxylon**

From St. John the species and varieties of *Claoxylon* are as follows:
Claoxylon
	helleri Sherff	end. Kauai
**	**Sandwicense** Muel-Arg. var. **sandwicense**	end. e. Maui
	var. **degeneri** Sherff	end. Kauai
	var. **glabrescens** (Sherff) Sherff	end. Oahu, Lanai, Maui, Hawaii
	var. **hillebrandii** Sherff	end. Hawaii
	var. **magnifolium**	end. H.I.
	var. **tomentosum**	Kauai

Thus the tree is represented on all the islands but not abundantly. As noted, *C. sandwicense* var. *sandwicense* is listed as endangered. If *C. helleri* is possibly extinct as stated by Degener, (FH, p. 190) it might well be added to the list of endangered or extinct species.

1. *Poola, C. sandwicensis, leaves and fruits, Kokee, Kauai.*

HNP

POOLA **Claoxylon sandwicensis** Muell-Arg.

Light green, bright and shining, finely toothed leaves are 3" (7.5cm) wide by 6" (15cm) long, obovate-oblong with a 1.5" petiole, pinnate veins and prominent midribs. They are clustered near the branch ends. Flowers are borne in axillary clusters or on short spikes along the twigs below the leaves. They are small, pretty, light yellowish-green, with parts in threes. The .5" (1cm) calyx is parted to the base in three triangular lobes. Fruit is three-parted capsule, purple with globose seeds. Spindly twigs are apically brownish, hispid. Bark is light grey or greenish, splotched light and dark, thin and smooth on 3" (7.5cm) trunks.

Wood is very light yellow, with filled pith, texture is very fine, figure plain, grain straight, density medium and medium hard. Vessels are very fine and scattered, rays very fine, closely spaced and somewhat wavy. Wood checks on drying but works well. There is no record of Hawaiian use.

This tree is an inconspicuous part of the moderately dry to dry forest.[4]

AKOKO **Euphorbia** L.

St. John lists 72 taxa of Euphorbia grouped under 16 species. This list is included here to emphasize the number of taxa now listed as endangered or extinct. The only species considered to be trees as listed by Rock are *E. lorifolia* (Gray) Hbd. now changed to *E. celastroides*, possibly varieties *amplectens* and *mauiensis*, *E. Lorifolia* var. *gracilis*, now changed to *E. olowaluana* var. *gracilis*, and *E. rockii* which has not been changed.

St. John's list of species and varieties of *Euphorbia* are:
Euphorbia L., 1754
  albimarginata T. &G., 1857. (as *albomarginata*). N:517. Rattlesnake weed.
  cult. s. Calif. to Mexico
    Chamaesyce albomarginata (T.&G.) Small, 1903
  antiquorum L., 1753. N:518. Cactus-like spurge, Malayan spurge tree.
  cult. India, s.e. Asia

** **Arnottiana** Endl., 1836, var. **Arnottiana** end. Oahu
    Hookeri Steud., 1841. H:396
    Chamaesyce Hookeri (Steud.) Arthur 1922.
**   var. **integrifolia** (Hbd.) St. John, 1940 end. w. Maui
    Hookeri var. *integrifolia* Hbd., 1888. H:397
    C. Arnottiana (Endl.) Deg.&Deg., 1959, var. *integrifolia* (Hbd.) Deg.&Deg., 1959. D:fam. 190, 12/28/59
** **atrococca** Heller, 1897, var. **atrococca** end. Kauai
    Chamaesyce atrococca (Heller) Croizat & Deg. in Deg.&Croizat, 1936. D:fam. 190, 12/9/36.
**   var. **kilaueana** Sherff, 1936 end. Kauai
    Chamaesyce atrococca var. *kilaueana* (Sherff) Deg.&Deg., 1959. D:fam. 190, 12/28/50.
**   var. **kokeeana** Sherff, 1936 end. Kauai
    Chamaesyce atrococca, var. *kokeeana* (Sherff) Deg.&Deg., 1959. D:fam. 190, 12/28/59

bifida H.&A., 1837 adv. China
    hypericifolia sensu Am. Bot., non L., 1753

canariensis L., 1753. N:518. Cardon cult. Canary Is.

celastroides Boiss. in A.DC., 1862, var. **celastroides** end. Nihoa, Kauai, Niihau
    multiformis Gaud., var. *celastroides* (Boiss. in A.DC.) Gray in Mann, 1867
    Chamaesyce celastroides (Boiss. in A.CD.) Croizat&Deg.in Deg.&Croizat, 1936. D:fam. 190, 12/9/36

    var. **amplectens** Sherff, 1936 end. H.I.
    Chamaesyce celastroides (Boiss.in A.DC.) Croizat&Deg.in Deg.&Croizat, 1936. var. *amplectens* (Sherff) Deg.&Deg., 1959. D:fam. 190, 12/28/59

**   var. **halawana** Sherff, 1936, F. **halawana** end. Molokai
    Chamaesyce celastroides, var. *halawana* (Sherff) Deg.&Deg., 1959. D:fam. 190, 12/28/59

    f. **kahanana** Sherff, 1936 end. Oahu
    Chamaesyce celastroides, var. *halawana*, f. *kahanana* (Sherff) Deg.&Deg., 1959. D:fam. 190, 12/28/59

    var. **hanapepensis** Sherff, 1936 end. Kauai
    Chamaesyce celastorides, var. *hanapepensis* (Sherff) Deg.&Deg., 1959. D:fam. 190, 12/28/59

    var. **Hathewayi** Sherff, 1951 end. Oahu

**   var. **haupuana** Sherff, 1936 end. Kauai
    Chamaesyce celastroides, var. *haupuana* (Sherff) Deg.&Deg., 1959. D:fam. 190, 12/28/59

***   var. **Humbertii** Sherff, 1936 end. Kauai
    Chamaesyce celastroides, var.*Humbertii* (Sherff) Deg.&Deg. 1959. D:fam. 190, 12/28/59

    var. **ingrata** Deg. & Sherff in Sherff, 1954 end. w. Maui
    Chamaesyce celastroides, var.*ingrata*(Deg.&Sherff) Deg.&Deg., 1959. D:fam. 190, 12/28/59

**   var. **kaenana** Sherff, 1936 end. Oahu
    Chamaesyce celastroides, var. *kaenana* Sherff) Deg.&Deg., 1959. D:fam. 190, 12/28/59

var. **kealiana Sherff, 1936 end. Kauai
    Chamaesyce celastroides, var. *kealiana* (Sherff) Deg.&Deg., 1959. D:fam. 190, 12/28/59

    var. **laehiensis** Deg. Deg.&Sherff in Sherff, 1964 end. Lanai
    var. **lorifolia** (Gray ex Mann) Sherff, 1936. Koko, 'akoko
    end. H.I., except Oahu
    lorifolia (Gray in Mann) Hbd., 1888. H:395; R:259.
    multiformis H.&A., var. *lorifolia* Gray ex Mann, 1867
    rivularis Heller, 1897
    Chamaesyce celastroides, var. *lorifolia* (Gray ex Mann) Deg.&Deg., 1959 D:fam. 190, 12/28/59
    Chamaesyce lorifolia (Hbd.) Croizat&Deg.in Deg.&Croizat, 1936. D:fam. 190, 12/9/36

  var. **mauiensis** Sherff, 1936   end. Lanai, Maui
   C. celastroides, var. *mauiensis* (Sherff) Deg.&Deg., 1959. D:fam.
   190, 12/28/59
** var. **moomoniana** Sherff, 1936   end. Molokai
   Chamaesyce celastroides, var. *moomoniana* (Sherff) Deg.&Deg., 1959.
   D:fam. 190, 12/28/59
** var. **nematopoda** Sherff, 1936   end. Kauai
   Chamaesyce celastroices, var. *nematopoda* (Sherff) Deg.&Deg., 1959.
   D:fam. 190, 12/28/59
*** var. **niuensis** Sherff, 1936   end. Oahu
   Chamaesyce celastroides, var. *niuensis* (Sherff) Deg.&Deg., 1959. D:fam.
   190, 12/28/59
  var. **odonatoides** Deg.&Sherff, 1951   end. Lanai
   Chamaesyce celastroides, var. *odonatoides* (Deg.&Sherff) Deg.&Deg., 1959.
   D:fam. 190, 12/28/59
  var. **pseudoniuensis** Deg.&Sherff in Sherff, 1956   end. Kauai
** var. **saxicola** Deg.&Sherff in Sherff, 1936   end. Hawaii
   Chamaesyce celastroides, var. *saxicola* (Deg.&Sherff in Sherff) Deg.&Deg.,
   1959. D:fam. 190, 12/28/59
** var. **Stokesii** (Forbes) Sherff, 1936   end. Kauai, Niihau
   Stokesii Forbes, 1913
   Chamaesyce celastroices, var. *Stokesii* (Forbes) Deg.&Deg., 1959. D:fam.
   190, 12/28/59
** var. **waikoluensis** Sherff, 1936   end. Molokai
   Chamaesyce celastroides, var. *waikoluensis* (Sherff) Deg.&Deg., 1959. D:fam.
   190, 12/28/59.
 clusiaefolia H.&A., 1832.H:394   end. Oahu
  Chamaesyce clusiaefolia (H.&A.) Arthur, 1922, D:fam. 190, 5/1/59
 cotinifolia L., 1753. N:517. Herba mala   cult. trop. Am.
 Cyparissias L., 1753. N:517. Cypress spurge   adv. Europe
  Tithymalus Cyparissias (L.) Scop., 1772
 Degeneri Sherff, 1936, var. **Degeneri**. Koko, 'akoko, beach spurge
          end. Kauai, Oahu, Molokai, Maui, Hawaii
  f. *minuscula* Sherff, 1954
  cordata Meyen, 1834, non Schrank, 1789
  Chamaesyce Degeneri (Sherff) Croizat & Deg. in Deg.& Croizat, 1936. D:fam.
   190, 12/9/36
  f. *minuscula* (Sherff) Deg.&Deg., 1959. D:fam. 190, 12/28/59
** var. **molokaiensis** Sherff, 1936   end. Molokai
   Chamaesyce Degeneri, var. *molokaiensis* (Sherff) Deg.&Croizat, 1946. D:fam.
   190, 9/15/46
 dentata Michx., 1803   adv. e. N.Am.
  Poinsettia dentata (Michx.) Small, 1903
*** **Deppeana** Boiss. in A.DC., 1862   end. Oahu
  festiva Sherff, 1936
  Chamaesyce Deppeana (Boiss.) Millsp., 1916
  C. festiva (Sherff) Croizat & Deg. in Deg.&Croizat, 1936. D:fam. 190, 12/9/36
 Forbesii Sherff, 1936   end. Oahu
  clusiaefolia H.&A., var. *grandifolia* Hbd., 1888. H:395
  Chamaesyce Forbesii (Sherff) Croizat & Deg., 1936. D:fam. 190, 12/9/36
 fulgens Karw. ex Klotzsch, 1834. N:517. Scarlet plume   cult. Mexico
 geniculata Ortega, 1797. H:398; N:516. Wild spurge, kaliko   adv. trop. Am.
  Poinsettia geniculata (Ortega) Klotzsch & Garcke, 1859. D:fam. 190, 7/14/59
 glomerifera (Sillsp) L.C. Wheeler, 1939. N:516   adv. warm regions, widespread
  hypericifolia sensu Haw. bot., non L., 1753. D:fam. 190. 5/14/37
  bifida sensu St. John, 1932, non H.&A., 1836
  C glomerifera Millsp., 1913
** **haeeleeleana** Herbst., 1971   end. Kauai
 heterophylla L., 1753, var. heterophylla. H:398. Fire plant, Mexican fire plant
  painted leaf, hypocrite plant   cult., esc. Mexico

Poinsettia heterophylla (L.) Klotzsch & Garcke ex Clotzsch, 1860
    var. cyathophora (Murr.) Griseb., 1859. N:516. Mexican fire plant
        cult., esc. temp.& trop. Am.
    cyathophora Murr., 1786
    Poinsettia cyathophora (Murr.) Klotzsch & Garcke ex Klotzsch, 1860.
        D:fam. 190, 6/30/32

** **halemanui** Sherff, 1936   end. Kauai
    Chamaesyce halemanui (Sherff) Croizat & Deg. in Deg.&Croizat, 1936.
        D:fam. 190, 12/9/36

    Hillebrandii Lévl., 1911. var. **Hilebrandii**   end. Oahu, w. Maui
    Chamaesyce Hillebrandii (Lévl.) Croizat & Deg. in Deg.& Croizat, 1936.
        D:fam. 190, 12/9/36

    var. **palikeana** Deg.& Sherff in Sherff, 1936   end. Oahu
    Chamaesyce Hillebrandii (Lévl.) Deg.&Deg., 1959, var. *palikeana* (Deg.&
        Sherff in Sherff) Deg.& Deg., 1959. D:fam. 190, 12/28/59

**   var. **waimanoana** Sherff, 1936. (as *wainianana*).   end. Oahu
    Chamaesyce Hillebrandii, var. *waimanoana* (Sherff) Deg.&Croizat, 1936
        D:fam. 190, 12/9/36

    hirta L., 1753. N:516. Garden spurge, hairy spurge, old blood, golondina,
        koko-kahiki   adv. Cosmopolitan
    pilulifera sensu Am. and Haw. authors, non L., 1753. H:397

    kuwaleana Deg.& Sherff in Sherff, 1949   end. Oahu
    lactea Haw., 1812. H:518. Mottled candlestick   cult. India
    lancifolia Schlecht., 1832. N:517. Ixbut   cult. Mexico, Cent. Am.
    leucocephala Lotsy, 1895. N:517. Punopuno   cult Cent. Am.
    marginata Pursh, 1814. N:516. Snow-on-the-mountain   cult. w. U.S.A.
    Milii des Moulin, var. splendens (Boj.) Ursch & Leandri, N:519.
        Crown of thorns   cult Madagascar
    splendens Boj., 1829

*** **multiformis** H.& A., 1832, var. **multiformis**. 'Akoko   end. Oahu
    Chamaesyce multiformis (H.& A.) Croizat & Deg. in Deg.&Croizat, 1936.
        D:fam. 190, 12/9/36

***   var. **haleakalana** Sherff, 1936   end. e. Maui
    Chamaesyce multiformis, var. *haleakalana* (Sherff) Deg.&Deg., 1959
        D:fam. 190, 12/28/59

***   var. **kaalana** Sherff, 1936   end. Oahu
    Chamaesyce multiformis, var. *kaalana* (Sherff) Deg.&Deg., 1959. D:fam.
        190, 12/28/59

**   var. kapuleiensis Deg.& Sherff in Sherff, 1936, f. **kapuleiensis**   end. Molokai
    Chamaesyce multiformis, var. *kapuleiensis* (Deg.&Sherff in Sherff) Deg.&
        Deg., 1959, f. *kapuleiensis*. D:fam. 190, 12/29/59

        f. **Pekelonis** Deg. Deg.& Sherff in Sherff, 1962   end. Molokai
    var. **manoana** Sherff, 1936   end. H.I.
    Chamaesyce multiformis, var. *manoana* (Sherff) Deg.&Deg., 1959
        D:fam. 190, 12/28/59

    var. **microphylla** Boiss. in A.DC., 1862   end. Oahu, Molokai, w. Maui
        var. *tenuior* Gray ex Mann, 1867
        var. *microphylla* Lévl., 1911 (dubious)
    Chamaesyce multiformis, var. *microphylla* (Boiss. in A.DC.) Deg.&Deg., 1959.
        D:fam. 190, 12/28/59

    var. **mohihiensis** Sherff, 1939   end. Kauai
***   var. **perdita**, Sherff, 1938   end. Oahu
    Chamaesyce multiformis var. *perdita* (Sherff) Deg.&Deg., 1959. D:fam.
        190, 12/28/59

**   var. **sparsiflora** (Heller) Sherff, 1936   end. Kauai
    sparsiflora Heller, 1897.
    Chamaesyce multiformis, var. *sparsiflora* (Heller) Deg.&Deg., 1959.
        D:fam. 190, 12/28/59

***   var. **tomentella** Boiss. in A.DC., 1862. H:396   end. Oahu
    Chamaesyce multiformis, var. *tomentella* (Boiss. in D.CD.) Deg.&Deg., 1959.
        190, 12/28/59

    neriifolia L., 1753. N:517. Indian spurge tree   cult. India, Malaya

**   **olowaluana** Sherff, 1936, var. **olowaluana**   end. w. Maui
    Chamaesyce olowaluana (Sherff) Croizat & Deg. in Deg.& Croizat, 1936.
      D:fam. 190, 12/9/36
   var. **gracilis** (Rock) Sherff, 1936, f. **gracilis**   **end. Hawaii**
     lorifolia (Gray) Hbd., var. *gracilis* Rock, 1913, R:259
      Chamaesyce olowaluana (Sherff) Deg.&Deg., 1959, var. *gracilis* (Rock)
        Deg.& Deg., 1959. D:fam. 190, 12/28/59
     f. **leiocarpa** Deg.& Sherff in Sherff, 1951   end. Hawaii
       Chamaesyce olowaluana, var. *gracilis*, f. *polycephala* (Deg.& Sherff in Sherff)
         Deg.& Deg., 1959 D:fam. 190, 12/28/59
   var. **lepidifolia** Deg.& Sherff in Sherff, 1951   end. w. Maui
     Chamaesyce olowaluana var. *lepidifolia* (Deg.& Sherff in Sherff) Deg.&
       Deg., 1959. D:fam. 190, 12/28/59
Peplus L., 1753. H:398; N:516. Petty spurge   adv. Eurasia
   Tithymalus Peplus (L.) Gaertn., 1790
prostrata Ait., 1789. N:517. Prostrate spurge   adv. Americas
pulcherrima Willd. ex Klotzsch, 1834, var. pulcherrima. H:398; N:518
   Poinsettia   cult. Mexico
   Poinsettia pulcherrima (Willd.) R. Grah., 1836. D:fam. 190, 8/8/60
   var. alba Hort. White Poinsettia   cult. Mexico
   var. plenissima Hort. Double Poinsettia   cult Mexico
*** **Remyi** Gray ex Boiss. in A.DC., 1866, var. **Remyi**. H:395   end. Kauai, Oahu
   Chamaesyce Remyi (Gray ex Boiss in A.DC.) Croizat & Deg. in Deg. & Croizat,
      1936. D:fam. 190, 12/9/36
*** var. **hanaleiensis** Sherff, 1936   end. Kauai
    Chamaesyce Remyi, var. *hanaleiensis* (Sherff) Deg.& Deg., 1959. D:fam.
      190, 7/14/59
**   var. **kahiliana** Sherff, 1936. (as *kalihiana*)   end Kauai
    Chamaesyce Remyi, var. *kahiliana* (Sherff) Deg. & Deg., 1959. D:fam.
      190, 7/14/59
**   var. **kauaiensis** Deg. & Sherff in Sherff, 1936   end. Kauai
    Chamaesyce Remyi, var. *kauaiensis* (Deg. & Sherff in Sherff) Deg. & Deg.,
      1959. D:fam. 190, 12/28/59
**   var. **leptopoda** Sherff, 1936   end. Kauai
    Chamaesyce Remyi, var. *leptopoda* (Sherff) Deg.& Deg., 1959. D:fam.
      190, 7/14/59
**   var. **Lydgatei** Sherff, 1936   end. Kauai
    Chamaesyce Remyi, var. *Lydgatei* (Sherff) Deg.& Deg., 1959. D:fam. 190,
      7/14/59
**   var. **molesta** Sherff, 1938   end. Kauai
    Chamaesyce Remyi (Sherff) Deg.& Deg., 1959. var. *molesta* (Sherff)
      Deg.& Deg., 1959. D:fam. 190, 7/14/59
**   var. **olokelensis** Skottsb.& Sherff in Sherff, 1936   end. Kauai
    Chamaesyce Remyi, var. *olokelensis* (Skottsb.& Sherff in Sherff) Deg.&
      Deg., 1959. D:fam. 190, 7/14/59
**   var. **pterpoda** Sherff, 1936   end. Kauai
    Chamaesyce Remyi, var. *pteropoda* (Sherff) Deg.& Deg., 1959. D:fam.
      190, 12/28/59
**   var. **wahiawana** Sherff, 1936   end. Kauai
    Chamaesyce Remyi, var. *wahiawana* (Sherff) Deg.& Deg., 1959. D:fam.
      190, 12/28/59
**   var. **waimeana** Sherff, 1936   end. Kauai
    Chamaesyce Remyi, var. *waimeana* (Sherff) Deg.& Deg., 1959. D:fam.
      190, 12/28/59
*** var. **Wilkesii** Sherff, 1936   end. Kauai
    Chamaesyce Remyi, var. *Wilkesii* (Sherff) Deg.& Deg., 1959. D:fam.
      190, 12/28/59
  Rockii Forbes, 1909. R:261. Koko, 'akoko, Rocks spurge   end. Oahu
    Chamaesyce Rockii (Forbes) Croizat & Deg. in Deg.& Croizat, 1936.
      D:fam. 190, 12/9/36

[5] See:
Hillebrand, p. 397.
Rock, p. 259.
Neal, p. 516.
St. John, p. 212.

1. Akoko, E. olowaluana v. gracilis. Small tree, South Kona, Hawaii.

2. Akoko, E. olowaluana, v. gracilis. Fruiting branch pinned against trunk of tree; bark is incise, note flow of latex. Growing on the lava fields of Puuwaawaa, North Kona, Hawaii; elevation 3,000 feet. Rock photo.

```
***Skottsbergii Sherff, 1936, var. Skottsbergii                    end. Oahu
       Chamaesyce Skottsbergii (Sherff) Croizat & Deg. in Deg.& Croizat, 1936.
         D:fam. 190, 12/9/36
    var. audens Sherff, 1936                                     end. Molokai
       Chamaesyce Skottsbergii, var. audens (Sherff) Deg.& Deg., 1959. D:fam.
         190, 12/28/59
***  var. kalaeloana Sherff, 1936                                  end. Oahu
       Chamaesyce Skottsbergii, var. kalaeloana (Sherff) Deg.& Deg. 1959
         D:fam. 190, 12/28/59
**   var. vaccinioides Sherff, 1936                              end. Molokai
```

Key to the tree-like species of *Euphorbia*

Leaves linear-oblong; flower heads terminal or axillary, single; capsule small
    Cocci broader at base . . . . **E. celastroides** Boiss
    Cocci width equal . . . . **E. olowaluana** Sherff
Leaves obovate-oblong; flower heads in open axillary cymes;
    capsules large . . . . **E. rockii**

AKOKO   Euphorbia cleastroides Boiss

The plant I saw above Milolii, Hawaii was not identified to variety and was a single stemmed shrub. Others are listed as trees 10 to 20' (3 to 6.3m) tall. The word AKOKO means blood colored.

Leaves are opposite, linear or oblong, .5 by 1" (1 to 2.5cm), fleshy, light green, with very short, reddish petiole. The tiny flowers occur in small clusters either axillary or terminal. Fruits are borne erect on a very short stalk, the cocci broader at the base. Twigs are stout, rough, light green, quickly aging to reddish brown. Bark is rough and exudes milky sap or latex copiously.

Wood is light straw colored, of medium texture, plain figure, straight grain, low density and soft. Small vessels occur in chains, rays are barely visible at 14x. The wood warps quite badly.

No Hawaiian uses are recorded except for firewood. AKOKO sap produces a very fine grade of rubber, according to Col. Bryan. The tree occurs in the dry forest where it is not an important element.[5]

AKOKO   Euphorbia olowaluana Sherff

This description is based on a specimen in HVNP herbarium identified by St. John. It was collected on Puu Kapele, Mauna Kea, Hawaii.

Leaves opposite and slender, 1.5 to 2" (3.5 to 5cm) long by .375 to .5" (.9 to 1.1cm) broad, very short petiole, distinct midrib, faint pinnate veins showing on the underside. The leaf nodes are enlarged, new stems very slender, reddish color. Older stems grey. Small tree with milky sap.

AKOKO   Euphorbia olowaluana var. gracilis (Rock) Sherff
                            Syn. **E. lorifolia** var. **gracilis** Rock

Rock found this AKOKO to be a tree 20' to 25' (6.3 to 7.8m) tall and nearly 1' (31.5cm) in diameter, with long slender leaves. It was growing in the very diverse and interesting mixed forest on the lava fields of Puuwaawaa, Kona, Hawaii at an elevation of 3,000' (945m).

AKOKO   Euphorbia rockii Forbes

This AKOKO, endemic to Oahu, is said to be a tree 15 to 20' (4.7 to 6.3m) tall and 8" (20cm) in diameter, with broad flat crown. Carlquist states it is the tallest of the AKOKOs but Rock found *E. olowaluana* var. *gracilis* to be taller. In any event these appear to be the largest of the species of *Euphor-*

bia. Dark green leaves are glossy, large and leathery, obovate-oblong, sessile, 1 by 3 to 5" (2.5 by 7.5 to 12.5cm) long, with prominent midrib and fine pinnate veins closely spaced. The very small flowers are borne in axillary clusters near the branch ends. Fruits, largest of the AKOKO, are three-cornered, bright pink or deep scarlet and 1" (2.5cm) long. Bark is smooth and whitish and exudes a thick sap when cut.[6]

MEHAMEHAME   **Drypetes phyllanthoides** (Rock) Sherff
Syn. **Neowawraea phyllanthoides** Hbd. St. John

Only one species of *Drypetes* is recognized as being native to the Hawaiian islands and it is endemic to all the islands except Lanai. It is generally a tree about 2' (6.3cm) in diameter and 30' (9.5m) tall but giant specimens are said to occur on Kauai, in one of the valleys below Kokee, that may be as much as 5' (1.5m) in diameter. The ones I saw at Honomolino, Hawaii were average size as given above, slender with sharply upright branches. State Forester Charles Judd measured a stump of this tree that was 10' (3m) in diameter at Walanea on Oahu.

Leaves are opposite, 1.5 by 3" to 3 by 6" (3.7 by 7.5cm to 7.5 to 15cm), heart shaped with prominent, light green midrib, distinct veins, pinnately arranged, .5" (1cm) reddish petiole, margin smooth, pale green above and underneath. Flowers are tiny and borne in tight clusters along the stem and in axils of leaves. Small red fruits are borne on short axillary stems about .25" (.5cm) in diameter, with juicy pulp around a 3-parted seed case, each section with two to four very small seeds. Twigs are slender, light brown, somewhat zigzag, covered with fine lenticles. Old trees are heavily buttressed and the bark is scaly, not furrowed.

Wood is dark reddish brown, fine texture, lightly streaked figure, straight grain, very dense and very hard. Vessels are very fine, numerous and scattered, rays are very fine and very numerous. Wood checks and must be hard to work.

Rock thought there were only three trees of MEHAMEHAME in existence when he found it in Kau on Hawaii, but since then it has been found to be more plentiful but still is not a conspicuous component of the mixed forest where it is found. St. John states that the placement of this genus will remain in doubt until pistillate flowers are found.[7]

[6] See:
Rock, p. 261

[7] See:
Rock, p. 245.
Neal, p. 504.
Carlquist, p. 259.
St. John, p. 212.

3. Akoko, E. rockii, showing fruiting branch and flowers. Rock photo.

1. Mehamehame, D. phyllanthoides, leaf detail.

2. Mehamehame bark detail.

4. Mehamehame trees in South Kona, Hawaii.

[1] See:
Hillebrand, p. 89.
Rock, p. 262.
Neal, p. 525.
Carlquist, p. 174.
St. John, p. 221.

CASHEW or MANGO FAMILY — Anacardaceae

This family is represented in Hawaii by only one genus with one species of native plants. It is endemic to all the Hawaiian Islands.

HVNP Kalapana Trail 2,300' (725m)

NENELEAU — **Rhus sandwicensis** Grey
Hawaiian Sumac — Syn. **Rhus semialata** var. **sandwicensis** (Grey) Hbd.
Syn. **Rhus chinensis** var. **sandwicensis** (Grey) Deg. & Greenw.

NENELEAU has been the subject of several name changes and it is refreshing to see that it has now been simplified. It is often a shrub but in better environment may be a tree 15 to 25' (4.7 to 7.8m) tall and 8 to 12" (20 to 30.5cm) in diameter. It is very abundant in places and looks very much like common staghorn sumac of continental U.S.A.

Leaves are pinnately odd compound with four to six pairs of leaflets and a terminal one, bright green with red veins and petioles, reddish when young. Leaves turn yellow in autumn and are shed, leaving the trees quite bare in winter. Flowers are very small, pale yellow but very numerous in terminal panicles that are rusty tomentose. The fruit occupies the same terminal structure, red and dense, each seed very small. Twigs are dark brown, somewhat flattened, tomentose, thick and with many large heart shaped leaf scars. The bark is smooth and dark brown to almost black.

Wood is yellowish accented with annular bands of steel grey, sometimes with greenish cast that may be annual rings. Texture is coarse, figure streaked or bold flame, grain straight, density light, wood soft. Vessels very fine and scattered but not in ring porous arrangement, rays visible where they cross the harder bands of steel grey wood that may be summer wood since growth must cease when the leaves are shed. Rays are fine and evenly spaced.

Wood is tough with fair workability. It is said that when saddle trees were needed by early cowboys (PANIOLAS) Hawaiians gathered this wood because of its toughness. Old uses were for plain calabashes and LOMI LOMI sticks used as back scratchers. Col. Bryan, in correspondence, states it was used for fence posts when available, as it was very durable.

NENELEAU surely must have been one of the trees that covered vast coastal and upper bench areas, now covered with cane fields, at least along the Hamakua coast of Hawaii. These plants can still be found in the gulches and along the roadside and, as one descends the narrow steep road into Waipio valley, the whole north facing cliff is densely forested with this small tree.[1]

1. Neneleau, R. sandwicensis, leaves.

2. Neneleau tree in winter with most of its leaves shed. Stainback Highway, Hawaii.

3. Kawau, Ilex anomala, leaves and small fruits in HVNP.

HOLLY FAMILY   Aquifoliaceae

Ilex anomala is the only native member of this family in the Hawaiian Islands and it is endemic.

HVNP Kipuka Puaulu
HNP

KAWAU   **Ilex anomala** H. & A.
Syn. **Ilex sandwicensis** (Endl.) Loess
Syn. **Byronia sandwicensis** Endl.

Although the genus name of this tree is the same as of the holly that grows in the eastern states the resemblance ends there. KAWAU is abundant in the OHIA forest in the Kilauea region of HVNP and also in wet forest areas of the other islands. It is a tall slender tree, often consisting of one upright stem 20' (6.3m) tall. In favorable environment in Honaunau Forest Reserve, Hawaii, L.W. Bryan found the biggest tree 3'11" (1.2m) in circumference, 45' (14m) tall and with a crown spread of 32' (10m).

Dark green leaves are closely clustered near the ends of the branches, ovate to inverted ovate, on 1" (2.5cm) petioles, .75 to 2.5" (1.8 to 6.1cm) wide and 3 to 5" (7.5 to 13cm) long. Petioles are 1.5" (3.7cm) long or less, red, midrib is also red part way and prominent on the underside, the pinnate veins also prominent. Flowers are white, borne in cymes in the axils of the leaves, small, 4-parted. Fruits are drupe, dark purple when ripe, in clusters near the ends of branches, each as 12 or more fine grooves when dry. The drupe is set in a shallow cup-like organ. Twigs are stout, green, aging to light brown with many wart-like leaf scars. Bark is smooth on small trunks, light grey in color. Wood is white streaked with green to greyish yellow, medium coarse, figure plain to streaked with a dense pattern of very fine ray ends showing on tangential section. Density is low and the wood is quite soft. Vessels are few, fine, and scattered, rays very fine and numerous. The tough wood warps and workability is only fair.

Hawaiians used the wood for TAPA anvils and canoe trim and rigging.

KAWAU is a very common component of the wet forest, entering the OHIA forest early in succession.

BITTERSWEET FAMILY   Celastraceae

This family is represented by only one genus with one species and one variety in the Hawaiian Islands where it is endemic to all the islands. St. John lists the variety *tomentosa* (Deg. & Greenw.) as endemic to Maui only.

HVNP Kipuka Puaulu
HNP

OLOMEA   **Perrottetia sandwicensis** Gray

OLOMEA is a common shrub or small tree of the Hawaiian forest. In the Honaunau Forest Reserve, where an extensive network of roads was cleared, OLOMEA is found very abundantly along the shoulders of these roads. This indicates that it is rather intolerant of shade and needs openings for its best development. It is suppressed or almost absent from the dense forest. It is 10 to 18' (3.1 to 5.6m) tall.

Ovate-oblong leaves are quite reddish, with red veins, petioles, midribs and pinnate veins. New leaves are bright red. Leaves are large, alternate, rough, edges toothed, shiny above and dull beneath. Flowers are small, greenish, very numerous, borne in large, loose compound panicles. Branches of the panicles are fine and droop. Flowers are 5-parted. Tiny bright red fruits

[1] See:
Hillebrand, p. 79.
Rock, p. 269.
Neal, p. 530.
Carlquist, p. 310.
St. John, p. 222.

1. Olomea, *P. sandwicensis*, leaf detail with red veins. Stainback Highway, Hawaii.

[1] See:
St. John, p. 222.

1. Mahoe leaf detail.

2. Mahoe bark detail.

3. Mahoe, A. mahoe, tree in Manuka State Park, Hawaii.

are densely clustered in drooping panicles noticeable in autumn. Twigs are short and stiff except at higher altitudes where they are longer and drooping, green or red, aging to light brown, smooth. Bark smooth and light brown in 2" (5cm) stems.

Wood is yellowish or golden brown with pinkish tint and with soft pith. Texture coarse, figure plain, grain straight, density low and wood is soft. Vessels are few and fine, rays very fine. Wood warps and workability is poor.

Hawaiians used the wood to rub against HAU wood to start a fire. It was also used for house battens. The shrub or tree appears very early in succession around the edges of clearnings or openings along road right-of-ways. It is abundant in some favorable environments.[1]

SOAPBERRY FAMILY   Sapindaceae

The Soapberry family includes three genera of native or indigenous Hawaiian woody shrubs or trees.

Key to the Genera

Petals present;
  Sepals and petals 5, fruit 1 to 3 cocci;
    leaves simple or abruptly pinnate . . . . **Sapindus** (Tourn.) L.
Petals absent;
  Sepals 5, fruit 1 or 2 cocci . . . . **Alectron** Gaertn.
  Sepals 2-5, fruit a winged capsule . . . . **Dodonaea** Mill.

MAHOE   Alectron mahoe St. John & Fred.

MAHOE is endemic to Oahu where it is a small to medium sized tree. Carquist postulates that the tree has lost its ability to disperse further because the seeds have become so large, thus accounting for its absence from the youngest island, Hawaii.

Alternate leaves are compound with up to 6 leaflets per rachis, 12" (31.5cm) long or more. The leaflets are large, 2.5 by 6" (6 by 15cm), dull green above and rusty green below, midrib very prominent, petioles short and thick. Apex is bluntly tipped, base quite blunt, the margins entire. Flowers are borne in axillary racemes, buds 3" (7.5cm) long. Fruits are round or misshapen, if twins. Husk splits to reveal a bright red shell, or aril, that in turn covers the large rough seeds. Twigs are stout, yellowish-green aging to brown and later to grey. Bark on a 3" (7.5cm) trunk is smooth and grey.

MAHOE literally means twins, referring to the many fruits that develop as twins. The wood is said to be very hard and tough but no use for it is recorded. The fruits were eaten and the seeds are said to be quite good.

This species is not mentioned in Hillebrand or Rock.[1]

MAHOE   Alectron macrococcum Radlk.

This MAHOE is more widely spread as it is endemic to Kauai, Molokai and Maui. On Maui, Rock found it in the very dry area of Auahi on the south slope of Haleakala where he found so many other species. It was fairly abundant at that time. The plant develops into an ungainly tree 20 to 30' (6.3 to 9.5m) tall with trunk 6 to 8" (15 to 20cm) in diameter. The branchlets, inflorescense and young fruits are all covered with silky brown hair.

Compound leaves are large with 2 to 4 leaflets per rachis, glabrous above, tomentose below. Flowers are small on axillary stems. Fruits are large and more often borne as twins, hanging in clusters. Fruit is smooth and brown. Shell splits to reveal a red, pulpy fruit with wrinkled seeds imbedded. Twigs are stout and somewhat rough. Bark is rough and brown. Wood is said to be very hard and tough. No known use was made of the wood but the fruits were eaten. Neal states that MAHOE in both species is very rare but it is not listed as endangered.[2]

[2.] See:
Rock, p. 277.
Neal, p. 531.
Carlquist, pp. 167-68.

AALII or KUMAKANI   **Dodonaea** Mill.

The nomenclature for the species of *Dodonaea* has become very confused. St. John has settled upon three species, 22 varieties and eight forms. The Species *D. viscosa* L. of Rock and Hillebrand is now *D. sandwicensis*, endemic to all the islands. The species *D. eriocarpa* stands unchanged. *D. spatulata* has been reduced to a variety of *D. sandwicensis*.

Key to the species adapted from Hillebrand

Capsule broadly winged, with wings projecting above:
    Capsule glabrous, flat, 2-winged, or in one variety,
        2 to 3 winged .... **D. sandwicensis** Sherff
    Capsule (or at least the ovary) pubescent, 3-4 winged, turgid . **D. eriocarpa** Sm.
    Capsule bladdery, with 4 narrow wings, evanescent above .. **D. stenoptera** Hbd.

Taxa of *Dodonaea* from St. John

Dodonaea Mill., 1754. N:536. A'ali'i.
    eriocarpa Sm., 1809, var. **eriocarpa**, f. **eriocarpa**. H:88; D:fam. 210, 10/26/56.
                                    end. Molokai, Lanai, Maui, Hawaii
        f. **bifurculata** Sherff, 1949. D:fam. 210, 10/26/56   end. Kauai
        var. **amphioxea** Deg. & Sherff in Sherff, 1951. D:fam. 210, 10/26/56
                                                        end. Maui
        var. **confertior** Sherff, 1945. D:fam. 210, 10/26/56   end. Hawaii
        var. **costulata** Deg. Deg. & Sherff in Sherff, 1964   end. Lanai
        var. **Degeneri** Sherff, f. **Degeneri**, 1945. D:fam. 210, 10/12/56
                                                       end. Kauai, Maui, Hawaii
            f. **decipiens** Sherff, 1945. D:fam. 210, 10/26/56   end. Oahu
            f. **heterocarpa** Deg. & Sherff in Sherff, 1951. D:fam. 210, 10/26/56
                                                            end. Lanai
        var. **Forbesii** Sherff, 1945, f. **Forbesii**. D:fam. 210, 10/26/56   end. Hawaii
            f. **straminea** Deg. & Sherff in Sherff, 1951. D:fam. 210, 10/26/56 end Lanai
        var. **glabrescens** Sherff, 1945. D:fam. 210, 10/26/56   end. Kauai, Oahu
        var. **Hillebrandii** Sherff, 1945.D:fam.210, 10/26/56   end. Maui, Hawaii
        var. **Hosakana** Sherff, 1945. D:fam. 210, 10/26/56   end. Hawaii
        var. **lanaiensis** Sherff, 1945. D:fam. 210, 10/26/56   end. Lanai
        var. **molokaiensis** Deg.& Sherff in Sherff, 1945.D:fam. 210, 10/26/56
                                                                    end. Molokai
        var. **oblonga** Sherff, 1045. D:fam. 210, 10/26/56   end. Lanai
        var. **obtusior** Sherff, 1045. D:fam. 210, 10/26/56   end. Kauai
        var. **pallida** Deg. & Sherff in Sherff, 1945, f. **pallida.** D:fam. 210, 10/26/56.
                                                                    end. Molokai
            f. **acuminatula** Deg. & Sherff in Sherff, 1945.D:fam. 210, 10/26/56.
                                                                    end. Molokai
        var. **Sherffii** Deg. & Deg., 1961   end. Molokai
        var. **Skottsbergii** Sherff, 1949. D:fam. 210, 10/26/56   end. Hawaii
        var. **vaccinioides** Sherff, 1945, f. **vaccinioides.** D:fam.210, 10/26/56
                                                            indig. Hawaii and Galapagos
            f. **oxyphylla** Deg. & Sherff in Sherff, 1951. D:fam. 210, 10/26/56
                                                                  end. Hawaii
            f. **salicifolia** Deg. & Sherff in Sherff, 1951. D:fam. 210, 10/26/56
                                                                  end. Hawaii
        var. **varians** Deg. & Sherff in Sherff, 1951. D:fam. 210, 10/26/56   end. Lanai
        var. **waimeana** Sherff, 1945. D:fam. 210, 10/26/56   end. Kauai, Oahu, Lanai
    sandwicensis Sherff, 1945, var. **sandwicensis** D:fam. 210, 3/15/59.
        A'ali'i, Dodonaea, Hawaiian hopseed bush   end. H.I.
        viscosa sensu Haw. bot., non Jacq., 1760. H:87; R:278.
        var. **latifolia** Deg. & Sherff in Sherff, 1954. D:fam. 210, 3/15/59   end. Lanai
        var. **simulans** Sherff, 1945. D:fam. 210, 3/15/59   end. Molokai
    stenoptera Hbd., 1888, var. **stenoptera**. H:88   end. Molokai
        var. *typica* Sherff, 1945.

3. See:
Hillebrand, p. 87.
Rock, p. 278.
Neal, p. 536.
Carlquist, p. 283.
Degener, PHNP, p. 200.
St. John, p. 224.

4. See:
Degener, PHNP, p. 199.
St. John, p. 223.

    var. **Fauriei** Sherff, 1945   end. Oahu
(viscosa Jacq., 1760, var. viscosa.) Not in H.I.   W.I.
    var. **arborescens**. (Cunn. ex Hook.) Sherff, 1945, f. **arborescens.** A'ali'i, kumakani, a'ali'i-ku-makani
        indig. Oahu, Lanai, Maui, Hawaii, and the World tropics
arborescens Cunn. ex Hook., 1840.
    f. **spatulata** (Sm.) Sherff, 1945   indig. Lanai, Maui, Pantropic
spatulata Sm., 1809.
    var. *spatulata* (Sm.) Benth., 1863. H:88, (as *spathulata*)

HVNP General. Both given as **D. viscosa**
HNP

AALII   **Dodonaea sandwicensis** Sherff
Syn. **D. viscosa** L.
Syn. **D. spatulata** Sm. in Deg. PHNP

    AALII occurs on all the islands often as a very conspicuous and abundant shrub or as a small tree with trunk 5 to 12" (12.5 to 25cm) in diameter. The one I saw at Kalalau Overlook on Kauai was 30' (9.5m) tall with conspicuous 2-winged capsules.
    Leaves are lanceolate, oblanceolate or obovate, entire, somewhat curled, alternate, with prominent midrib and often with sticky varnish-like coating. Many small flowers are borne in terminal and axillary panicles 2. to 2.5" (2.5 to 5cm) long. Fruits are often very numerous, bright red, pale yellowish or brownish, viscid and 2-winged or 3-winged in the variety at Kilauea. Twigs slender, reddish brown showing striations; bark rough for a small tree.
    Leaves were used for medicine and a red dye was made from the capsules. The wood from AALII in general may have been used for tools such as OO, spears and weapons because of its extreme hardness.
    Heart wood is golden brown streaked with brown, with black core. Sapwood is light brown and thin, texture is fine, figure streaked, grain straight to crossed, wood very dense and extremely hard. Vessels are very fine, few and scattered, rays barely visible at 14x. Wood warps and is hard to work.
    AALII invades open areas rapidly following fire and is a pioneer on lava flows in dryer sites.[3]

HVNP Mauna Loa Strip
HNP (Undetermined species at Paliku)

AALII KUMAKANI   **Dodonaea eriocarpa** Sm.
    Degener found *D. eriocarpa* var. *skottsbergii* Sherff along the Mauna Loa Truck Trail at an elevation of 6000' (1890m), and an unspecified variety near the junction of the belt highway and the road that leads to Punaluu, Hawaii. He gives the variety found on Haleakala as *hillebrandii* Sherff which apparently is also found on Mt. Hualalai, Kona, Hawaii.
    Degener states that variety *hosakana* Sherff, found near Punaluu, Hawaii, differs from the Kilauea AALII in that the leaves are distinctly hairy, fruits in 3-4 winged capsules, somewhat hairy and borne in compact almost spherical clusters. AALII that have the compact spherical clusters about 2" (5cm) across have been seen frequently by the writer along the road between Kipuka Nene and Hiliana Pali in HVNP. The shrubs are about 5' (1.5m) tall. The flowers form a dull red terminal panicle 2" (5cm) long with each flower very small. Leaves are .5 by 2-2.5" (1 by 5-6cm), tapererd both ends, quite wavy margins, twigs quite brown.[4]

AALII   **Dodonaea stenoptera** Hbd.
    Rock describes this AALII as being a shrub growing on Molokai above

1. *Aalii leaves and fruit.*

2. *Aalii bark detail.*

3. *Aalii, Dodonea sandwicensis. Trees along Mauna loa strip road, HVNP.*

Kamalo where Hillebrand also found it. This could be *D. Stenoptera* var. *stenoptera* that St. John lists as endemic to Molokai.[5]

MANELE, AULU & KAULU on Oahu   **Sapindus** (Tourn) L.
Soapberry

The genus *Sapindus* is represented in the Hawaiian Islands by *S. oahuensis* Hbd., endemic to Oahu and *S. saponaria* forma *inequalis* indigenous to Maui, Hawaii and tropical America.

Key to the species from Rock

Leaves abruptly pinnate . . . . **Sapindus saponaria**
Leaves simple, entire . . . . **Sapindus oahuensis**

HVNP Kipuka Puaulu and Kipuka Ki

MANELE   **Sapindus saponaria f. inequalis** (DC) Radlk.

MANELE is a large to very large and beautiful tree of the old climax forest where it grows in the middle forest zone at about 4000' (1260m). Rock found it growing on the lava fields of Puuwaawaa and near Kilauea on the Island of Hawaii. There are now many fine specimens in Kipuka Puaulu and a beautiful large grove in Kipuka Ki a short way up the Mauna Loa strip road.

The odd-compound leaves are made up of 4-6 or more pairs of leaflets and a terminal one. Each leaflet is 2-4" (5 to 10cm) long and about 1" (2.5cm) wide, bright yellowish-green with prominent midrib, pinnate veins, margins entire and leaflet not flat. The rachis is somewhat winged between leaflets. Leaves are shed in winter. The yellowish, very numerous flowers are borne in terminal panicles about 6" (15cm) long. Fruit forms a large, dense cluster of berries, often in pairs or triplets, or with one or two aborted. Each berry consists of a yellowish to greenish pulpy outer coat that covers the round black seed about .375 (1cm) in diameter. The outer coat exudes a very sticky material called sapinon that forms a lather when mixed with water, thus the name *sapindus*. Twigs are slender, smooth and greenish-grey. Bark is smooth and light grey, scaling off in large patches on older trees.

Wood is nearly white with black irregular lines, texture fine, figure plain, grain straight, density low, soft. Vessels scattered but with a tendency to form a ring porous pattern, perhaps related to the fact that the trees shed their leaves. likely causing an annual ring to form. Rays are very fine. Stability good, workability good. No use is recorded for the wood but the black seeds were used for LEIs and the sapinon for medicine for fever and rheumatism. L.W. Bryan's big tree measures 10'1" (3.1m) in circumference, 106' (32m) tall with 84' (26m) crown spread, located in Kipuka Ki in HVNP.[6]

[5.] See:
Hillebrand, p. 88.
Rock, p. 281.
St. John, p. 225.

[6.] See:
Rock, p. 271.
Neal, p. 532.
St. John, p. 225.

3. *Aalii, D. eriocarpa v. hosakana,* tree with terminal panicles and balled fruit.

4. *Aalii,* balled fruit on left; leaves and terminal panicles on right, HVNP.

1. *Manele* trunks showing bark detail.

2. *Manele* leaves and fruit.

5. *Manele, S. saponaria,* large tree, HVNP.

7. See:
Hillebrand, p. 85.
Rock, p. 273.
Carlquist, p. 283.
St. John, p. 225.

1. *Kauila bark detail on large tree, South Kona, Hawaii.*
2. *Kauila, A. ponderosa tree in HVNP.*
3. *Kauila flower enlarged to show detail; pale yellow.*
4. *Kauila leaf, flower and fruit.*

AULU or KEULU
LONOMEA   **Sapindus oahuensis** Hbd.

St. John lists this tree for Oahu only, but Neal and Rock list it for Kauai also, giving it a Hawaiian name peculiar to Kauai. It is a small tree 20 to 30' (6.3 to 9.5m) tall in the lower forest zone on the leeward side of the mountains.

Leaves are simple in contrast to the compound leaves of MANELE. They are oblong, entire, with prominent veins. The small yellow flowers are borne in long terminal panicles covered with rusty tomentum. Fruit is a rough capsule 1 to 1.5" (2.5 to 3.7cm) in diameter containing one large seed. Twigs are smooth, bark is whitish with lenticles. Wood is greyish white with straight grain, used for spears and house building. Seeds were used as a cathartic.[7]

BUCKTHORN FAMILY   **Rhamnaceae**

The buckthorn family is represented by two genera in the native flora, *Alphitonia* and *Colubrina*.

Key to the genera
Fruit 3-grooved at the apex, calcine cup
   not extending beyond the base . . . . **Colubrina** L.C. Rich, ex Bromg.
Fruit not grooved, globose, the calcine cup extending
   to the middle . . . . **Alphitonia** Reissek in Endl.

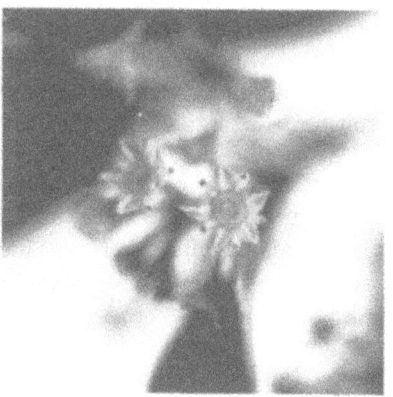

HVNP Listed as endangered

KAUILA or O'A   **Alphitonia ponderosa** Hbd.
                                       Syn. **A. excelsa** Reiss

Early Hawaiians used the same name for *A. ponderosa* and *Colubrina oppositifolia*. It is sometimes spelled KAUWILA. It is endemic to Kauai, Molokai, Lanai and Hawaii. It is a tree of the dry forest, on into the moderately wet forest where it is found in the vicinity of Manuka State Park, Kau, Hawaii. Rock reported it also from Maui and Oahu. It may grow as tall as 80' (24.4m) in best habitat but L.W. Bryan's big tree is 7' (2.1m) in circumference, 62' (19.5m) tall with a 54' (17m) crown spread in Kokee State Park, Kauai. Alternate leaves are thick, oblong to narrow, 6" (15cm) long on 1" (2.5cm) petiole, greyish or rusty-wooly below, veins pinnate and very prominent underside. Pale greenish flowers, not more than .25" (.6cm) across, with parts in fives, occur in axillary clusters near the branch ends. The petals are like points of a star, with stamens nearly as long, positioned between the star points. Spherical, woody fruit capsules with a circular ring above the base, borne in culsters, are about .5" (1.1cm) in diameter. Twigs are long, slender and brown. Bark is whitish and deeply corrugated on large trunks.

Wood is very hard, reddish brown with black streaks. Sapwood is pinkish straw colored, texture is fine, figure plain or slightly streaked, grain straight, density very high so it sinks in water. Vessels are few, fine and scattered, rays are very fine. Shrinkage is moderate and workability fair. This fine hard wood was used for spears, javelins, daggers, carrying poles, OO, TAPA beaters, the anvil on which to beat TAPA, LAAU LOMI LOMI to massage the back, weights for fish lines and some part of the plant was used medicinally. One modern use is in making beautiful statuettes in the round.

Although not abundant, the tree is well represented in the forest and not endangered. It is a minor component of the complex forest in which it grows.[1]

KAUILA   **Colubrina** L.C. Rich ex Brong

Two species of Colubrina occur in Hawaii, *C. oppositifolia* Brong ex Mann, endemic to Oahu and Hawaii, and *C. asiatica* (l) Brong indigenous to Niihau, Kauai, Oahu, Molokai, Africa, India, Australia to Polynesia.

Key to the species
Leaves alternate, 2-3" (5 to 7.5cm) long . . . . **C asiatica**
Leaves opposite, to 7" (18cm) long . . . . **C oppositifolia**

KAUILA, listed as endangered   **Colubrina oppositifolia** Brong ex Mann

This KAUILA is a smaller tree than *Alphitonia ponderosa*. Bryan's big tree is 8'6" (2.7m) in circumference, 47' (15m) tall with a 44' (14m) crown spread, located at Puuwaawaa, Kona, Hawaii. The generic name derives from Colubar, a serpent, perhaps due to the twisting furrows in the bark of some species. This tree occurs on the very rough lava flows between Puuwaawaa and Huehue in North Kona where it is quite common even though it is listed as endangered.

[1] See:
Hillebrand, p. 81.
Rock, p. 285.
Neal, p. 511.
Carlquist, pp. 287-90.
St. John, p. 225.

[2] See:
Hillebrand, p. 80.
Rock, p. 283.
Neal, p. 541.
Carlquist, pp. 169, 281-85, 294.
St. John, p. 225.

3. *Kauila bark detail.*

1. *Leaves and fruit of Kauila.*

2. *Pale green Kauila flowers.*

4. *Kauila, C. oppositifolia, grove of small trees, Kapulehu, Hawaii. Bryan photo.*

Leaves are opposite, which gives the plant is specific name. They are 3.5 to 4" (9 to 10cm) long and up to 2" (5cm) wide with 1" (2.5cm) petiole or longer, ovate or oblong, underside with glands along midrib, petiole reddish, veins light green, distinct on upper side, veins pinnate, tipped at apex and blunt at base. Flowers in leaf axils, in clusters of three or more, small, greenish, .25" (.6cm) in diameter or less, five petals, five sepals as a crown around a small ovary, very similar to *Alphitonia ponderosa*. Fruit angular, brown, 3-parted capsule about .5" (1.2cm) in diameter with a shallow cup. Several seeds per fruit. New twig growth reddish aging to light brown and rough with leaf scars. Bark light brown to grey, scales off in large round flakes.

Heart wood dark red to black without dark streaks, sapwood straw colored, texture very fine, figure plain, grain straight, so dense it sinks in water. Vessels fine, scattered and very numerous, rays very fine. Very hard and durable; good workability; takes a high polish. KAUILA was used for spears, TAPA beaters, OOs and is a conspicuous component of the dry forest.[2]

[1] See:
Hillebrand, p. 53.
Rock, p. 289.
Neal, p. 545.
Carlquist, p. 312.
St. John, p. 227.

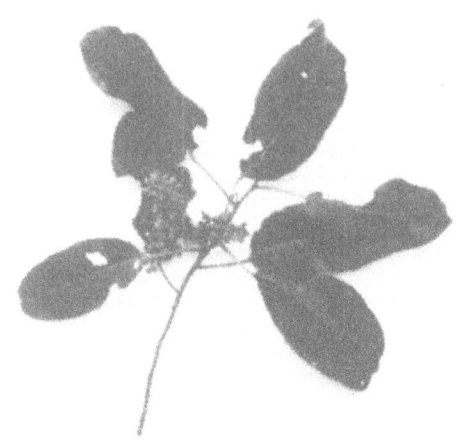

1. Kalia, E. bifidus, leaves and enlarged insect damaged flower cluster, Kokee, Kauai.

ANAPANAPA **Colubrina asiatica** (l) Brong.

ANAPANAPA is usually a shrup with rambling or twinning stems but sometimes a tree to 20' (6.3m) tall. It is widely distributed throughout the tropical regions of the world.

In contrast to C. Oppositifolia its leaves are alternate, shiny, pointed, 2 to 3" (5 to 7.5cm) long ovate to heart shaped, edges toothed or scalloped. Flowers are tiny, yellow-green, borne in short broad axillary clusters. The brown, 3-grooved, fruit is only about .33" (.8cm) in diameter, opening to show three black, angular seeds. The name means glistening. The habitat of this plant is near the coast in Hawaii and on all the islands where it grows.

LINDEN FAMILY **Tilaceae** including **Eleaocarpaceae**

This family is represented in Hawaii by only one native species of the genus *Elaeocarpus*, *E. bifidus* H. & A.

KALIA **Eleaocarpus bifidus**

KALIA is endemic to Kauai and Oahu where, on Kauai, it is very common in the wet forest at 3500 to 4000' (1200 to 1260m). It can be seen in the Kokee area where it is a tree 30 to 40' (9.5 to 12.6m) tall and up to 1' (31.5cm) in diameter.

Dark green leaves are about 2" by 4-7" (5cm by 10-18cm), smooth, ovate with 2" (5cm) yellow petioles. Margins toothed, midrib light green and prominent, pinnate veins few and less distinct. Flowers are five petaled, greenish with petals forked at tip. Often a mite injures the flower cluster causing a malformed, gall-like growth that turns red. Fruit is a drupe over 1" (2.5cm) long, generally one-seeded, shiny and brown. Branches that tend to droop are sticky at the ends. Bark is dark grey and roughened with small, wheat sized warts over the whole surface of a 3" (7.5cm) tree trunk.

Wood is medium hard, very light yellow, texture fine, figure none, grain straight, density medium, vessels few, very fine and scattered, rays barely visible at 10x and closely spaced. Wood checks in curing, workability is low because of the long, tough fibers that make it hard to saw. Long slender branches were used for thatch rods in house construction. Fibers from the bark were used in cordage.

This tree makes up as much as 30% of the forest in wet situations on Kauai. It has never moved down the island chain beyond Oahu perhaps because of the size and weight of the seeds or, one might speculate, perhaps the environment on the newer islands is not ready for it yet. The seed sinks in water and thus would not be carried by ocean currents.[1]

MALLOW FAMILY **Malvaceae**

The mallow family is well represented in Hawaii with five genera of shrubs or trees, two with endemic species, two with endemic or indigenous species and the fifth, a Polynesian introduction.

Key to the genera

Shrubs, woody at least at the base
    Flowers small, fruits 5-to-many lobed, each lobe with one seed ...... **Sida** L.
Trees, erect
    Flowers curved on one side, not opening .... **Hibiscadelphus** Rock
    Flowers not curved, opening
        Flowers white, pink or yellow .... **Hibiscus** L.

        Flowers not white or pink
            Flowers yellow with purple centers
                Leaves heart shaped, entire . . . . **Thespesia** Soland. ex Correa
            Flowers red
                Leaves heart shaped with 3 to 7 shallow, pointed lobes . . **Kokia** Lewt.

HVNP Wahaulu

ILIMA   **Sida falax** Walp.
                                               S. falax var. **kauaiensis** Hochr.

1. *Hau Kuahiwi leaves and fruit.*

ILIMA is the flower of Oahu. It is a shrub to 4' (1.25m) in height and never becomes a tree. However, it is a conspicuous shrub in coastal areas and inland as high as 2000' (630m). The flowers are about 1" (2.5cm) in diameter, bright yellow or rich orange to dull red, or rarely greenish, 5-parted. There were several forms known to Hawaiians, each with its own name. Neal gives a good account, on pages 552-53, of the plant and of making LEIs from the flowers.

HAU KUAHIWI   **Hibiscadelphus** Rock

The species of *Hibiscadelphus* are as follows:

***H. bombycinus** Forbes	end. Hawaii
H. hualaliensis Rock	end. Hawaii
H. giffardianus Rock	end. Hawaii
H. wilderianus Rock	end. e. Maui

H. bombycinus was found near Kawaihae, Hawaii long ago but has never been relocated in modern times so it is presumed to be extinct.

H. wilderianus was found by Rock in 1910 on the dry southern slope of Haleakala on the island of Mauai. It was decadent then and is either endangered or most likely extinct, unless preserved in a garden or arboretum.

2. *Hau Kuahiwi bark detail.*

HVNP

HAU KUAHIWI   **Hibiscadelphus giffardianus** Rock

The story of this HAU KUAHIWI has a happier ending than the previous two. Although reduced to a single known tree that died in the summer of 1936 except for a root sucker that persisted until 1940, seed had been gathered and the tree propagated to the extent that the species survives, thanks to the efforts of Mr. Giffard, for whom the species is named, and Colonel Bryan. Now it is included in the endangered plant project of Hawaii Volcanoes National Park and it is doing well where it has been planted in Kipuka Puaulu and Kipuka Ki.

The planted trees are straight and slender with sharply upright branches but have not reached full size. Leaves are 6 to 8" (15 to 20cm) in diameter, roughly round but slightly lobed. Veins are palmate, distinct on the upper surface, a vein leading out to the apex of each lobe. Leaves are cordate, giving the appearance of the petiole being attached to the under surface of the leaf, rather than to the base. Petiole green; flowers are greenish to deep magenta with petals lightly rolled into a tube, never fully opening, stamens and pistil protruding one-third the length of the petals. Tube formed by the petals is curved. Fruits are yellowish, rough and five valved. Twigs are stout, bark on a 3" (7.5cm) trunk is smooth and light tan. As the tree is known only in the National Park no wood was available for study but it may be quite similar to *H. hualaliensis*. The largest tree measured by the author is 1'8" (45cm) in circumference, 42' (12m) tall with a 22' (6m) crown spread and still growing. It is located in Kipuka Ki in HVNP.

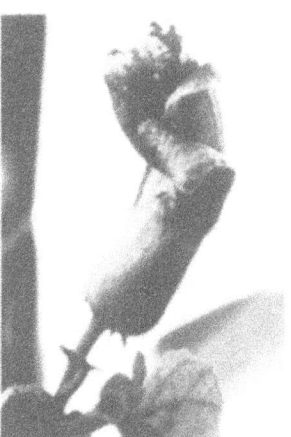

3. *Enlarged Hau Kuahiwi flower, rolled reddish petals. Seekins photo.*

[1] See:
Rock, p. 301.
Neal, p. 567.
St. John, p. 229.

HVNP

HAU KUAHIWI   Hibiscadelphus hualaliensis Rock

This species is more abundant and widely spread but still listed as endangered. It occurs in the Kona district of Hawaii on Mt. Hualalai very sparingly. It is also being propagated in HVNP in the endangered species project on the assumption that it may have occurred in the Park at some time. Good specimens are developing well in Kipuka Puaulu and Kipuka Ki. This is also a small, upright branching tree hard to distinguish from **H. giffardianus**. and appears to reach about the same size.

Leaves appear to be a little more rounded and glossy than those of *H. giffardianus*. Flowers appear more tightly rolled and smaller, yellow or green. The woody or leathery capsule, 1.25" (3cm) in diameter and 1.5" (4cm) long, longitudinally 5-parted, is filled with seeds covered with long grey hairs. Twigs are stout, bark smooth on 6" (15cm) trunk.

Wood, as studied from a dead limb, is steel grey with a small filled pith, texture fine, figure plain, grain straight and close, density high and wood hard. Vessels are medium sized, few and scattered, rays very fine, closely spaced and somewhat wavy. There are strong annular rings about three times as far apart as the rays, but irregular. No Hawaiian uses were recorded for such a rare tree.[1]

1. Hau Kuahiwi, H. giffardianus, small planted tree, HVNP.

2. Hau Kuahiwi, H. hualalaiensis, vigorous planted tree, HVNP

3. Hau Kuahiwi leaves

4. Hau Kuahiwi fruit.

KOKIO   Hibiscus L.

Table of Species of Hibiscus

Species	Common name	Color	Size	Location
H. arnottianus Gray	Kokio'o-ke'oke'o	white	10-15'	Oahu
H. a. parviflorus		white		Oahu
H. a. punaluuensis		white	30' tree	Oahu
**H. immaculatus Roe	Molokai white	white		Molokai
**H. waimeae Heller	Kokio'o-ke'oke'o	white		Kauai
H. w. hannerae Deg.		white		Kauai
H. youngianus Gaud.	Hau-hele	pink		Kauai, Oahu, Maui
**H. clayi Deg. & Deg.	Clay hibiscus	red	9	Kauai
**H. kokio Hbd ex wawra	Kokio-ula'ula	red		Oahu
**H. k. pukoonis Caum		red		Molokai
**H. newhousei Roe		red	20'	Kauai
**H. saintjohnianus Roe	St. John hibiscus	orar red	15'	Kauai
**H. breckenridgei Gray	Ma o hau hele	yellow	4-5'	Lanai, Maui
H. b. molokaianus Rock		yellow		Molokai
**H. b. mokuleiana Roe		yellow		Oahu
H. rockii Deg. & Deg.	Rock's hibiscus	yellow		Kauai
H. tiliaceus L.	Hau	yellow	tree	Ind.Trop.Pacific & Old World
H. t.t. f. immaculatus Deg. & Greenw.	Hau	yellow		ind. India to Hawaii

1. Kokio, poor, decadent tree, K. drynarioides, Kapulehu, Hawaii.

2. Kokio, H. breckenridgei, bush in Manuka State Park, Hawaii.

5. Aloalo, white hibiscus bush, Manuka State Park, Hawaii.

3. Kokio ula, H. kokio, flower and leaf detail of native red hibiscus. Carlson photo.

4. Kokio, may be H. breckenridgei. Carlson photo.

6. Aloalo, H. arnottianus v. punaluuensis, native white hibiscus, Manuka State Park, Hawaii.

Many of the Hibiscus species listed have been very rare but seeds were collected and propagated in nurseries so that many of them are now used as ornamentals. In that way they have been spared from extinction. The only abundant tree species, *H. tiliaceus*, is the only species treated fully in this book. Neal, pages 560-61, Degener, *FH*, page 221 and Rock, pages 291-95 have good descriptions of several of the other species.[2]

HVNP

HAU   **Hibiscus tiliaceus** L.
Syn. **Partium tilliaceum** (l) Britton

HAU is a much branched tree that sprawls in all directions making an impenetrable mass of long limbs. Some branches may be sufficiently upright for the tree to be said to be 20' (6.3m) tall. These jungle areas occur on the coasts of all the islands and throughout much of the tropical Pacific. They are very abundant. Leaves are alternate, heart shaped, 2 to 12" (5 to 30cm) in diameter, dark green above, light grey-green below with 2" (5cm) petiole. Prominent veins are palmate and lighter colored than leaf, and distinct. Large yellow flowers, 4" (10cm) in diameter, fade during the day or second day to magenta or brownish pink. The flower center may be yellow or nearly purple. Fruit is a downy, ovoid, capsule 1" (2.5cm) long, 5-valved with three seeds in each compartment. Twigs are light grey, browning with age, smooth with tough bark. Smaller trunks are smooth, light yellowish-grey, with bark broken into thin irregular plates on larger trunks.

7. A tangle of trunks of Hau, H. tiliaceus, Hilo, Hawaii.

[2] See:
St. John, p. 230.

[3] See:
Hillebrand, p. 49.
Rock, p. 293.
Neal, p. 559.
St. John, p. 230.

[4] See:
Hillebrand, p. 49.
Rock, p. 302.
Neal, p. 563.
St. John, p. 232.

1. Milo leaves, flower and fruit.

2. Hau, new yellow flower at top, old red flower at right and leaves.

3. Hau bark detail.

Heart wood is light brown, sapwood white with pinkish cast, pith soft. Texture medium, figure plain or streaked, grain straight, density very low and wood very light; stability is good with low shrinkage, workability excellent.

Hawaiians used the tough wood for adz handles, in fire making and for fish floats. The curved branches were sought to use for IAKO or arms for attaching the AMA or float of WILIWILI wood to the body of the dugout canoe. Bast fibers from the bark were used for coarse TAPA cloth, sandals, twine for rope and netted bags.

HAU is a very conspicuous part of the coastal forest.[3]

HVNP Wahaulu

MILO, Portia Tree **Thespesia populnea** (l) Corr.

MILO is another member of the Mallow family that is indigenous to Hawaii but also occurs around the world in tropical countries. In Hawaii it is not a forest tree but was grown mostly as a shade tree around houses and temples, although small groves may be found near beaches. It is a large sprawling, many branched tree but is more apt to develop a straight, sturdy trunk that HAU. It may be 40' (12.6m) tall and 3; (90cm) in diameter.

Leaves are heart shaped, margins entire, with long slender, green petiole, apex is more pointed than in HAU, palmate veins quite prominent. Bell shaped flowers, 2-3" (5 to 7.5cm) in diameter are pale yellow with purple centers, fading to pinkish later in the day. Flowers are borne much of the year. Fruit is a globose, woody, 5-celled capsule 1 to 1.5" (2.5 to 3.7cm) in diameter, flattened at the ends. Capsule contains up to 12 or more seeds, elongated, downy covered. Twigs are scaly, stout, rough with leaf scars, light brown with fine red scales. Bark is thick and corrugated, light to dark grey.

Wood reddish brown to black with occasional yellow streaks, fades with exposure to light, to golden brown. Sapwood is light straw colored, texture fine, figure streaked, grain straight to curly, medium density and hardness. Vessels are few and scattered, rays many and very fine. Shrinkage very low and workability very good. Takes a high polish and is very beautiful.

Hawaiians made POI calabashes, platters and dishes of the wood and sometimes used bast from the bark for cordage. MILO may be seen growing wild on the beaches of all the islands. The wood is highly prized by modern bowl makers. L.W. Bryan's big tree is 9' (2.8m) in circumference, 42' (13m) tall and with a crown spread of 69' (22m) located at Kokaha, Hawaii.[4]

This same tree is called Portia tree in Florida.

4. Milo, T. populnea, large tree, HVNP.

KOKIA or KOKIO
HAU-HELE-ULA

Kokia Lewt.

St. John lists four species of *Kokia* as follows:
- *****Kokia cookei** Deg. — end. Molokai
- ****Kokia drynarioides** (Seem) Lewt. — end. Hawaii
- ****Kokia kauaiensis** (Rock) Deg. & Duvel — end. Kauai
- ****Kokia lanceolata** Lewt. — end. Kauai

Even though *K. cookei* is listed as extinct, other information indicates there is one plant in Fleming Arboretum, Molokai, two trees at Kaulawai, Molokai and one in Waimea Arboretum, Oahu. *K. drynarioides* was propagated by the Hawaii Forest Service and several plants are to be found on the island of Hawaii. Rock states that *K. lanceolata* was endemic to Oahu and had long been extinct when his book was published in 1913. *K. kauaiensis* is being propagated by Pacific Tropical Botanical Garden and wild plants are said to occur in Paaiki, Mahaunaloa and Koaie valleys on Kauai.

KOKIO

Kokia drynarioides (Seem) Lewt.
Syn. **K. rockii** Lewt.

KOKIA is normally a small tree about 12 to 15' (3.8 to 4.7m) tall, gnarled and poorly shaped. One growing at Kipuka Puaulu in HVNP is about 20' (6.3m) tall, straight and slender and still growing rapidly. Another one at Kaupulehu preserve, and a couple growing along the belt highway in Kona, better fit the general description. These trees are rare at best and need to be protected and propagated vigorously if they are to survive.

Leaves are round or roughly heart shaped with three to seven shallow lobes, with prominent palmate veins that extend to the tip of each lobe. Base deeply incised and the petiole as long as the leaf. Leaves are clustered near the ends of branches. Bright red, hibiscus-like flowers are very showy with petals slightly twisted. Fruit is a woody capsule in the center of three large persistent bracts, like a saucer. Seeds are .5" (1.2cm) long covered with brownish wooly hair. Long, relatively stout twigs are light grey and smooth except for leaf scars. Bark is thin greyish-brown, slightly warty in 6" (15cm) diameter trees to very warty on a large, older trunk at Kaupulehu.

Wood is reddish brown, texture coarse, figure plain, grain straight. Density is low and wood is soft. Vessels are large, open and scattered, rays very fine, barely visible at 10x. Wood is brittle and easily broken, grain tears easily.

Hawaiians extracted a reddish brown juice from the bark for use in dying fish nets. This is one old practice that has lived on resulting in much damage to planted trees. The tree is too rare to be of any importance in the native forest but deserves propagation for the beauty of its flowers and leaves. Big tree is 5'4" (1.63m) in circumference, 27' (8.23m) tall with a 23' (7m) crown spread located at Puuwaawaa, Hawaii.[5]

[5] See:
Rock, p. 303.
Neal, p. 567.
St. John, p. 231.

1. Kokio leaf and flower detail, HVNP

2. Kokio bark detail.

3. Kokio, K. kauaiensis, leaf detail, PTBG, Kauai.

[1] See:
Hillebrand, p. 41.
Rock, p. 308.
Neal, p. 582.
Carlquist, p. 315.
St. John, p. 235.

TEA FAMILY   **Theaceae**

The tea family is represented in Hawaii by one native genus, *Eurya*, with one species endemic to the Hawaiian islands, *E. sandwicensis*, and a variety, *grandifolia*, endemic to Kauai and Oahu.

ANINI   **Eurya sandwicensis** Gray

ANINI is a shrub or small tree 15 to 20' (4.7 to 6.3m) tall and 6 to 8" (15 to 20cm) in diameter, of the upper wet OHIA forest around 4000' (1260m) elevation. It is fairly common along the Stainback highway on the island of Hawaii above the first prison perimeter gate.

Leaves are finely toothed, obovate, oblong or oval, blunt at apex, .75 to 1.5" (1.8 to 3.6cm) long, prominent midrib, dense network of pinnate veins, petioles so short lower leaves appear to clasp the one above. Flowers solitary in leaf axils, sepals purplish, petals yellowish, on short pedicles. Fruit is a berry, dryish, globose, black, .25 to .5" (.6 to 1.2cm) in diameter, crowned by the styles, with 12 small seeds in each cell. Stout pubescent twigs are smooth except for leaf scars. Bark is whitish and smooth.

Wood is light reddish-brown, texture fine, figure plain, medium density and hardness, grain straight, vessels few and fine, rays very fine, indistinct and closely spaced. Stability and workability good. ANINI is a minor component of the mature OHIA forest.[1]

1. Anini, *E. sandwicensis*, leaf and fruit detail.

2. Slender Anini tree in fern forest, Stainback Highway, Hawaii.

4. Kamani, *C. inophyllum*, grove along Puna Coast, Hawaii.

3. Kamani leaves and fruit on long stems (not shown).

MANGOSTEEN FAMILY   **Guttiferae**

The Mangosteen family is represented in Hawaii by only one genus, *Calophyllum*, and one indigenous species, *inophyllum* L., found in all the islands and in tropical Asia and the Pacific islands. It is thought by some to have been introduced to these islands by the early Hawaiians. The case for this viewpoint is strengthened by the fact that present groves appear to be near old sea shore habitation sites. It has never spread widely like the HAU for example. One of the best known groves is located at Halawa, Molokai. There are very impressive groves along the Puna coast of Hawaii and the writer saw one tree in a grove of False Kamani, *Terminalia catappa* on windward Oahu.

KAMANI   Calophyllum inophyllum L.

KAMINI forms rather large groves of trees 4 to 5' (1.2 to 1.5m) in diameter and 60' (19m) tall. L.W. Bryan's big tree is 18'6" (5.8m) in circumference, 59' (18.8m) tall with 81' (25m) crown spread, located in Malama-ki Forest Reserve, Puna, Hawaii. The wide crown spread indicates the extent of its sprawling growth habit. Very large limbs lie along, or close to, the ground for long distances.

Dark green leaves are shiny, leathery, oblong and blunt tipped at apex, have a heavy greenish or reddish petiole about 1" (2.5cm) long. The yellowish midrib is prominent but the straight, closely spaced, pinnate veins are indistinct. White flowers resemble orange blossoms, are 1" (2.5cm) in diameter, fragrant and borne in small axillary racemes. Stamens are many and long. Long stemmed fruit are globose, green or somewhat wrinkled and leathery when dry, about 1" (2.5cm) in diameter or more. Bony covering of fruit is somewhat poisonous, the kernal is surrounded by cork, giving the seeds good flotation. Twigs are light green with longitudinal striations, aging to smooth brown with a small, filled pith. The rough bark on large trunks is longitudinally corrugated.

Wood is very pretty, reddish brown, with some purplish tint, coarse texture, figure showing fine stripe with bold feather pattern, grain curly, moderately dense and moderately hard. The few large vessels are scattered, no rays are visible at 10x. Shrinkage is moderate, workability is fair.

The wood was used for calabashes and an oil was extracted from the nut to be used medicinally. The round fruit hanging on a long stem readily distinguishes this KAMANI from false kamani.[1]

[1] See:
Hillebrand, p. 40.
Rock, p. 309
Neal, p. 385.
Carlquist, p. 104.
St. John, p. 236.

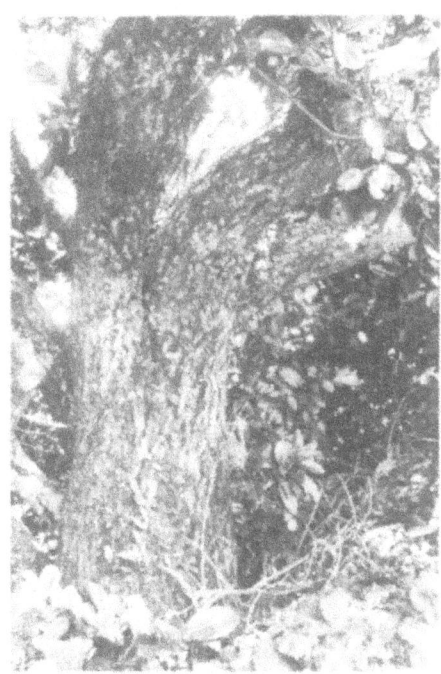

1. Bark of large Kamani.

FLACOURTIA FAMILY   Flacourtiaceae

This family is represented in Hawaii by one genus of native trees, *Xylosma*, which has one species, *hawaiiensis* Seem. and one variety, *hillebrandii* (Wawra) Sleumer. The full species is endemic to Kauai, Oahu and Lanai while the variety is endemic to Molokai, Lanai, Maui and Hawaii.

Key to the Taxa

Leaves entire, stigma sessile, generally 3 .... **X. hawaiiensis**
Leaves with blunt pointed teeth (crenate or sinuate), or broad,
   stigmas raised on style, generally 2 .... **X. hawaiiensis** var. **hillebrandii**

MAUA   Xylosma hawaiiensis Seem.

This MAUA grows on Oahu in the leeward valleys and on Kauai in the forests above Waimea to Kokee. It may be as tall as 30' (9.5m) with a trunk 1' (31.5cm) in diameter.

Leaves are entire, smooth, shiny, large, ovate or rounded and red tinted. New growth leaves are red, which gives a fast growing tree a reddish tint. Yellowish midrib is very prominent on the underside, veins few and pinnate, petiole short and heavy. Flowers are borne in small axillary and terminal clusters, .5 to .75" (1.2 to 1.8cm) in diameter, star shaped, white, with four to five petals and five light brown stamens. Fruits are globose to oblong, up to 1" (2.5cm) long and .75" (1.8cm) in diameter, permanently beaked, attached by inch-long dark red stems. Nut single seeded. Twigs are rough, light brown, slender and crooked, bark is smooth on 4" (10cm) tree, light brown.

Wood is light reddish brown with very faint annular zones of lighter and darker wood resembling very faint, closely spaced growth rings, texture very fine, figure plain, grain straight and very close, no vessels visible at 10x, rays very numerous, very closely spaced, barely visible at 10x. Wood is very dense and very hard, checks in curing. Boards upon which to pound POI may have been made of this wood.

2. Decadent Maua tree, X. hawaiiensis v. hillebrandi, South Kohala, Hawaii.

[1] See:
Hillebrand, p. 20.
Rock, p. 311.
St. John, p. 239.

[2] See:
Hillebrand, p. 20.
Rock, p. 313.
St. John, p. 239.

The tree occurs in the mixed forest late in succession and is not a very conspicuous element.[1]

HVNP Kipuka Puaulu
HNP

MAUA   **Xylosma hawaiiensis** var. **hillebrandii**

This MAUA is a tree 15' (4.7m) tall on the lava flows of the dry areas to nearly 60' (19m) tall and 1'6" (46cm) in diameter in the wetter forests of South Kona where L.W. Bryan measured his big tree 5'1" (1.5m) in circumference, 58' (18m) tall with 43' (13.5m) crown spread, located on Hoomau Ranch, Honomolino, Hawaii.

Leaves are 1.5 to 3.5" (3.8 to 8.8cm) wide by 2 to 5" (5 to 12.5cm) long, broadly rounded base, apex blunt pointed, edges coarsely notched or crenate. Petiole is .5 to 1" (1.3 to 2.5cm) long, flattened so that the leaves flutter in the breeze. Flowers have the same description as the species. Small oval fruits are .375" (1cm) in diameter, in small clusters along the twig, black outer shell, red soft pulp, two seeds per fruit. Fruits are permanently beaked. Twigs are slender, roughened by leaf scars, somewhat warty and flexible. Bark is smooth and light colored in contrast to the flaky bark of KAUILA, in whose company these trees grow.

Wood is light red with brownish streaks, texture fine, figure plain to flame, grain straight, density medium and hardness medium. Vessels are numerous and very fine, rays barely visible at 14x. The wood warps and workability is poor.[2]

1. Leaf, bud and flower detail, Maua, X. hawaiiensis, Kokee, Kauai. Terminal leaves red.

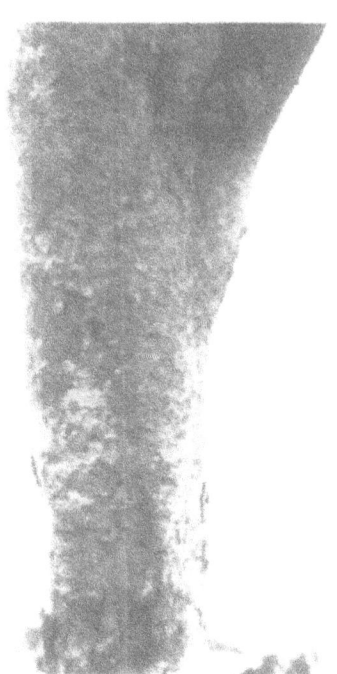

2. Bark detail Maua, X. hawaiiensis v. hillebrandi, Kouth Kohala, Hawaii.

3. Leaves and fruit of Maua, X. hawaiiensis, Kokee, Kauai.

4. Leaf and fruit detail, Maua, X. hawaiiensis v. hillebrandi.

AKIA FAMILY   **Thymeliaceae**

AKIA family is represented in Hawaii by a total of 40 taxa. One or more of these is endemic to each of the islands. Although most are shrubs some of them become quite tree-like.

Taxa of *Wikstroemia* from St. John:

Wikstroemia Endl., 1833. 'Akia, false 'ohelo.
    basicordata Skottsb., 1972   end. Oahu
    bicornuta Hbd., 1888, subsp. **bicornuta**, f. **bicornuta**   end. Lanai
        Diplomorpha bicornuta (Hbd.) Heller, 1897
        f. **glabra** Skottsb., 1972   end. Lanai
    subsp. **montis-eke** Skottsb., 1972 (as *montis-Eke*)   end. w. Maui
    bicornuta x lanaiensis Skottsb., 1972. A natural hybrid   end. Lanai
    Caumii Skottsb., 1936   end. e. Maui
    Degeneri Skottsb., 1972   end. Oahu
    foetida (L.f.) Gray, var. *oahuensis* Gray, 1865, in part

elongata Gray, 1865. H:385	end. Molokai, Maui
Diplomorpha elongata (Gray) Heller, 1897	
eugenioides Skottsb., 1964	end. w. Maui
Forbesii Skottsb., 1964	end. Molokai
furcata (Hbd.) Rock, 1913. R:319	end. Kauai
sandwicensis Meisn. in A.CD., var. *furcata* Hbd., 1888. H:386	
furcata x **palustris**, var. **major**, fide Skottsb., 1972. A natural hybrid	end Kauai
sandwicensis Meisn., var. *longiflora* Hochr., 1925	
Diplomorpha longepedunculata Heller, 1897, nomen	
haleakalensis Skottsb., 1936	end. e. Maui
hanalei Wawra, 1875	end. Kauai
Isae Skottsb., 1964	end. Oahu
lanaiensis Skottsb., 1964, var. **lanaiensis**	end. Lanai
var. **acutifolia** Skottsb., 1936	end. Lanai
laptantha Skottsb., 1936	end. Oahu
macrosiphon Skottsb., 1972	end. Oahu
monticola Skottsb., 1972, var. **monticola**	end. e. Maui
var. **occidentalis** Skottsb., 1972	end. w. Maui
oahuensis (Gray) Rock, 1913. R:316. 'Akia, asasa	end. Oahu
foetida (L.f.) Gray, var. *?oahuensis* Gray, 1865. H:385	
Diplomorpha oahuensis (Gray) Heller, 1897, as to basionym and Oahu plant	
oahuensis x **recurva**, fide Skottsb., 1972	end. Oahu
palustris Hochr., 1925, var. **palustris**, f. **palustris**	end. Kauai
furcata (Hbd.? Rock, var. *palustris* Skottsb., 1944	
f. **hirtella** Skottsb., 1972	end. Kauai
var. **major** Skottsb., 1972, f. **major**	end. Kauai
f. **oblonga** Skottsb., 1972	end. Kauai
phillyroefolia Gray, 1865, var. **phillyroefolia**	end. Hawaii
Diplomorpha phillyreifolia (Gray) Heller, 1897	
var. **buxifolia** (Gray) Skottsb., 1972	end. Hawaii
buxifolia Gray, 1865	
Uva-ursi Gray, var. *buxifolia* (Gray) Hbd., 1888. H:387	
Diplomorpha buxifolia (Gray) Heller, 1897	
var. **rigida** Gray, 1865	end. Hawaii
pulcherrima Skottsb., 1936	end. Hawaii
recurva (Hbd.) Skottsb., 1936, var. **recurva**	end. Oahu
elongata Gray, var. *recurva* Hbd., 1888. H:386	
var. **neriifolia** Skottsb., 1972	end. Oahu, e. Maui
sandwicensis Meisn. in A.DC., 1857	end. Hawaii
Fauriei Levl., 1911	
Diplomorpha sandwicensis (Meisn. in A.DC.) Heller, 1897	
Sellingii Skottsb., 1944	end. Oahu
Skottsbergiana Sparre, 1964	end. Kauai
caudata Skottsb., 1964, non J.W. Moore, 1940	
Uva-ursi Gray, 1865, var. **Uva-ursi** H:387; N:616. 'Akia	
	end., also cult. Oahu, Molokai, Maui
Diplomorpha Uva-ursi (Gray) Heller, 1897	
var. **kauaiensis** Skottsb., 1972	end. Kauai
vacciniifolia Skottsb., 1964	end. Kauai, Oahu, Molokai, Maui
villosa Hbd., 1888. H:386	end. w. Maui

HVNP General
HNP Species not identified

AKIA   **Wikstroemia sandwicensis** Meisn
                    or **W. phillyroefolia** Gray

With such an array of taxa it takes an expert on AKIA to know which one is at hand. The plants vary widely from small shrubs with small leaves in the Kilauea region, to small trees with large leaves in the Wahaulu area on the

1. Akia shrub, Kamoamoa, Hawaii, HVNP.

[1] See:
Hillebrand, p. 386.
Rock, p. 317.
Neal, p. 615.
St. John, p. 245.

1. Leaves and fruit of Akia, W. sandwicensis. Red berries.

2. Bark and trunk detail, Akia.

coast, all in HVNP. Leaf size seems to be the chief distinction in labeling the specimens in HVNP herbarium. Again Hillebrand separates these two species mainly on the basis of leaf size.

Rock lists W. oahuensis, W. sandwicensis and W. furcata as reaching tree size.

Leaves are dark green, opposite, short petioled, small and ovate or longer and narrow, or pubescent in some. Flowers occur in clusters of tiny, 4-petaled blossoms at or near the ends of the branches, yellowish green, with each flower .25" (.7cm) or less in diameter. Fruit is a drupe, bright red, orange or yellow, juicy, thin skinned, with red pulp around the seed, which is black and about the size of a kernel of wheat. Twigs are repeatedly forked in pairs, slender new growth yellowish-green grading to light brown with age. Bark is reddish brown, smooth except for light rings around the trunk, and very tough.

Wood is white with very light greenish tint, streaked with brown, texture medium, figure plain to streaked, grain straight, density low and wood soft. Vessels numerous, very fine, scattered rays very fine. Stability and workability are good.

The very tough bark is one characteristic that made this plant valuable. The bast fibers were used in making one of the best grades of rope and in TAPA making. The branches, leaves and berries were beaten and the pulp carried down into fish ponds where the poison contained in the plant stupified the fish, making them easy to catch. The stupifying agent did not appear to hurt the fish for human food nor does it appear to hurt grazing animals. Wood was used as AUAMO or beating sticks.

AKIA is a conspicuous part of the shrub forest in the dry areas of the islands. The profuse crops of red berries make it stand out on the rather drab terrain where it is often associated with native LAMA and ALAHEE and introduced guava and lantana in the lowlands. Around Kilauea it grows associated with AALII and PUKIAWE in sparse OHIA forest.[1]

MYRTLE FAMILY   **Myrtaceae**

The Myrtle family is represented in Hawaii by two genera of native trees, *Eugenia* and *Metrosideros*.

Key to the Species

Fruit a capsule .... **Metrosideros** Banks ex Gaertn.
Fruit a berry .... **Eugenia** (Mich) L.

It is interesting to note that the species of *Metrosideros* include the most numerous trees of the Hawaiian forest and two introduced genera of the Myrtle family, *Eucalyptus* and *Psidium*, are among the most common introduced trees in the islands.

OHIA-AI, NIOI and OHIA HA   Eugenia (Mich) L.

St. John includes under *Eugenia* three endemic species, *E. sandwicensis* Gray, endemic to Kauai and Maui, *E. molokaiana* Wilson and Rock, endemic to Molokai and *E. koolauensis* Deg., endemic to Oahu. In addition he lists *E. malaccensis* L., and *E. reinwardtiana* (Bl) D.C., as Polynesian introductions or indigenous, and the final taxa, *E. malaccensis* f. *cericarpa* as endemic to Oahu.

OHIA-AI   **Eugenia malaccensis** L.
Syn. **Jambosa malaccensis** (l) D.C.

OHIA-AI is considered to be an early Hawaiian introduction to the islands where it has spread and is now locally common in the gulches on the windward sides of some of the islands. It is a tree up to 60' (19m) tall.

Leaves are large, opposite, 2.5 by 6" (6 by 15cm) with short, heavy petioles, distinct midrib and prominent pinnate veins. Flowers are borne in open clusters of 12 to 15, in the axils of the leaves or along the stem below. Petals fall off singly rather than cohering as in *E. sandwicensis*. Fruits are 3 to 4" (7.5 to 10cm) in diameter, red and watery, with generally one seed. Smooth grey twigs have a large pith. Bark is rough.

Wood is straw colored, streaked with brown, texture coarse, figure streaked, grain straight, density low and soft. Vessels are very numerous and large, rays barely visible at 14x. Wood warps.

OHIA-AI of the form *E. malaccensis* forma *cericarpa*, endemic to Oahu, differs in that the fruit is white.

OHIA-AI was considered to be sacred by the Hawaiians. The wood was chosen for the carving of idols. Trunks of trees were hewn into posts and rafters for houses, for making enclosures around temples, and for coupling two hulls together to make a double canoe. L.W. Bryan's big tree measures 4'9" (1.45m) in circumference, 35' (11m) tall, with crown spread of 20' (6.3m) and is located at Kaelekehe, Kona, Hawaii. William Ellis saw this as a common tree in Kona in 1823.[1]

[1] See:
Hillebrand, p. 128.
Rock, p. 321.
Neal, p. 635.
St. John, p. 252.

[2] See:
Hillebrand, p. 129.
Rock, p. 323.
St. John, p. 252.
Degener, FH, p. 273.

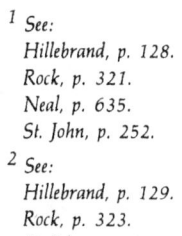

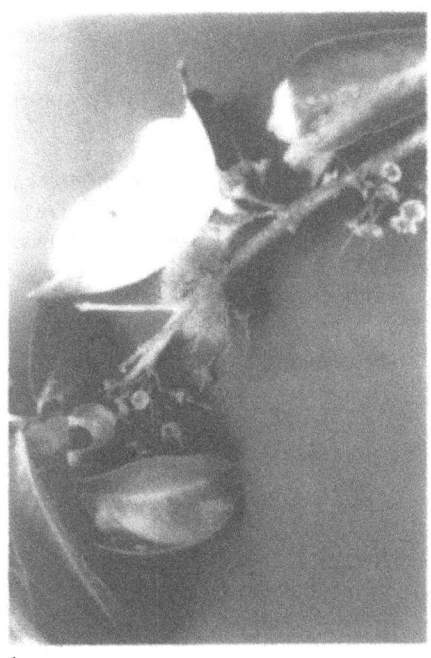

1. Flowers (bright red) and leaves of Ohia-ai, *E. malaccensis*, Polynesian introduction.
2. Bark detail of Ohia-ai North Kona, Hawaii.
3. Ohia-ai tree. Also called mountain apple. North Kona, Hawaii.

HNP

OHIA-HA   **Eugenia sandwicensis** Gray
Syn. **Syzygium sandwicensis** (Gray) Ndz.

OHIA-HA differs from OHIA-AI in that in the former the petals adhere, and fall together while in the latter they fall singly. OHIA-HA is endemic on the islands from Kauai to Maui, where it is a forest tree 60' (19m) tall and 1. to 1.5' (31.5 to 45.5cm) in diameter.

Dark green or yellowish-green, glossy leaves are 3 to 6" (7.5 to 15cm) long, opposite, pinnate veins faint, apex pointed, petiole very short. Flowers are pinkish to red, small and culstered along the branches. Fruits are bright red, edible berries .33" (.6cm) in diameter. Seeds are hard, durable and reddish. Twigs are stout, greenish-brown, smooth between the leaf scars. Bark is reddish-brown and smooth. Wood reddish brown, difuse, porous, irregular grain, quite hard and durable.

This is a tree of the rain forest, quite conspicuous when in bloom.[2]

1. Trunk of largest Ohia in Kipuka Puaulu, HVNP with author.

2. Grove of Ohia in Kipuka Puaulu, HVNP. Some are nearly 100 feet tall. Rock photo.

OHIA   **Metrosideros** Banks ex Gaertn.

St. John lists six species, 11 varieties and four forms or 21 taxa. In doing so he omits all the taxa under *M. polymorpha* which he states have not been correlated with taxa under *M. collina* and appear to be largely duplications.

Taxa of *Metrosideros* according to St. John:

Metrosideros Banks ex Gaertn., 1788
  collina (J.R. & G. Forst) Gray, 1854, subsp.**polymorpha** (Gaud.) Rock.
    1917, var. **polymorpha**. N:637. 'Ohi'a-lehua, lehua   end. H.I.
    var. *typica* Rock, 1917
    ploymorpha Gaud., 1830. H:125; R:325
      Note: See also under *M. polymorpha*
    var. **Fauriei** (Lévl.) Rock, 1917   end. Molokai
      ploymorpha, subsp. *incana*, var. *Fauriei* (Lévl.) Skottsb., 1944
      Nania Fauriei Lévl., 1911
    var. **glaberrima** (Lévl.) Rock, 1917, f. **glaberrima**. Lehuahamae,
      'ohi'a hamau, 'ohi'a-ku-makua   end. Kauai, Oahu, Hawaii
      Nania polymorpha (Gaud.) Heller, var. *glaberrima* Lévl., 1911
      f. **sericea** Rock, 1917   end. Kauai, Oahu, Molokai, Lanai, Hawaii
    var. **glabrifolia** (Heller) Rock, 1917   end. Kauai
      Nani(a) glabrifolia Heller, 1897
    var. **haleakalensis** Rock, 1917   end Maui
    var. **hemilanata** Hochr., 1925   end. Kauai
    var. **imbricata** Rock, 1917   end. Oahu
    var. **incana** (Lévl.) Rock, 1917, f. **incana**   end. H.I.
      Nania polymorpha (Gaud.) Heller, var. *incana* Lévl., 1911
      f. **lurida** Rock, 1917   end. Molokai
    var. **macrophylla** Rock, 1917   end. Hawaii
    var. **Newellii** Rock, 1917   end. Maui, Hawaii
    var. **prostrata Rock, 1917, f. prostrata**   end. Kauai, Molokai, Maui
      polymorpha, var *prostrata* (Rock) Skottsb., 1944
      f. **strigosa** Rock, 1917   end. Hawaii
    var. **pumila** (Heller) Rock, 1917. Lehua-maka-noe, misty eyed lehua
               end. Kauai
      Nani(a) pumila Heller, 1897
      polymorpha subsp. *incana* (Lévl.) Skottsb., var. *pumila* (Heller) Skottsb., 1944,
        f. *pumila*
  excelsa Soland. ex Gaertn., 1788. N:638 Pohutukawa,
New Zealand christmas tree   cult. New Zealand
    tomentosa A. Rich., 1832-34
  macropus H.& A., 1832, f. **macropus**. H:127;R:336. 'Ohi'a-lehua
               end. Kauai, Oahu, Molokai
    f. **ruber** St. John, 1935   end. Oahu
  pumila (Heller) Hochr., var. **makanoiensis** Hochr., 1925   end. Kauai
  robusta A. Cunn., 1839   cult. New Zealand
  rugosa Gray, 1854. H:127;R:335. Lehua-papa   end. Oahu
  tremuloides (Heller) Knuth, 1898-9. R:333. Lehua-'ahihi   end. Oahu
    Nani(a) tremuloides Heller, 1897
    M. polymorpha, var. *tremuloides* (Heller) Skottsb., 1944
  waialealea (Rock) Rock, 1917   end. Kauai
    M. tremuloides (Heller) P. Knuth, var. *waialealea* Rock, 1913. R:335.

Key to the Species of *Metrosideros* adapted from Rock

Large shrubs or trees:
  Leaves on short petioles:
    Leaves suborbicular, cordate ovate or oblong;
      Capsule almost free . . . . **M. collina**
    Laeaves linear or elliptical, acute at both ends . . . . **M. tremuloides**
    Leaves rugose and impressed above;
      Capsule adnate to near the apex . . . . **M. rugosa**
  Leaves on long petioles of .75 to 2" (2 to 5cm)
    Leaves ovate to ovate-oblong

Capsule hidden in the calyx tube .... **M. macropus**
　Leaves acuminate-caudate;
　　Capsule projecting beyond the calyx-tube .... **M. waialealae**
Dwarf shrubs .... **M. pumula**

[3] See:
Hillebrand, p. 125.
Rock, p. 331.
Neal, p. 637.
Carlquist, pp. 114-18, 177.
Degener, PHNP, pp. 230-36.
St. John, p. 253.

HVNP General
HNP Paliku, Hosmer Grove

OHIA　　　　**Metrosideros collina** var. **polymorpha** (Gaud) Rock

Rather than getting involved in the problems of nomenclature surrounding *Metrosideros* I have chosen the above scientific name for the OHIA that is endemic to all the islands and cited in much of the literature as the OHIA of general occurrence. For the purpose of this book it is not considered necessary to determine the identity of any given tree further nor to consider the validity of the name *polymorpha* as a species name.

OHIA occurs from near sea level to 9000' (2835m) in the mountains. That it develops into a very large tree in good environment is shown by L.W. Bryan's big tree that is 17'10" (5.6m) in circumference, 84' (27.5m) tall with crown spread of 78' (25m), found growing at Waipunalei, Hilo, Hawaii. The big OHIA in Kipuka Puaulu is 18'6" in circumference.

The native name for this tree is confusing. The tree is called OHIA and the flower is LEHUA, certainly an early and interesting instance of 'binomial nomenclature.'

Opposite leaves are dull green on the upper surface and whitish below, shiny, often red when new, leathery, oval, rounded or elongated, often quite closely spaced on the twig so that they appear to be cupped together. Flowers generally red, but may be orange or yellow, pompom like clusters of many individual florets, the whole cluster 2 to 3" (5 to 7.5cm) in diameter, terminal. Fruit a 3-parted capsule .25" (.6cm) in diameter, the calyx persists as 5-pointed ring around the equator of the capsule which is light grey-green when new, dark brown when mature. Twigs light brown aging to medium brown, new growth smooth, older growth roughened to scaly. Bark loose and shreddy on older trunks.

Wood light to deep red, texture medium, figure streaked, grain straight to curly or interlocked, very dense and very hard. Vessels open, numerous, fine scattered, rays barely visible at 14x. Stability fair, hard to work, harsh and brittle. Flowers were used for special LEIs, a black dye was made from the bark and various parts were used medicinally. The wood, often the most common kind available, was used for idols, POI boards, poor quality houses, enclosures around temples, coupling and gunwales for canoes, anvils for beating TAPA and weapons. In modern times railroad ties, posts, flooring, lumber, etc., are made of OHIA.

OHIA is most abundant tree in vast areas of the Hawaiian forest. It comes in as a pioneer on fresh lava flows, forming pure stands. As the process of natural succession begins to work OHIA is gradually replaced by other species until the ultimate climax forest is a mixture of a few very large, old OHIAs intermixed with up to 40 other kinds of trees.

The over abundant OHIAs are killed in various ways such as by disease, insect attack, starvation due to over crowding, etc. At times large areas of OHIAs are killed in a short time. It is possible that this is largely a natural process. In places it may be triggered by some sort of human activity and in other places it has been known to have been caused because the ground became too warm, due to underground volcanic activity. Whatever the causes, the process of conversion from a pure stand of OHIA to the ultimate mixed forest is not fully understood. It is a very long process and scientists have only recently begun to chart it.[3]

1. *Flower, leaves and fruits of Ohia.*

2. *Pompom-like flower of Ohia, M. collina v. polymorpha. Generally the flower is bright red, it may be yellow.*

Other OHIA

M. collina subsp. *polymorpha* var. *pulima* (Heller) Rock, not to be confused with *M. pumila* (Heller) Hochr., is called LEHUA-MAKA-NOE, misty-eyed LEHUA, said by St. John to be endemic to Kauai swamps, but Neal includes the Maui and Hawaii swamps in its range. This is a dwarf form of OHIA.

M. tremuloides, LEHUA-AHIHI, endemic to Oahu, is an interesting form with long slender leaves, acute at both ends, bright green and graceful. It occurs on the lower slopes of Tantalus back of Honolulu and in the neighboring valleys at about 1000 to 2000' (315 to 630m) elevation if its habitat has not been completely preempted by housing developments since Rock's time.

M. waialealae Rock, endemic to Kauai, was described by Rock as a variety but it has since been raised to species rank. Rock states that it occupies the summit ridge of Mt. Waialeale, the crest of the island of Kauai. Here it forms a pure stand of the most beautiful of all the forms of OHIA. It is a small tree, about 25' (7.8m) in height.

M. rugosa Gray, LEHUA PAPA, endemic to Oahu, is found at the summit of the main range and on the vertical cliffs on the windward side of the island, according to Rock. It is readily identified by the small deeply rugose leaves, wrinkled or marked with deeply impressed midrib and veins, thickly tomentose on the underside, as are the buds. Flowers are red and about the size of common LEHUA flowers. It is a shrub or small tree about 10 to 15' (3 to 4.7m) tall.

M. macropus H. & A., also called OHIA LEHUA, is endemic to Kauai, Oahu and Molokai and the form *ruber* St. John, is endemic to Oahu. *M. macropus* has long-petioled leaves, large floral scales and much larger flowers, either red or yellow. It is a good sized tree found in the Koolau range of Oahu as well as on Kauai and Molokai. It is glabrous throughout.

M. pumila (Heller) Hochr. is listed as endemic to Kauai as variety *makanoiensis*.

GINSENG FAMILY   Araliaceae

This family is represented in Hawaii by three endemic genera of trees along with many species, varieties and forms.

Key to the Genera
Leaves in digitate arrangement, opposite . . . . **Cheirodendron** Nutt ex seem.
Leaves in pinnate arrangement
    Leaves sinuate crenate (toothed) . . . . **Reynoldsia** Gray
    Leaves entire . . . . **Tetraplasandra** Gray

These trees are all heavy seeders, generally with large masses of fruits in terminal clusters. *Tetraplasandra* and *Cheirodendron* prefer wet habitat in older OHIA forest while *Reynoldsia* is found in dryer areas often in company with such dry area species as LAMA, WILIWILI and A'IAHEE.

OLAPA and LAPALAPA   **Cheirodendron** Nutt ex Seem.

St John lists six species, 20 varieties and three forms of *Cheirodendron* showing it to be a very variable genus. Degener in *Flora Hawaiiensis*, page 281 gives a full key to all of the taxa.

List of the taxa of Cheirodendron

Cheirodendron Nutt. ex Seem., 1867
  Dominii Krajina, 1931. D:fam. 281, 3/15/56 — end. Kauai
  Fauriei Hockr., 1925. var. **Fauriei**. D:fam. 281, 3/15/56 — end. Kauai
    wahiawaense Krajina, 1931
      (? and var. *populneum* Krajina, 1931?)
    trigynum (Gaud.) Heller, var. *kauaiense* Lévl., 1911
    var. **Macdanielsii** Sherff. 1951. D:fam. 281, 3/15/56 — end Kauai

1. Leaf detail, Olapa, C. helleri, Kokee, Kauai.

**	**Helleri** Sherff, 1951, var. **Helleri**. D:fam. 281, 3/15/56	end. Kauai
**	var. **microcarpus** Sherff, 1951. D:fam. 281, 3/15/56	end. Kauai
	var. **multiflorum** (Skottsb.) Sherff, 1954. D:fam. 281, 3/15/56	end. Kauai
	trygynum (Gaud.) Heller, var. *multiflorum* Skottsb., 1944	
	var. *sodalium* Sherff, 1952. D:fam. 281, 3/15/56	end. Kauai
	kauaiense Krajina, 1931, var. **kauaiense**. D:fam. 281, 3/15/56	end. Kauai
	var. **Forbesii** Sherff, 1951	end. Kauai
	var. **keakuense** Krajina, 1931	end. Kauai
	platyphyllum (H. & A.) Seem., 1867. H:149;D:fam. 281, 3/15/56. Lapalapa	end. Oahu
	Panax platyphyllum H. & A., 1832	
	trigynum Gaud.) Heller, 1897, var. **trigynum**. D:fam. 281, 3/15/56. Olapa, olapalapa, common cheirodendron, mahu, kauila mahu	end. Hawaii
	Gaudichaudii (DC) Seem., 1867. H: 148; R:361	
	Aralia trigyna Gaud., 1826	
	Panax? Gaudichaudii DC., 1830.	
	var. **acuminatum** Skottsb., 1944. D:fam. 281, 3/15/56	end. n.w. Hawaii
	var. **confertiflorum** Sherff, 1951. D:FAM. 281, 3/15/56	end. Maui
	var. **Degeneri Sherff**, 1951, f. **Degeneri**.D:fam. 281, 3/15/56	end. Hawaii
	f. **pauciflorum** Sherff. 1951. D:fam. 281, 3/15/56	end. Hawaii
	var. **Fosbergii** Sherff, 1951. D:fam. 281, 3/15/56	end. Oahu
	var. **halawanum** Sherff, 1951. D:fam. 281, 3/15/56	end. Oahu, Molokai, Lanai
	var. **Hillebrandii** Sherff, 1951. D:fam. 281, 3/15/56	end. Oahu
	var. **ilicoides** Sherff, 1951. D:fam. 281, 3/15/56	end. Hawaii
	var. **mauiens** Lévl., 1911, f. **molokaiense**. D:fam. 281, 3/15/56	end. e. Molokai
	f. **angustius** Sherff, 1951. D:fam. 281, 3/15/56	end. Molokai
	var. **oblogum** Sherff, 1951, f. **oblongum**. D:fam. 281, 3/15/56	end. e. Maui
	f. **latius** Sherff, 1951. D:fam. 281, 3/15/56	end. e. Maui
	var. **osteostigma** Sherff, 1951. D:fam. 281, 3/15/56	end. Molokai
**	var. **Rockii** Sherff, 1951. D:fam. 281, 3/15/56	end. Lanai
	var. **Skottsbergii** Sherff, 1951. D:fam. 281, 3/15/56	end. Lanai, Maui
**	var. **subcordatum** Sherff, 1951. D:fam. 281, 3/15/56	end. n.w. Hawaii

[1] See: St. John, p. 258.

1. *Olapa tree rising above tree fern understory. Stainback Highway, Hawaii.*

2. *Leaf and bud detail, Lapalapa, C. platyphyllum, Kokee, Kauai.*

OLAPA   **Cheirodendron helleri** Sherff

This OLAPA, endemic to Kauai, is a small understory tree, 20' (6.3m) tall, of the mixed forest common in the wetter part of the Kokee area.

The striking feature is the large size of the shiny, dark green, leathery leaves, light underneath, about 3" (7.5cm) wide and 9" (22.5cm) long, pointed at both ends. Leaves are arranged digitally in threes. Digital arrangement is like the fingers of the hand, from which the tree gets its name, *Cheiro*, from Greek for hand and *dendron*, for tree. Leaf stems are 6" (15cm) long and each leaflet is attached with a 2" (5cm) petiole. Veins are same color as the leaves. Leaves have a strong carroty odor when crushed. Flowers are tiny, in terminal clusters as are the fruit. Twigs are light grey with prominent leaf scars. Bark is moderately rough on 3" (7.5cm) trunks.[1]

LAPALAPA   **Cheirodendrom platyphyllum** (H&A) Seem.

Rock found this species on Kauai in the high mountains as well as Oahu but St. John states it is endemic to Oahu. The material the writer collected at the Kalalau Overlook on Kauai fits Rock's description. It is a good sized tree, 25 to 30' (7.8 to 9.5m) tall and 1' (31.5cm) in diameter.

The trees stand out clearly in the OHIA forest as their leaves are light green and shiny, always fluttering in the lightest breeze. Leaflets, in threes, are attached to the long slender petiole by flattened stems as long as the leaves. These flattened stems allow the leaf to flutter much more readily than would a round stem. Leaflets have a prominent light midrib and closely spaced, light pinnate veins are broader than long, and have toothed margins.

3. *Lapalapa tree, Kokee, Kauai. Leaves light green, glossy and stirred by lightest breeze.*

[2] See:
Hillebrand, p. 149, Oahu only.
Rock, p. 363, Oahu and Kauai.
Carlquist, p. 307, Oahu only.
Neal, p. 652
St. John, p. 258, Oahu only.

[3] See:
Hillebrand, p. 148.
Rock, p. 361.
Neal, p. 652.
Degener, FH, p. 281.
St. John, p. 258.

Flowers are borne in single panicles or three together, with many small flowers per panicle. Fruit is a very small drupe, borne profusely in the panicles, four- or five-angled when dry. Twigs are light tan with large leaf scars, branches grey and smooth, bark on larger trunks mottled light and dark green.

Wood is whitish tinged with yellow. The fresh cut wood is said to have a spicy odor and burns while still green.

This OLAPA is a minor component of the very complex mixed wet forest where it occurs at an elevation of 3500 to 4000' (1100 to 1250m).[2]

HVNP Variety not specified, Kilauea area & Kipuka Puaalu
HNP C.t. var. *confertiflorum*, also unspecified var. at Paliku

OLAPA   **Cheirodendron trigynum** (Gaud) Heller
                                        Syn. **C. gaudichaudii** (DC) Seem

There are five additional varieties or forms of *C. trigynum* endemic to Hawaii. It is difficult to determine in the field which name to give an individual specimen. For practical purposes it is sufficient to name only the species. OLAPAs are conspicuous in the wet OHIA forest on the island of Hawaii. Seeds fall on trunks of OHIAs and tree ferns where they sprout and extend roots to the ground. OLAPA, in best environment, is a medium sized tree. Bryan's big tree is 4'6" (1.37m) in circumference, 37' (11.6m) tall, with crown spread of 28' (8.8m) located in HVNP.

Opposite leaves are compound, leaflets in threes or fives, palmately arranged, with long petioles and short, flattened stems to individual leaflets, midrib light green and prominent, fine pinnate veins closely spaced. Some leaflets have finely denticulate margins. Small, inconspicuous flowers are arranged in large terminal panicles. Small, deep purple fruits are very numerous in open branching panicles that are quite conspicuous, commonly three seeds per drupe. Twigs smooth, new growth green, aging to light brown. Bark smooth, yellowish.

1. Olapa tree, C. trigynum, Auahi, Maui. Rock photo.

2. Fruiting cluster of Olapa, C. trigynum.

3. Leaves of Olapa, C. trigynum.

Heart wood is straw colored with grey streaks, sapwood white, large soft pith. Wood texture medium, figure plain, grain straight, density low and medium hard. Vessels very fine and scattered, rays fine and few. Stability very poor, wood warps badly, workability fair.

Hawaiian uses: poles were cut, smeared with sticky material and placed to catch small birds; bark and leaves produced a bluish dye. The fluttering leaves inspired the OLAPA hula. Young graceful girls were called OLAPA.

OLAPA is one of the most common trees, after the OHIA, in the wet forest. They invade pure stands of OHIA as the seeds are able to germinate on trunks of larger trees, thus assuring the seedling a place in the sunlight. Crushed leaves have a carroty odor.[3]

OTHER OLAPAs

Cheirodendron faureu Hochr., endemic to Kauai, has been identified along the trail to the TV relay station on Mt. Kahili and *C. kauaiensis* var. *forbesii* Sherff, has been found along the same road. Stone found *C. trigynum* var. *degeneri* forma *pauciflora* along the trail to Napau Crater in HVNP, and *C.t.* var. *degeneri* Sherff has been identified along the Stainback Highway, 11 miles above the junction with Highway 11 in unit N of Waikea Forest Reserve at 2500' (762m) elevation. *C.t.* var. *confertiflorum* grows in Waihoi Valley, Maui and Carlquist found *C.t.* var. *acuminatum* at Kehena, Hawaii.

OHE, and OHE MAKAI   **Reynoldsia** Gray

1. *Leaf and bud detail, Ohe Makai, R. hillebrandi, Puna, Hawaii.*

St. John recognizes eight species and six added varieties of *Reynoldsia* in the Hawaiian Islands, all as endemic and almost all of them are also listed as endangered or extinct.

List of species and varieties of *Reynoldsia*:

Reynoldsia Gray, 1854
**	**Degeneri** Sherff, 1952	end. Molokai
**	**Hillebrandii** Sherff, 1952. D:fam. 281, 7/5/71	end. Hawaii
	Hosakana Sherff, 1952	end. Oahu
**	**huehuensis** Sherff, 1952, var. **huehuensis**	end. Hawaii
**	var. **brevipes** Sherff, 1052	end Hawaii
**	var. **intermedia** Sherff, 1952	end. Hawaii
**	**mauiensis** Sherff, 1952, var. **mauiensis**	end. Maui
**	var. **macrocarpa** Deg.& Sherff, 1952	end. Maui
	oblonga Sherff, 1952	end. Hawaii
	sandwicensis Gray, 1854, var. **sandwicensis**. H:156;R:351; D:fam. 281, 3/3/39. 'Ohe, 'ohe'ohe makai, Hawaiian reynoldsia	end. Oahu
**	var. **intercedens** Sherff, 1952	end. Oahu
***	var. **molokaiensis** Sherff, 1952	end. Molokai
**	**venusta** Sherff, 1952, var. **venusta**	end. Oahu
**	var. **lanaiensis** Sherff, 1952. 'Ohe kukuluae'o	end Lanai

Hillebrand, Rock and Degener (*FH*) have listed *R. sandwicensis* as the species found on all islands. Herbst, in his 1974 revised edition of Rock, identifies Rock's pictures as illustrating *R. Hillebrandi* Sherff, and *R. mauiensis*.

2. *Bark detail, Ohe Makai.*

HVNP Wahaulu

OHE MAKAI   **Reynoldsia hillebrandi** Sherff

Many writers consider the **Reynoldsia** on the island of Hawaii, to be *R. sandwicensis* Gray, but for the sake of uniformity this writer follows St. John, even though the list of endangered trees shows *R. hillebrandi* to be endangered whereas it is plentiful. It is a tree of medium size, L.W. Bryan's big tree measures 6'8" (2m) in circumference, 48' (15m) tall, with crown spread of 23' (7.2m), found at Puuwaawaa, Kona, Hawaii. Glossy, bright green leaves are pinnately compound with 7 to 11 scalloped leaflets per leaf. Apex is bluntly rounded, base almost square across, midribs light green, petioles short, whole leaf about 10" (25cm) long. Leaves shed in winter. Many greenish or brownish flowers come forth in spring before the leaves, on stiff erect terminal panicles. Fruit is a drupe, dark purple, juicy, not sweet, with a circular ring or scar near apex. Twigs are very stout, .5" (1.2cm) in diameter out to the end, grey, with a large filled pith. Bark bluish-grey to dark grey, smooth, exudes a yellowish-golden gum.

Wood is white, texture coarse, figure streaked, grain straight, density low and very soft. Vessels few and fine, rays not visible. Workability fair.

The gum was used in some manner and the wood was used for stilts or KUKULUAEO. OHE MAKAI means the OHE by the sea which describes its habitat although it occurs inland for considerable distances. It grows in

3. *Ohe Makai tree, Puna, Hawaii.*

[4] See:
Hillebrand, p. 156.
Rock, p. 351.
Neal, p. 652.
Carlquist, pp. 277-85.
St. John, p. 260.

the company with WILI WILI at Puuwaawaa, Hawaii, and on the dry side of Haleakala, Maui, and with LAMA near Wahaulu Ranger Station in Puna, Hawaii. Its light green foliage makes it conspicuous.[4]

OHE OHE   **Tetraplasandra** Gray

The genus **Tetraplasandra** Gray, combines the trees listed by Hillebrand under *Pterotropia, Triplasandra* Seem and *Tetraplasandra* Gray. Rock combined *Triplasandra* and *Tetraplasandra*. St. John lists 84 taxa. His list of varieties looks like a Who's Who of Hawaiian botany. A large number of the taxa are also listed as threatened, endangered or extinct.

List of taxa of *Tetraplasandra*:

Tetraplasandra Gray, 1854
****bisattenuata** Sherff, 1952   end. Kauai
   gymnocarpa (Hbd.) Sherff, 1952, var. **gymnocarpa**. D:fam. 281, 7/16/62.
      Ohe, Koolau tetraplasandra   end. Oahu
      Ptertropia gymnocarpa Hbd., 1888. H:151;R:355; D:fam. 281, 8/24/38
      var. **leptocarpa** Sherff, 1952. D:fam. 281, 7/16/62   end. Oahu
      var. **megalocarpa** Sherff, D:fam. 281, 7/16/62
**   var. **pupukeensis** (Deg.) Sherff, 1953. D:fam. 281, 7/16/62   end. Oahu
      Pterotropia gymnocarpa Hbd., var. *pupukeensis* Deg. 1938. D:fam. 218, 8/24/38
  ***hawaiensis** Grey, 1854, var. **hawaiensis**. H:154; R:339.'Ohe   end. Hawaii
     var. **awiniensis** Sherff, 1952   end. Hawaii
     var. **gracilis** Sherff, 1952   end. Hawaii
**   var. **microcarpa** Sherff, 1952   end. Molokai
  kaalae (hbd.) Harms, 1898, var. **kaalae**. R:345   end. Oahu
    Triplasandra kaalae Hbd., 1888. H:154
**   var. **multiplex** Sherff, 1953   end. Oahu
****kahanana** Deg. & Sherff, 1953   end. Oahu
  kavaiensis (Mann) Sherff, 1952, var. **kavaiensis** (as *kauaiensis*). 'Ohe'ohe
                                                                         end. Kauai
    Heptapleurum kavaiense Mann, 1867
**   var. **dipyrena** (Mann) Sherff, 1952   end. Lanai (Maui, Hawaii?)
    Heptapleurum dipyrenum Mann, 1867
    Pterotropia dipyrena (Mann) Hbd., 1888. H:150;R:357
**   var. **grandis** Sherff, 1952   end. Hawaii
**   var. **intercedens** Sherff, 1952   end. e. Maui
    var. **koloana** Sherff, 1952   end. Kauai
**   var. **nahikuensis** Sherff, 1952   end. e. Maui
**   var. **occidua** Deg. & Sherff in Sherff, 1953   end. w. Maui
    var. **robustior** Sherff, 1952   end. Kauai
****kohalae** Skottsb., 1944   end. Hawaii
*****lanaiensis** Rock, 1911. R:341   end. Lanai
  lihuensis Sherff, 1953, var. **lihuensis**   end. Kauai
*   var. **gracilipes** Sherff, 1953   end. Kauai
*****Lydgatei** (Hbd.) Harms, 1898, var. **Lydgatei**   end. Oahu
    Triplasandra Lydgatei Hbd., 1888. H:153
*** var. **brachypoda** Sherff, 1952   end. Oahu
*** var. **coriacea** Sherff, 1952   end. Oahu
    var. **Forbesii** Sherff, 1952   end. Oahu
**   var. **leptorhachis** Deg. & Sherff in Sherff, 1952   end. Oahu
  meiandra (Hbd.) Harms, 1898, var. **meiandra**   end. Oahu
    Triplasandra meiandra Hbd., 1888. H:152
    Heptapleurum waimeae Wawra, 1873
*   var. **bisobtusa** Sherff, 1952   end. Hawaii
    var. **Bryanii** Sherff, 1953   end. Oahu
*** var. **Degeneri** Sherff, 1952   end. Kauai
**   var. **Hillebrandii** Sherff, 1952   end. Lanai
**   var. **hiloensis** Sherff, 1952   end. Hawaii
**   var. **leptomera** Sherff, 1952   end. e. Maui
    var. **longipedunculata** Skottsb., 1944   end. Oahu

**	var. **makalehana** Sherff, 1952	end. Oahu
	var. **mauiensis** Sherff, 1952	end. e. Maui
	var. **molokaiensis** Skottsb., 1944	end. Molokai
	var. **occidentalis** Skottsb., 1944	end. w. Maui
	var. **olowaluana** Sherff, 1952	end. w. Maui
	var. **ovalis** Sherff, 1952	end. Maui
	var. **polyantha** Sherff, 1952	end. Molokia
	var. **polystigmata** Sherff, 1952	end. e. Maui
	var. **prolifica** Sherff, 1952	end. Hawaii
	var. **prolificoides** Sherff, 1952	end. Hawaii
	var. **ramosior** Sherff, 1952	end. w. Maui
	var. **rhynchocarpa** Sherff, 1952	end. Hawaii
*	var. **rhynchocarpoides** Deg.& Sherff in Sherff, 1952	end. Hawaii
	var. **Rockii** Sherff, 1952	end. Hawaii
*	var. **simulans** Sherff, 1952	end. Hawaii
	var. **Skottsbergii** Sherff, 1952	end. Molokai
	var. **tenuistylis** Sherff, 1952	end. Hawaii
	var. **tenuistyloides** Deg.& Sherff in Sherff, 1953	end. Hawaii

micrantha Sherff, 1952 — end. Oahu
    Pterotropia kaalae sensu Skottsb., 1936, non (Hbd.) Harms, 1898

***Munroi** Sherff, 1952 — end. Lanai

oahuensis (Gray) Harms, 1898, var. **oahuensis**. R:345 — end. Oahu
    Gastonia oahuensis Gray, 1854
    Triplasandra oahuensis (Gray)Seem, 1868. H:153

***	var. **eradiata** Sherff, 1953	end. Oahu
*	var. **Fauriei** Sherff, 1953	end. Oahu
*	var. **hailiensis** (Deg.& Sherff in Sherff) Deg.& Sherff in Sherff, 1953	end. Oahu
	meiandra (hbd.) Harms, var. *hailiensis* Deg. & Sherff in Sherff, 1952	
*	var. **logipes** Sherff, 1953	end. Oahu
	var. **subglobosa** Deg. Deg. & Sherff in Sherff, 1962	end. Oahu
	var. **pseudolongipes** Deg. & Sherff, 1953	end. Oahu
*	var. **pseudorhachis** Sherff 1953	end. Oahu
	var. **venulosior** Sherff 1953	end. Oahu

pupukeensis Skottsb., 1936, var. **pupukeensis** — end. Oahu
    gymnocarpa (Hbd.) Sherff, var. *pupukeensis* (Deg.) Sherff, 1955

	var. **decipiens** Deg. & Sherff in Sherff, 1953. D:fam. 281, 11/15/62	end. Oahu
	var. **megalopoda** Sherff, 1952 F. **megalopoda** D:fam. 281, 11/15/62	
		end. Oahu
	f. **trigona** Deg. & Sherff in Sherff, 1952. D:fam. 281, 11/15/62	end. Oahu
*	var. **nitida** Deg. & Sherff, 1952. D:fam. 281, 11/15/62	end. Oahu
*	var. **venosa** Deg. & Sherff, 1952. D:fam. 281, 11/15/62	end. Oahu

Sherffi Deg. & Deg., 1962. D:fam. 281, 11/15/62. 'Ohe, Sherff's tetraplasandra
    end. Kauai

*turbans** Sherff, 1952 — end. Oahu

waialealae Rock, 1911, var. **waialealae**. R:341 — end. Kauai

	var. **acrior** Sherff, 1952	end. Kauai
	var. **kokuana** Deg. & Sherff in Sherff, 1956	end. Kauai
	var. **pluricostata** Deg. & Sherff in Sherff, 1956	end. Kauai
	var. **subsessilis** Sherff, 1952	end. Kauai
*	var. **urceolata** Sherff, 1952	end. Kauai
	var. **wahiawensis** Sherff, 1952	end. Kauai

*waianesis** Deg., 1938, var. **waianesis** D:fam, 281, 2/11/38 — Waianae
    tetraplasandra — end. Oahu

** var. **palehuana** Sherff, 1953 — end. Oahu

waimeae Wawra, 1873, var. **waimeae**. H:155; R:339. 'Ohe-kiko'ola — end. Kauai

[5] See:
Hillebrand, p. 152.
St. John, p. 261.
Rock, p. 348.
Carlquist, pp. 96, 167, 303.

[6] See:
Hillebrand, p. 154.
Rock, p. 339.
St. John, p. 261.

1. Ohe Ohe, T. meiandra, leaf and fruit detail.

2. Bark detail of large Ohe Ohe tree.

3. Small Ohe Ohe tree rising above fern and brush understory. Stainback Highway, Hawaii.

HVNP
HNP var. *mauiensis*

OHE OHE   **Tetraplasandra meiandra** (Hbd.) Harms
Syn. **Triplasandra meiandra** Hbd.

Of this one species St. John lists 25 varieties. It thus becomes very difficult to distinguish the varieties in the field and no attempt is made here to do so. OHE OHE are large trees of the wet to moderately dry forest. It is a tree of shapely ascending branches and a rather flat crown that frequently rises well above the surrounding trees.

Pinnately compound leaves are alternate, 1 to 1.5' (30 to 45cm) long with 2 to 13 oblong leaflets, rounded at each end, dark above, light brown below, with heavy tomentum, stems of leaflets short, leaf margins smooth. Midribs are light green, the pinnate veins are distinct. Flowers are borne in large complex clusters, called double umbels, 1' (31.5cm) or more long. Each individual flower is small. Very abundant fruits are many ribbed, small, globose, purplish-black, each fruit flattened at top. Seeds are small and wedge shaped. Twigs are very stout, .75" (1.8cm) in diameter at the start of the new growth, rachis of the leaf clasps the stem half way around. Bark is whitish and fairly smooth.

Wood is very light tan to white, coarse textured, figure plain, grain straight, density low and soft. Vessels few, fine and light tan in color, gives tannish tint to wood, rays numerous but very fine. Stability and workability good. No known use was made of the wood by Hawaiians.

OHE OHE is represented by varieties in both wet and dry forest. It is conspicuous for its growth habit as mentioned, and appears to be a rather early invader of the OHIA forest.[5]

HVNP Wahaulu

OHE OHE   **Tetraplasandra hawaiiensis** Gray

This OHE OHE is a medium sized tree of the deep, damp OHIA forest, generally upright with stiff, ascending, candalabra like branches, but may be twisted and with decumbent branches. L.W. Bryan's big tree is 14'2" (4.25m) in circumference, 67' (20.4m) tall and with crown spread of 69' (21.03m) located on Hoomau Ranch, Honomolino, South Kona, Hawaii.

Alternate or whorled, even or mostly odd compound leaves are all on current growth, 12 to 18" (31.5 to 45cm) long with 6 to 8 pairs of leaflets per rachis. Leaflets 1.5 to 2" by 3 to 5" (3.7 to 5 by 7.5 to 13cm), tomentose underneath. Flowers tiny, borne in paniculate inflorescence with stamens four times as many as petals. Fruits are borne very abundantly in large axillary clusters near the ends of the branches, panicle and stalk 12" (31.5cm) long or longer, buds and fruit covered with grey tomentum. Fruits somewhat resemble very small acorns set half way in the cups, up to .5" (1.2cm) in diameter. Twigs are very stout, .75" (1.8cm) in diameter, green aging to grey-green. Bark smooth except for numerous lenticles in parallel rows, grey, light and dark speckled. Wood is light straw colored with brown streaks, texture medium coarse, figure plain to streaked, grain straight, density low and wood soft. Vessels few and scattered, rays few and distinct. Wood was not good for any particular use.

This OHE OHE can be found quite plentifully in the edge of the Kalapana section of HVNP and specially across the boundary in the adjacent subdivision, where very large specimens can be seen. Here some of the queer, decumbent-limbed trees are found. Several instances were seen where limbs had broken off and the bark had grown over the stub, healing it completely. This is one of the more common trees of the older OHIA forest in a reasonably moist area.[6]

1. Ohe Ohe, T. hawaiiensis, leaf and flowering habit.
2. Large Ohe Ohe, T. hawaiiensis, in Manuka State Park, Hawaii.

HEATH FAMILY   Ericaceae

Heath is represented in Hawaii by the genus *Vaccinium* L. The most common species is *V. reticulatum* Sm., the OHELO, so common as a low shrub around Kilauea Crater and said to be sacred to the Goddess PELE.

List of Taxa of *Vacinnium*:

Vaccinium L. 1754
   berberifolium (Gray) Skottsb., 1927, (as *berberidifolium*). D:fam. 287, 3/30/34.
      'Ohelo, barbery-leaved 'ohelo   end. Maui, Hawaii
     penduliflorum Gaud., var. *berberifolium* Gray, 1862
   calycinum Sm., 1819, var. **calycinum**, f. **calycinum**. 'Ohelo-kau-la'au.
                                                                  end. Molokai, Maui, Hawaii
     reticulatum Sm., f. *calycina* (Sm.) Wawra, 1873
     grandifloium (Wawra) Fosb., 1942, f. *grandifolium*
     reticulatum Sm. f. *grandifolium* Wawra, 1873
       f. **Fauriei** (Lévl.) Skottsb., 1937. 'Ohelo kau-kau-la-au   end. Hawaii
          Fauriei Lévl., 1912   1912
       f. **fimbriatum** Skottsb., 1937   end. Hawaii
       f. **glaucum** Skottsb., 1944   end. w. Maui
       f. **hamatidens** (Lévl.) Fosb., 1942   end. Kauai
          hamatidens Lévl., 1911
       f. **Meyenianum** (Klotzsch) Skottsb., 1937   end. Oahu
          Meyenianum Klotzsch, 1851
      var. **montanum** (Wawra) Skottsb., 1937   end. e. Maui
         reticulatum Sm., f. *montana* Wawra, 1873
   dentatum Sm., 1819, var. **dentatum**. D:fam. 287, 5/20/40
                                          end. Kauai, Oahu, Molokai, Lanai, Maui
     cereum Cham., 1826
     reticulatum Sm., F. *cereum* (Cham.) Wawra, 1873
     var. **argutidens** Skottsb., 1927. D:fam. 287, 5/20/40   end. Kauai
     var. **lanceolatum** (Gray) Skottsb., 1927. D:fam. 287, 5/20/40   end. Kauai, Oahu
       reticulatum Sm., var.? *lanceolatum* Gray, 1862. H:272
         f. *lanceolata* (Gray) Wawra, 1873
     var. **minutifolium** Skottsb., 1944. D:fam. 287, 11/11/60   end. Kauai
Oxycoccus L., 1753. Smaller cranberry   cult. Nearctic
   pahalae Skottsb., 1927. D:fam. 287, 3/15/40. 'Ohelo, Pahala, 'ohelo
                                                                 end. Oahu, Hawaii
   peleanum Skottsb., 1927   end. Hawaii
   reticulatum Sm., 1819, f. **reticulatum** H:271; N:662. 'Ohelo   end. Maui, Hawaii
     f. *parvifolia* Wawra, 1873
     f. **hirsutius** Skottsb., 1927   end. Hawaii
     f. **longiflorum** Skottsb., 1937 (as *longiflora*)   end. Maui

[1] See:
Neal, p. 662 for OHELO.
Degener, PHNP, pp. 240-45.
St. John, p. 266.

HVNP Kilauea
HNP

OHELO KAULAAU   **Vaccinium calycinum** Sm.

Although Rock does not list any of the *Vacciniums* as being trees, I have noticed that this species is almost tree-like, 10' (3.1m) or more tall.

It has alternate leaves 1 by 3" (2.5 by 7.5cm), short pointed at the apex, elongated at base, with short petiole, thin, light green and shiny above, dull below, veins prominent on the underside. Small flowers are greenish. Large, sour, bright red, cranberry-like fruits, .5" (1.2cm) in diameter or more, are attached by long stems in the leaf axils. New twig growth is 4-angled and green, aging to stout dark brown and rough. Bark is smooth on 1" (2.5cm) stems.

Wood is very light tan with rings of darker tan, texture very fine, figure plain, grain straight and close, density high, quite hard. Vessels very fine, rays prominent, light colored and closely spaced. Very small pith, Good stability. Too small to work.

No uses are known. It is quite abundant in the Kilauea region of HVNP and in other areas of older OHIA forests.[1]

EPACRIS FAMILY   Epacridaceae

Hawaii has one native genus in Epacris family, *Styphelia*, with two species and one variety.

List of taxa of *Styphelia*

Styphelia douglasii (Gray) F. Muell. ex. Skottsb.
                                        end. Kauai, Molodai, Maui, Hawaii

Styphelia tameiameiae (Cham) F. Muell. var. **tameiameiae** ind. HI, Marquesas Is.
var. **brownii** (Gray) St. John   end. HI

Key to the species adapted from Hillebrand

Leaves glabrous with most nerves forking;
  tall shrubs or trees . . . . **S. tameiameiae**
Leaves ciliate at the margins, nerves all simple or outer pair dividing;
  low, often trailing shrubs . . . . **S. douglasii**

HVNP Kilauea region
HNP Paliku

PUKIAWE or KAWAU   **Styphelia tameiameiae** (Cham) F. Muell.
                                              Syn. **Cyathoides tameiameiae** Cham

PUKIAWE is a very common large shrub in dryer areas and becomes a shrubby tree 15' (4.6m) tall in good environment in Kau and South Kona.

Very small leaves are about .06 by .5" (.2 by 1.2cm), stiff, alternate, leathery, very short stemmed, oblong, dark green above, light green below. The very small, white flowers are borne in the leaf axils singly or in small clusters. The petals are united forming a 5-pointed star. Greenish calyx tube a little longer than the diameter of the flowers which is barely .0625" (.2cm). Fruit is a small, red or white drupe hardly .25" (.6cm) in diameter, dry, globose, with one hard seed. Twigs are slender, brown and scaly. Bark finely corrugated, brown to black, and rough on larger stems.

Heart wood dark brown, sapwood light brown, texture fine, figure slightly curly and streaked, grain not straight, close; density high and wood hard. Vessels numerous, very fine, scattered, no rays visible at 10x. Wood is quite stable but brittle.

Red and brown dyes were made from the bark; the smoke from a fire of the wood cleansed chiefs who had been put under a TABU. A fire of the wood was used in cremating bodies of outlaws.

1. Clustered pink, red and white berries of Pukiawe. HVNP, Hawaii. Seekins photo.

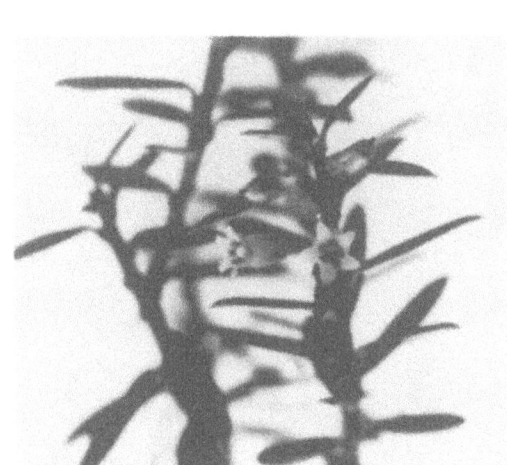

2. Closeup of Pukiawe flowers and leaves. Kokee, Kauai.

PUKIAWE is a very conspicuous component of the shrubby areas around Kialuea and Mauna Loa where it is mixed with AALII and OHELO.[1]

PUKIAWE   **Styphelia Douglassii** (Gray) F. Muell.

This PUKIAWE is a shrub of the high mountains of several islands up to the upper limit of plant growth.

[1] See:
Hillebrand, p. 272.
Rock, p. 366.
Neal, p. 663.
Degener, PHNP, pp. 245-47, (good account).
St. John, p. 267.

MYRSINE FAMILY   **Myrsinaceae**

Myrsine is the only native shrub and tree genus of the *Myrsine* family in the Hawaiian Islands. All taxa of the genus are endemic to the Islands. One other native genus is found here, *Embelia*, but it is a vine only.

List of the taxa of *Myrsine*:

Myrsine L., 1754
  alyxifolia Hosaka, 1940   end. Kauai
    sandwicensis A. DC., var. *buxifolia* Wawra, 1874
    Rapanea alyxifolia (Hosaka) Deg. & Deg., 1971
  Degeneri Hosaka, 1940   end. Oahu
    Rapanea degeneri (Hosaka) Deg. & Deg., 1971
  denticulata (Wawra) Hosaka, 1940   ßend. Kauai
    sandwicensis A.DC. var. *denticulata* Wawra, 1874
    Rapanea Hosakana Deg. & Deg., 1971
  emarginata (Rock) Hosaka, 1940   end. Oahu, Molokai, Maui
    Rapanea emarginata (Rock) Deg. & Deg., 1971
    Suttonia Hillebrandii Mez, var. *emarginata* Rock, 1913. R:373
  **Fernseei (Mex) Hosaka, 1940, Kolea   end. Oahu
    Suttonia Fernseei Mez, 1902. R:370
    Rapanea Fernseei (Mez) Deg. & Hosaka, 1939. D:fam. 290, 4/21/39
    M. Gaudichaudii A.DC., var. *grandifolia* Wawra, 1874
  Hosakae Wilbur, 1965. 'Oliko   end. Kauai
    angustifolia (Mez) Hosaka, 1940, non D. Dietr., 1839
    Rapanea Helleri Deg. & Deg., 1971
  Juddii Hosaka, 1940   end. Oahu
    Rapanea Juddii (Hosaka) Deg. & Deg., 1971
  kauaiensis Hbd., 1888. H:280. Kolea   end. Kauai
    Suttonia kauaiensis (Hbd.) Mez, 1902, F:368
    (?) *S. kauaiensis*, var. *petiolata* Hochr., 1925
    Rapanea kauaiensis (Hbd.) Deg. & Hosaka, 1939. D:fam.290, 4/21/39
    R. Hillebrandii (Mez) Deg. & Hosaka, 1939. D:fam. 290, 4/21/39
  Knudsenii (Rock) Hosaka, 1940   end. Kauai
    Suttonia Knudsenii Rock, 1913. R:373
    Rapanea Knudsenii (Rock) Deg. & Hosaka, 1939

1. Pukiawe, *S. kameiameiae*, shrub near Mauna Loa Road, HVNP, Hawaii.

1. Kolea bark detail.

2. Kolea tree, South Kohala, Hawaii.

   kokeeana Hosaka, 1940   end. Kauai
      Rapanea kokeensis (Hosaka) Deg. & Deg., 1971
   lanaiensis Hbd., 1888, var. **lanaiensis**.H:281. Kolea   end. H.I.
      Suttonia lanaiensis (Hbd.) Mez, 1902. R:369
      S. lanaiensis, var. *coriacea* Rock, 1913. R:369
      S. volcanica Rock, 1913
      S. volcanica, var. *lavarum* Rock, 1913. R:371
      Rapanea lanaiensis (Hbd.) Deg. & Hosaka, 1939, D:fam. 290, 4/21/39
      R. volcanica (Rock, Deg. & Hosaka, 1939. D:fam. 190, 4/21/39
**   var. **oahuensis** Hosaka, 1940   end. Oahu
   Lessertiana A. DC., 1841. H:271, N:664. Kolea-lau-nui   end. H.I.
      Fauriei Lévl., 1911
      Suttonia Lessertiana (A.DC.) Mez, 1902. R:375
      S. Lessertiana, f. *ovicarpa* Rock, 1913. R:377
      S. spathulata Rock, 1913. R:370
      Rapanea Lessertiana (A.DC) Deg. & Hosaka, 1939. D:fam. 190, 4/21/39
      R. spathulata (Rock) Deg. & Hosaka, 1939. D:fam. 290, 4/21/39
****linearifolia** Hosaka, 1940, var. **linearifolia**   end. Kauai
      Rapanea linearifolia (Hosaka) Deg. & Deg., 1971
     var. **Nittae** Hosaka, 1940   end. Kauai
   Meziana (Lévl.) Wilbur, 1965, var. **Meziana**   end. Oahu
      Gaudichaudiana A.DC., f. *acuminata* Wawra, 1874
      Fosbergii Hosaka, var. *acuminata* (Wawra) Hosaka, 1940
      Suttonia Meziana Lévl., 1912
     var. **Fosbergii** (Hosaka) Wilbur, 1965   end. Oahu
        Fosbergii Hosaka, 1940
        Rapanea Fosbergii (Hosaka) Deg. & Deg., 1971
****Mezii** Hosaka, 1940   end. Kauai
      Rapanea Mezii (Hosaka) Deg. & Deg., 1971
****petiolata** Hosaka, 1940   end. Kauai
      Rapanea petiolata (Hosaka) Deg. & Deg., 1971
   pukooensis (Lévl.) Hosaka, 1940   end. Kauai, Oahu, Molokai
      Rapanea pukooensis (Hosaka) Deg. & Deg., 1971
      Suttonia pukooensis Lévl., 1912
   punctata (Lévl.) Wilbur, 1965   end. Lanai, Maui
      Suttonia punctata (Lévl.) Lévl., 1912
      S. lanceolata (Wawra) Rock, 1913
      M. Rockii (Deg. & Hosaka) Hosaka, 1940
      Rapanea Rockii Deg. & Hosaka, 1939. D:fam. 290, 4/21/39
      M. sandwicensis A.DC., var. *lanceolata* Wawra, 1874
      M. sandwicensis, var. *punctata* Lévl., 1911
      S. lanceolata (Wawra) Rock, 1913
****St. Johnii** Hosaka, 1940   end. Kauai
      Rapanea St. Johnii (Hosaka) Deg. & Deg., 1971
   salicina (Hook.f.) Heward ex Hook, 1842. H:664. Toro.   cult. New Zealand
   sandwicensis A.DC., 1841, var. **sandwicensis** R:377. Kolea-lau-li'i
                                                                   end. Oahu, Hawaii
     var. *grandifolia* Wawra, 1874
     Rapanea sandwicensis (A.DC.) Deg. & Hosaka, 1939. D:fam. 290, 4/21/39
     var. **mauiensis** Lévl., 1911   end. Oahu, Molokai, Lanai, Maui
        Rapanea sandwicensis, var. *mauiensis* (Lévl.) Deg. & Deg., 1963. D:fam. 290, 1/18/63
   Wawraea (Mez) Hosaka, 1940   end. Kauai
      Gaudichaudii A.DC., var. *hirsuta*Wawra, 1874
      kauaiensis Hbd., var. *hirsuta* Hbd., 1888. H:280
      Suttonia Wawraea Mez, 1902. R: 368
      Rapanea Wawraea (Mez) Deg. & Hosaka, 1939. D:fam. 290, 4/21/39

   Rock gives a key to eight of the species listed here but it is not very helpful in working with 20 species.

HVNP Kilauea
HNP Paliku

KOLEA   **Myrsine lessertiana** A.DC
Syn. **Suttonia lessertiana** (A.DC) Mez.
Syn. **Rapanea lessertiana** (A.DC) Deg. & Hosaka

[1] See:
Hillebrand, p. 279.
Rock, p. 375.
Neal, p. 664.
Carlquist, p. 314.
St. John, p. 268.

This KOLEA is endemic to all the islands, thus it is one of the species most apt to be found where it is a tree of the wet OHIA forest, invading this forest quite early in succession. The tree is tall, straight and slender.
L.W. Bryan's big tree is 6'9" (2m) in circumference, 67' (20.4m) tall with crown spread of 25' (7.8m), found in HVNP. Most trees are more like 30 to 50' (9.5 to 15.75m) tall and 1 to 2' (31.5 to 63cm) in diameter.

Leaves alternate but closely bunched at ends of branches, petioles very short. New leaves quite red, later becoming green with red midrib and pinnate veins, still later dark green. Leaves are up to 6" (15cm) long and 1.5" (3.7cm) wide, with acute apex, but varying widely from tree to tree. Tiny light lavender flowers occur in dense rows along stems below leaves. Small purple fruit on short stems are very numerous, one seeded. Twigs slender to stout and rough. Bark on young trunks smooth but later breaks into small sections, giving a warty appearance. If the bark is cut, the tree freely exudes deep red sap.

2.

1.

1. Leaf, fruit and twig of Kolea.
2. Closeup of Kolea, M. lessertiana, flower detail with pink petals. Seekins photo.
3. Bark detail, Kolea.
4. Small Kolea, M. lessertiana, HVNP, Hawaii

3.

4.

Wood is pinkish and mottled, texture coarse, figure plain to streaked, grain straight, density medium and quite hard. Vessels numerous, medium sized, rays fine, numerous, sometimes showing on cut surface as dense pattern of ray ends. Resinous wood warps, but works well.

Hawaiians used the red sap as dye for TAPA, charcoal used in making black dye, logs used in house construction and for TAPA anvils.

KOLEA is quite common in the OHIA forest and is wide spread in the wetter areas of the islands. It is so variable that it is not possible to give a description to fit all the trees that may be found.[1]

HVNP Chain of Craters area
HNP var. *mauiensis* Lévl.

KOLEA-LAULII   **Myrsine sandwicensis** A.DC
Syn. **Rapanea sandwicensis** (A.DC) Deg. & Hosaka
Syn. **Suttonia sandwicensis** (A.DC) Mez.

LAULII literally means little leaf so this is 'little leaf KOLEA' and the leaves are indeed small. Plant is readily found along the Chain of Craters Road in HVNP as a tall shrub or small tree with long projecting limbs profusely covered with small leaves, particularly toward the ends. St. John says endemic to Oahu and Hawaii only but Rock states endemic to all the islands. It may be 25' (7.8m) tall in favorable environment.

[2] See:
Hillebrand, p. 281.
Rock, p. 377.
Carlquist, p. 315.
St. John, p. 269.

[3] See:
Rock, p. 371.
St. John, p. 268.

[4] See:
St. John, p. 267.

1. *Kolea, M. lanaiensis*, buds, leaves and fruit on right.

2. *Kolea Laulii, M. sandwicensis*, small leaves and twig. HVNP, Hawaii.

3. *Kolea, M. alyxifolia*, leaves and slender branches. Kokee, Kauai.

Leaves are usually less than 1" (2.5cm) long, green above and pale beneath, round at apex, pointed at base, petiole very short. New leaves may be red. Leaves have small notch at apex and are very closely attached to the twig with a short petiole. Midrib and veins not prominent. Small 6-parted, light lavender, yellowish or reddish flowers, with petals veined with darker lines, are about .375" (.95cm) across, borne in small clusters of three to seven in axils of leaves and on the bare twig below the leaves. Fruit is a drupe, black or bluish, globose, about .125 to .25" (.3 to .6cm) in diameter, thickly clustered close to the twig. Twigs dark green aging to dark brown, rough with leaf scars. Bark smooth on 2" (5cm) stems. No wood was available for study.[2]

KOLEA **Myrsine lanaiensis** Hb.d
Syn. **Rapanea lanaiensis** (Hbd.) Deg. & Hosaka
Syn. **Suttonia volcanica** Rock

This KOLEA is endemic to all the islands of the group with one added variety, *M. lanaiensis* var. *oahuensis* Hosaka, endemic to Oahu. It is a small tree 12 to 15' (3.8 to 4.7m) tall or taller found in dryer parts of the islands.

Thin, opposite leaves have prominent midrib sometimes red or light green, prominent pinnate veins and spots on the leaves (punctate). Upper surface glossy and dark green, under surface dull and light green. Flowers two to eight in a cluster, axillary, or mostly along the twig below the leaves. Fruit very small, clustered around twigs on .5" (1.2cm) stems, depressed globose, blue-black when ripe. Bark light greyish brown and smooth to warty on largest trunks. Wood not studied.

This is an occasional tree in the forests of the dryer parts of the islands. The var. *oahuensis* is listed as endangered.[3]

KOLEA **Myrsine alyxifolia** Hosaka
Syn. **Rapanea alyxifolia** (Hosaka) Deg. & Deg.

This KOLEA is a shrub or small tree with short trunk distinguished by its slender, almost twining branches. It is endemic to Kauai where it may been seen in Kokee.

Leaves dark green, slightly rolled at edges, apex and base both blunt, petiole .25" (.6cm) long, opposite, with terminal leaves larger than lower ones. Large leaves 1.25 to 1.5 by 2 to 2.5" (3 to 3.6 by 5 to 6.3cm). No flowers or fruits seen. Twigs very slender and long, smooth and medium brown.

Wood is white, fine texture, plain figure, straight, close grain, moderately dense and hard. Vessels very small and scattered, rays prominent, lighter than other wood and closely spaced. Stability good, too small to use.

This is an occasional shrub or small tree of the mixed forest of the Kokee area of Kauai.[4]

'OLIKO   **Myrsine hosakae** Wilbur

This is a very outstanding shrub or small tree that does not appear to resemble in any way the other KOLEAs described. One beautiful specimen was seen near the Kalalau lookout at about 4000' (1260m) on Kauai in very wet forest.

Leaves are long and very slender, about .5 by 8" (1.2 by 20cm) clustered near the ends of the branches. New leaves light yellowish-green with red midrib. Tiny six parted flowers are borne axillary on short stems, yellowish or greenish white. Fruit not seen. Slender twigs rough. Wood not seen.

This plant would make a beautiful addition to the landscaping of parks and residential areas. It is not common.[5]

SAPODILLA FAMILY   **Sapotaceae**

The Sapodilla family is represented in the Hawaiian Islands by two genera of native woody plants, *Nesoluma* Baill, and *Planchonella* Pierre. St. John combines under the latter the plants previously listed under *Sideroxylon* L. by Rock and *Pouteria* by some writers.

Key to the genera of *Sapotaceae* adapted from Hillebrand:

Corolla 8-10 lobed, without staminodia, fruit small, black,
   olive shaped with generally 1 seed . . . . **Nesoluma**
Corolla 5-lobed with staminodia within the sinuses of its lobes:
   fruit large, globose with 2-5 seeds . . . . **Planchonella**

KEAHI   **Nesoluma polynesicum** (Hbd.) Baill
                                                                Syn. **Chrysophyllum polynesicum** Hbd.

KEAHI is a medium sized tree with rounded crown, rough, drooping branches and milky sap, endemic to Oahu, Molokai, Lanai, Maui and St. John includes Hawaii. The genus has one form, *glabrum* H.J.Lam., indigenous to Kauai, Oahu, Molokai, Raivavae and Rapa.

Leaves entire, broadly acute or rounded at base, apex bluntly rounded, veins pinnate. Flowers borne all along the stem and axillary, fragrant, white to greenish-white, parts in fives. Fruit black, olive shaped, shiny, about .75" (1.6cm) long, borne abundantly along the branch below the leaves. Thin flesh not edible, seeds shorter but almost as wide as fruit, brown. Twigs rough. Wood not seen but said to be hard and durable.[1]

'ALA'A, AULU or KAULU   **Planchonella** Pierre
                                                               Sideroxylon of Haw. Botanists

Planchonella is another of those genera whose nomenclature has gone through a series of changes. The genus as now constituted by St. John consists of 18 taxa. All are endemic to the Hawaiian Islands.

List of taxa of *Planchonella*:

Planchonella Pierre, 1890. (*Sideroxylon* of Haw. botanists)
****auahiensis** (Rock) Skottsb. 1926, var. **auahiensis** 'Ala'a   end. Maui
   Sideroxylon auahiense Rock, 1911
   Pouteria auahiensis (Rock) Fosb., 1962
   Planchonella sandwicensis (Gray) Pierre, var. *sandwicensis*, f. *sandwicensis*,
     sensu H.J. Lam, 1942, in part.
  var. **aurantia** (Rock) Skottsb., 1926   end. Maui
   aurantium (Rock) Skottsb., 1936
   sandwicensis (Gray) Pierre, var. *sandwicensis*, f. *sandwicensis* sensu H.J. Lam,
     1942, in part.
   Pouteria aurantia (Rock) Fosb., 1962
   Sideroxylon auahiense Rock, var. *aurantium* Rock, 1913

[5] See:
St. John, p. 268.

[1] See:
Hillebrand, p. 277.
Rock, p. 380.
Degener, FH, p. 293.
St. John, p. 272.

1. Oliko, M. hosakae, detail of light pink flowers and slender leaves.

2. Oliko, M. hosakae, leaf and flower habit.

3. Tall Oliko shrub, Kalalau Lookout, Kauai.

Ceresolii (Rock) St. John, comb. nov. end. Mauai
  sandwicensis (Gray) Pierre, var. *spathulata* (Hbd.) H.J. Lam, f. *spathulata*
    sensu H.J. Lam, 1942, in part
  Sideroxylon Ceresolii Rock, Indig. Trees Haw. Is, 385, 387, 1913
  Pouteria Ceresolii (Rock) Fosb., 1962
puulupensis Baehni & Deg., 1938. 'Ala'a, kaulu, aulu, puulupe planchonella
                                                                    end. Oahu
  sandwicensis (Gray) Pierre, var. *sandwicensis* f. *puulupensis* (Baehni & Deg.)
    H.J. Lam, 1942
****rhynchosperma** (Rock) St. John. n. comb. end. e. Maui
  sandwicensis (Gray) Pierre, var. *sandwicensis*, f. *sandwicensis* H.J. Lam, 1942, in part
  Sideroxylon rhynchospermum Rock, Torrey, Bot. Club, Bull., 37: 297, 300,
    fig. 2.3, a, b, 1910
  Pouteria rhynchosperma (Rock) Fosb., 1962
sandwicensis (Gray) Pierre, 1890. Aulu, kaulu, 'ala'a end. H.I.
  Sapota sandwicensis Gray, 1862
  Sideroxylon sandwicense (Gray) B.& H. ex Hbd., 1888. H:276, R:383.
  S. sandwicense (Gray) B.& H., var. *auratum* Hbd. 1888. H:277
  Pouteria sandwicensis (Gray) Baehni & Deg., 1938. D:fam. 293, 12/23/38
  Planchonella sandwicensis (Gray) Pierre, 1912, var. *sandwicensis*, f. *sandwicensis*
spathulata (Hbd. Pierre, 1890, var. **spathulata** end. Oahu, Lanai, Maui
  sandwicensis (Gray) Pierre, var. *spathulata* (Hbd.) H.J. Lam, f. *spathulata*
    H.J. Lam, 1942
  Sideroxylon spathulatum Hbd., 1888. H:277
  Pouteria spathulata (Hbd.) Fosb., 1962
  var. **densiflora** (Hbd.) St. John, comb. nov. end. Oahu, Hawaii
    sandwicensis (Gray) Pierre, var. *sandwicensis*, f.*densiflora* (Hbd.) H.J. Lam, 1942
    Sideroxylon spathulatum Hbd., var. *densiflorum* Hbd., F. Haw. Is., 277, 1888
  var. **molokaiensis** (Lévl.) St. John, comb. nov. end. Molokai
    Myrsine molokaiensis Lévl., Fedde Repert. 10:154, 1911

Key to the species of *Planchonella* from Rock, modified:

Flowers single
  Flowers sessile
    Fruits globose, citron or orange yellow
      Seeds as in *P. sandwicensis* but smaller .... **P. auahiensis**
  Flowers pedicellate
    Fruits large, conical, greyish-white
      Seeds elliptical elongate, dull; radicle long and protruding .... **P. ceresolii**
Flowers 2-3, pedicellate
    Fruits conical, brownish yellow
      Seeds small, linear-elongate, dull .... **P. spathulatum**
Flowers 2-4, pedicellate
    Fruits globose, ovoid to obovate, purplish-black
      Seeds thick, rounded at both ends, yellowish-brown ..... **P. sandwicensis**
      Seeds thick, flat, beaked at both ends, light brown .... **P. rhynchosperma**
    Fruits globose, with persistent calyx at base
      Seeds 2-4, clear yellow .... **P. puulupensis**

HNP

AULU, 'ALA'A   **Planchonella sandwicensis** (Gray) Pierre
Syn. **Sideroxylon sandwicensis** Gray) B&H ex Hbd.
Syn. **Pouteria sandwicensis** (Gray) Baehni & Deg.

AULU, 'ALA'A is endemic to the Hawaiian Islands. Some botanists have failed to list it for the island of Hawaii, but L.W. Bryan found his big tree near Puuwaawaa, Kona, Hawaii. It measured 5'3" (1.6m) in circumference, 38' (12.5m) tall and with crown spread of 29' (9.4m). According to Rock the distinction between *P. sandwicensis* and *P. auahensis* is that the former has purple fruits and the latter yellow fruits. Yet the trees seen by the writer at Puuwaawaa had yellow fruits. The writer saw *P. sandwicensis* at Kokee, Kauai, up to 50' (15m) tall. Such inconsistencies make specific identification difficult.

1. *Alaa, roadside tree in South Kohala, Hawaii.*

Leaves alternate, 2 to 5" (5 to 13cm) long by 1.25 to 2.5" (3 to 6cm) wide, with heavy petioles .5 to 1" (1.2 to 2.5cm) long, covered with brown tomentum, upper surface shiny green, lower surface covered with brown to reddish tomentum. Small flowers in small axillary clusters of two to four on short pedicles. Fruits purplish-black, closely attached to the stem. Twigs quite smooth, light grey, sap milky. Bark grey, divided into segments by deep grooves. Wood light yellow, texture fine, figure plain, grain straight. Vessels very small and arranged in annular chains, rays very fine and closely spaced, density medium, wood quite hard. Stability good, workability good, small closed pith.

Hawaiians used the wood for house building, OO handles and spears.[2]

'ALA'A   **Planchonella auahensis** var. **aurantia** (Rock) Skottsb.
Syn. **Sideroxylon auahensis** var. *aurantum* Rock
Syn. **Pouteria aurantia** (Rock) Fosb.

This 'ALA'A does not occur on Hawaii according to St. John but Rock found it common in the Puuwaawaa, Kona, Hawaii area as this yellow fruited 'ALA'A is today. It is a tree 25 to 50' (7.8 to 15.25m) tall, up to 2' (60cm) in diameter with straight ascending branches. These trees are also found in Ocean View Estates area of South Kona. A beautiful small grove was seen on the edge of an opening in the OHIA forest.

Alternate leaves are 1.25" (3cm) wide by 2.5 to 3" (6 to 7.5cm) long, slender new leaves roufous, aging to dark green with prominent light green midrib and fine pinnate veins, pointed at each end and on 1" (2.5cm) petiole. Small cream colored flowers borne in leaf axils singly. Fruit citron yellow, globose to top shaped, sessile, about 1" (2.5cm) in diameter, yellow pulp with one large yellowish brown or brown seed .5" (1.2cm) in diameter. New twig growth roufous brown, aging to light grey, smooth except for leaf scars. Bark with moderately deep furrows on large trunks.

Wood light yellow with brown streaks, texture medium fine, figure moderate flame or plain, grain somewhat wavy, density high, wood quite hard. Vessels fine in long closely spaced annular chains, rays fine, closely spaced. Stability only fair, wood warps and checks, workability poor.

Hawaiian uses are probably the same as for *P. sandwicensis*.[3]

[2] See:
Hillebrand, p. 276.
Rock, p. 383.
Carlquist, p. 279.
St. John, p. 272.

[3] See:
Rock, p. 391.
St. John, p. 272.

1. Alaa, P. sandwicensis, leaves, Kokee, Kauai.

2. Alaa, P. auahiense, v. aurantium, fruit (yellow) and leaves.

EBONY FAMILY   Ebenaceae

Hawaii has only one genus of native trees of the Ebony family, *Diospyros*. This is a wide spread genus with representatives on the North American continent, the common persimmon, for one.

The list of taxa in Hawaii is as follows:

Diospyros L., 1754
   discolor Willd., 1806. N:674 Mabolo   cult. P.I.
   Ebenaster Retz., 1788. N:674. Black sapote, sapote negro   cult. W.I.
   Ebenum Koenig, 1776. N:672. Macassar ebony   cult. India, Malaya
   ferrea (Willd.) Bakh., 1933, subsp. **sandwicensis** (A.DC.) Fosb., 1939, var.
      sandwicensis (A.DC) Bakh, 1937. f. B.F. Lama   end. H.I.
        Maba sandwicensis A.DC., 1844
         f. **obtusa** Fosb., 1939   end. Oahu
         f. **ovata** Fosb., 1939   end. Kauai
         f. **subcoriacea** Fosb., 1939   end. Kauai
         f. **wailauensis** Fosb., 1939   end. Molokai
      var. **Degeneri** Fosb., 1939, f. **Degeneri**   end. e. Maui
         f. **lanaiensis** Fosb. 1939
      var. **lauaiensis** Fosb., 1939, f. **kauaiensis**   end. Kauai, Oahu
         f. **Wiebkie** Fosb., 1939   end. Kauai
      var. **pubescens** (Skottsb.) Fosb., 1939, f. **pubescens**   end. Hawaii

3. Alaa bark detail.

[1] See:
Hillebrand, p. 274.
Rock, p. 393.
Neal, p. 673.
Carlquist, pp. 276-85.
St. John, p. 273.

Maba sandwicensis A.DC., var. *pubescens* Skottsb., 1926
 f. **sclerophylla** Fosb., 1939   end. Hawaii
 var. **Toppingii** Fosb., 1939   end. Oahu
Hillebrandii (Seem.) Fosb., 1936. D:fam. 295, 4/7/60. Lama, Hillebrand end. Oahu

HVNP Dry forest

LAMA   **Diospyros ferrea** var. **sandwicenses** (A.DC.) Fosb.
     Syn. **Maba sandwicensis** A.DC.

Since this is the LAMA that is common to all the islands it is the one most apt to be seen except in local situations where one of the other varieties or forms might be seen. It is generally a tree 20 to 35' (6.3 to 11m) tall with a well rounded crown. The writer measured a big tree near Wahaulu Ranger Station, just outside the Park with the following measurements: circumference, 5'4.5" (1.6m), height 25' (7.8m), crown spread 34' (11m). Although this tree lacks 10' (3m) from being as tall as the champion LAMA measured by L.W. Bryan at Puuwaawaa it is much larger in circumference and crown spread, a very beautiful tree.

Alternate leaves thick, leathery, dull green, arranged in opposite rows giving a flat aspect to the branches. They are oblong or oval, about 2" (5cm) long by .5" (1.2cm) wide on a short petiole. Flowers borne close to the twig, axillary, and single, on a very short peduncle, covered with about six small bracts, with three greenish-white or pink petals, united with tiny antlers at base of small green cup. Edible fruit bright reddish or yellow, .66" (1.6cm) long, set in cup like an acorn, one or two brown seeds. Twigs slender, new growth smooth grey-green, aging to light brown, rough and scaly. Bark black and rather smooth on small trunks but quite rough on large old trunks.

1.

2.

3.

4.

1. Lama big tree found by Lamb, Seekins and Usagawa in Puna, Hawaii. Seekins photo.
2. Big Lama tree, Puna, Hawaii.
3. Lama bark detail.
4. Lama, D. ferrea, leaf and fruit detail.

Wood very light reddish brown to rich reddish brown with black accents, texture fine, figure plain to light flame, grain straight and close, very dense and very hard. Vessels very fine and scattered, rays very fine and very numerous, stability not good and hard to work.

Hawaiians used the wood for timbers for houses of the gods, as well as for very durable tide gates for fish ponds. An enclosure made of LAMA wood was called a PALAMA.

LAMA is very plentiful in dry areas such as the area back of Wahaulu Ranger Station near KALAPANA, in the Puuwaawaa area of Kona and the Ocean View Estates region of South Kona.

The species *D. hillebrandi* is found only on Oahu where Rock found it in the hills of Kahuku and Waialua and in Niu valley at 2000' (630m). The leaves are much larger than in *D. ferrea*.[1]

OLIVE FAMILY — Oleaceae

The Olive family is represented by only one native tree species, *Osmanthus sandwicensis* Gray) Knobl.

HVNP Kipuka Puaulu

OLOPUA **Osmanthus sandwicensis** (Gray) Knobl.

OLOPUA is endemic to all the Hawaiian Islands and in some localities quite abundant. Preferred habitat is the relatively dry forest on the lee sides of all the islands and into the edge of the wet forest. It may become a very large tree, the L.W. Bryan big tree is 10'2" (3.1m) in circumference, 54' (17m) tall with crown spread of 31' (9.8m), located on Hoomau Ranch, Honomolino, Hawaii. The writer saw a tremendous stump in this same area that must have been 24' (7.8m) in circumference.

Leaves large, opposite, quite variable in size and appearance. Leaves from trees in Kipuka Puaulu in HVNP are about 3 by 6" (7.5 by 15cm) or larger, with deeply impressed midrib and pinnate veins, very shiny and crinkled in appearance. Leaves from Kokee on Kauai were more slender and more sharply pointed at both ends, with more prominent yellow midrib but with much less shiny, crinkled appearance. Some leaves have a reddish cast and the petioles are short. Flowers are 4-parted, inconspicuous, pale yellow, borne in the leaf axils in 1 to 2.5" (2.5 to 6 cm) long racemes. Fruit a purplish drupe very similar to a ripe olive in appearance, flesh thin, .5 to 1" (1.2 to 2.5cm) long, borne axillary or just below the leaves on short peduncle. Twigs stout, light brown, bark thick, very corrugated in older trees, often divided into large scales.

Heart wood light reddish to yellowish-brown with black streaks, sapwood yellow, texture fine, figure striped, grain straight, and close, very dense and very hard. Vessels few, small in short radial chains, rays very numerous and very fine. Stability fair, the wood checks but is durable, hard to work.

Hawaiians used the wood for adz handles, for fuel since it will burn with a hot flame even when green, fish spears, as a rasp to use in shaping fish hooks and for OO.

It is interesting to note that in Kipuku Puaulu in 1934-38 the writer found the forest understory almost devoid of shrubs or tree seedlings as livestock had grazed the area until just a few years before. When I visited the area again in 1960 the understory was crowded with a rank growth of KOPIKO. Then when I returned again in 1974 and 1976, much of the KOPIKO had given way to OLOPUA. It is possible that this is normal succession in Hawaiian forests as KOPIKO is one of the early invaders of new OHIA forests while OLOPUA is much more prominent in old OHIA forests that are a mixture of many species so noticeable in Kipuka Puaulu and in the moderately wet forests of South Kona.[1]

[1] See:
Hillebrand, p. 301.
Rock, p. 397.
Neal, p. 676.
Degener, FH, p. 300.
St. John, p. 275.

1. Leaf detail, Olopua, *O. sandwicensis*, HVNP, Hawaii.

2. Bark detail of Olopua.

STRICHNINE or LOGANIA FAMILY — Loganaceae

Hawaii has only one native woody genus of the Strichnine family, *Labordia* Gaud., but it makes up in species what it lacks in genera. St. John lists a total of 83 taxa. Rock lists only four species as trees but all are listed here because so many are threatened, endangered or extinct. All taxa are endemic to the Hawaiian Islands.

List of taxa of *Labordia*:

Labordia Gaud., 1829
*****Baillonii** St. John, 1936 — end. Hawaii
   cyrtandrae (Baill.) St. John, 1936, var. **cyrtandrae**. Kamakahala, pale labordia
      end. Oahu
     hypoleuca Deg., 1932. D:fam. 302, 8/10/32
     Geniostoma cyrtandrae Baill., 1880
 *   var. **nahikuana** Sherff, 1939 — end. e. Maui
     hypoleuca Deg., var. *nahikuana* (Sherff) Deg. & Deg., 1957. D:fam. 302, 2/15/57
*****decurrens** Sherff, 1938, var. **decurrens** — end. Oahu
   var. **pocillata** Sherff, 1944 — end. Kauai
  Degeneri Sherff, 1938, var. **Degeneri** D:fam. 302, 8/24/38. Kamakahala, Degener labordia — end. Kauai
   var. **subcarinata** Sherff, 1939 — end. Kauai
****fagraeoidea** Gaud., 1829, var. **fagraeoidia** H:290, D:fam. 302, 3/15/40
   Kamakahala, fagraea laborida — end. Oahu
   var. **conferta** Sherff, 1938. D:fam. 302, 3/15/40 — end. Oahu
   var. **Hillebrandii** Sherff, 1939, f. **Hillebrandii**. D:fam. 302, 3/15/40 — end. Oahu
    f. **subcalva** Deg.& Sherff in Deg., 1940. D:fam. 302, 3/15/40 — end. Oahu
   var. **Humei** Sherff, 1938, f. **Humei** D:fam. 302, 3/15/40 — end. Oahu
    f. **paniculata** Sherff, 1938. D:fam. 302, 3/15/40 — end. Oahu
   var. **jugorum** Sherff, 1938. D:fam. 302, 3/15/40 — end. Oahu
**   var. **longisepala** Sherff, 1938, D:fam. 302, 3/15/40 — end. Oahu
   var. **multinervia** Sherff, 1951 — end. Oahu
*   var. **St.-Johniana** Sherff, 1938. D:fam. 302, 3/15/40 — end. Oahu
   var. **septentrionalis** Sherff, 1938. D:fam. 302, 3/15/40 — end. Oahu
   var. **sessilis** (Gray) Sherff, 1938, f. **sessilis** D:fam. 302, 3/15/40 — end. Oahu
    sessilis Gray, 1860
    f. **glabrescens** Sherff, 1939. D:fam. 302, 3/15/40; R:406 — end. Oahu
   var. **simulans** Deg. & Sherff in Sherff, 1939. D:fam. 302, 3/15/40 — end. Oahu
**   var. **waianaeana** Sherff, 1938. D:fam. 302, 3/15/40 — end. Oahu
*****glabra** Hbd., 1888, var. **glabra**, H:291 — end. Maui
**   var. **latisepala** Sherff, 1939 — end. Oahu
**   var. **orientalis** Sherff, 1938 — end. Maui
  hedyosmifolia Baill., 1880, var. **hedyosmifloia** — end. Hawaii
   var. **centralis** (Skottsb.) St. John, 1936 — end. Molokai, Lanai, Maui
    Grayana Hbd., var. *centralis* Skottsb., 1936
   var. **Grayana** (Hbd.) Sherff, 1938, f. **Grayana** Kamakahala — end. Hawaii
    Grayana Hbd., 1888
    f. **angustisepala** Deb. & Sherff in Sherff, 1951 — end. Hawaii
   var. **Hosakana** Sherff, 1938 — end. Oahu
**   var. **kilaueana** Sherff, 1938 — end. Hawaii
**   var. **magnifolia** Deg. & Sherff, in Sherff, 1939 — end. Hawaii
**   var. **robusta** Sherff, 1938 — end. Hawaii
**   var. **Rockii** Sherff, 1A938 — end. Maui
**   var. **Skottsbergii** Sherff, 1938 — end. Hawaii
  Helleri Sherff, 1938, var. **Helleri** — end. Kauai
   var. **macrocarpa** Sherff, 1938 — end. Kauai
  hirtella Mann, 1867, var. **hirtella**. H:292 — end. Lanai, Molokai, Maui
   var. **haleakalana** Sherff, 1938 — end. Maui
   var. **hispidior** Sherff, 1938 — end. Maui
**   var. **imbricata** Deg. & Sherff in Sherff, 1939 — end. Hawaii
**   var. **laevis** Sherff, 1938 — end. Molokai
**   var. **laevisepala** Sherff, 1939 — end. Molokai

***	var. **microcalyx** Hbd., 1888. H:292	end. Hawaii
***	var. **microphylla** Hbd., 1888. H:292	end. Maui
	var. **soroia** Sherff, 1938	end. Maui
	hymenopoda Deg. & Sherff in Sherff, 1951	end. Oahu
	kaalae Forbes, 1916, var. **kaalae**	end. Oahu
**	var. **brachypoda** Sherff, 1938	end. Oahu
**	var. **Fosbergii** Sherff, 1938	end. Oahu
**	var. **kauaiensis** Sherff, 1939	end. Kauai
**	var. *mendax* Sherff, 1938	end. Oahu
*	**Lydgatei** Forbes, 1916	end. Kauai
	mauiensis Sherff, 1938	end. Maui
**	**membranacea** Mann, 1867, var. **membranacea** H:291, R:405. Kamakahala	end. Oahu
**	var. **exigua** Sherff, 1938	end. Maui
**	**molokaiana** Baill, 1880, var. **molokaiana**	end. Molokai
	lophocarpa Hbd., var. *plurifolia* Hbd., 1888. H:290	
	var. **Bryanii** Sherff, 1938	end. Oahu
	var. **congesta** Deg. & Sherff in Sherff, 1938	end. Molokai
	var. **lophocarpa** (Hbd.) Sherff, 1938	end. Molokai
	lophocarpa Hbd., 1888, in part. H:289	
**	var. **Munroi** Sherff, 1938	end. Lanai
	lophocarpa Hbd., 1888, in part	
	var. **phyllocalyx** (Hbd.) Sherff, 1938	
	lophocarpa Hbd., var. **phyllocalyx** Hbd., 1888. H:290	
	waiolani Wawra, 1872ç	
**	var. **setosa** Deg. & Sherff in Sherff, 1938	end. Molokai
**	**olympiana** Sherff, 1938	end. Oahu
	membranacea sensu Rock, non Mann, 1867	
	pallida Mann, 1867, var. **pallida**	end. Kauai
**	var. **hispidula** Sherff, 1939	end. Kauai
***	**pedunculata** Sherff, 1939	end. e. Maui?
	pumila (Hbd.) Skottsb., 1936	end. Kauai
	fagracoidea Gaud., var. *pumila* Hbd., 1888	
	pallida Mann, f. *alpina* Wawra, 1872	
	tinifolia Gray, 1860, var. **tinifolia** H:292, R:406; D:fam. 302, 3/15/40.	
	Kamakahala, pale-flowered labordia	end. Oahu, Molokai, Maui, Hawaii
*	var. **euphorbioidea** Sherff, 1938. D:fam. 302, 3/15/40	end. e. Maui
**	var. **Forbesii** Sherff, 1938. D:fam. 302, 3/15/40	end. Molokai
	var. **haupuensis** Sherff, 1944	end. Kauai
***	var. **honoluluensis** Sherff, 1938. D:fam. 302, 3/15/40	end. Oahu
*	var. **lanaiensis** Sherff, 1938. D:fam. 302, 3/15/40	end. Lanai, Maui, Hawaii
	var. **leptantha** Sherff, 1938. D:fam. 302, 3/15/40	end. Oahu, Molokai
**	var. **microgyna** Deg. & Sherff in Sherff, 1939. D:fam. 302, 3/15/40	end. Kauai
***	var. **parvifolia** Sherff, 1938. D;fam. 302, 3/15/40	end. Molokai
**	var. **tenuifolia** Deg. & Sherff in Sherff, 1938. D:fam. 302, 3/15/40	end. Molokai
	var. **waialuana** Sherff, 1938. D:fam. 302, 3/15/40	end. Oahu
***	**triflora** Hbd., 1888. H:293	end. Molokai
	venosa Sherff, 1938	end. Maui
	waialealae Wawra, 1872. H:292. Kamakahala-lau-li'i	end. Kauai
*	**Wawrana** Sherff, 1938	end. Kauai

Key to the tree species, adapted from Rock:

Corolla yellow
    Flowers single, enclosed within the foliaceous calyx lobes.
        Capsule small, crested . . . . **L. molokaiana** Baill.
    Flowers several in a sessile cyme
        Capsule .4cm long, not crested . . . . **L. olympiana** Sherff
        Capsule .5cm high, 3-valved, minutely pedunculate . . . **L. fagraeoidea** Gaud
                                                       Syn. **L. sessilis** Gray
Corolla greenish
    Flowers in a paniculate cyme . . . . **L. tinifolia** Gray

[1] See:
Rock, p. 406.
Degener, FH, p. 302.
St. John, p. 276.

[2] See:
Rock, p. 406.
St. John, p. 278.

[3] See:
St. John, p. 277.

1. Stem and leaves of Kamakahala, Hawaii.

KAMAKAHALA   **Labordia fagraeoidea** var. **sessilis** (Gray) Sherff
Syn. **L. sessilis** Gray

Degener's *Flora Hawaiiensis* gives a key to the varieties and forms of *L. fagraeoidea*. Rock describes it as attaining tree-like stature, often as much as 35 to 40' (11 to 12.6m) high, found only in the wet rain forest of Oahu.

Leaves subsessile, thick and leathery, oblong or lanceolate-oblong, acute at apex, cunate at base, 3 to 6" (7.5 to 15cm) long and 2" (5cm) wide, pale underneath, veins transparent and pinnate, stipules united and long, tubular. Flowers 3-parted, borne sessile in axils of the leaves in small clusters of two to five, corolla fleshy, deep yellow. Fruit a 3-valved capsule, glabrous, up to 1" (2.5cm) long. Twigs smooth except for leaf scars. Wood not seen.

For many varieties the only known specimen may have been the plant from which the original description was made. This may account for so many taxa being listed as threatened, endangered or extinct.[1]

HVNP Kilauea Iki determined by St. John to species
HNP var. *centralis*

KAMAKAHALA   **Labordia hedyosmifolia** Baill

Variety *centralis* is listed as endemic to Maui and var. *grayana* and its form *angustisepala* are endemic to Hawaii. Thus likely the HVNP plant is the latter variety. The specimen was listed as a shrub 10' (3.1m) tall with small, opposite, short petioled leaves, .75 by 2" (2 by 5cm), midrib and veins prominent. Small yellow flowers in terminal clusters. Twigs slender. No wood seen.

KAMAKAHALA   **Labordia tinifolia** Gray

Plants identified as *L. tinifolia* were seen by the writer in Honaunau Forest Reserve and south of Manuka State Park, South Kona, Hawaii. The one in Honaunau Forest Reserve was about 15' (4.7m) tall, growing on the side of an OHIA tree in quite wet forest. Rock states the trees may be 15 to 20' (4.7 to 6.3m) tall but he did not find the species on Hawaii. Col. Bryan found a grove of 20 trees at Manuka, South Kona in 1933. They were up to 50' (15m) tall.

Leaves 1.5 by 3" (3.7 by 7.5cm), blunt apex, elongated to a point at the base, attached to a short green petiole. Leaves opposite, pinnate veins prominent. Buds in terminal clusters. Twigs slender, brown and somewhat twining. Bark smooth on 2" (5cm) trunk.[2]

KAMAKAHALA   **Labordia molokaiana** var. **bryanii** Sherff

L.W. Bryan gathered wood that he labeled *L. bryanii*. From St. John's list it appears the species has been reduced to a variety. I did not see the plant.

Wood is light tan, texture fine, grain straight and close, figure plain, density medium, wood soft. Vessels few, medium large, scattered and open, rays very light and thin.[3]

An interesting note: *L. bailloni*, endemic to Hawaii, is listed as extinct yet Carlquist includes a picture of it on page 318 of his recently published book.

PERIWINKLE FAMILY   Apocynaceae

The Periwinkle family is represented in Hawaiian Islands by three genera of native trees, *Ochrosia* Juss, *Pteralyxia* K. Schum, and *Rauvolfia* (Plum) L. The generic name for *Ochrosia* changes back and forth between *Ochrosia* and *Bleekeria* but St. John has settled upon *Ochrosia*.

Key to the genera of *Apocynaceae* from Rock:

Discus wanting
    Endocarp winged, drupe always 1-celled,
        large, bright red . . . . **Pteralyxia** K. Schum
    Endocarp compressed, deeply furrowed underneath, drupe 2-celled,
        large, yellow . . . . **Ochrosia** Juss.
Discus present
    Leaves whorled, drupe smooth, small, black, obcordate . . . **Rauvolfia** (Plum) L.

HVNP Kipuka Puaulu

HOLEI   **Ochrosia compta** K. Schum.

Ochrosia is represented by only this one endemic species in the native flora. It is so scarce that it is listed as endangered. Efforts to increase its numbers are being made by HVNP and Pacific Tropical Botanical Garden, both of which are growing plants. It is a small tree 10 to 15' (3.1 to 4.7m) tall with long drooping branches. A vigorously growing specimen in Kipuka Puaulu is 2'8" (82cm) in circumference, 18' (5.5m) tall, with crown spread of 25' (7.7m).

Whorled leaves are elongate-oblong about 1.5 by 6" (3.7 by 15cm), 3-to-4-to many leaves per whorl near ends of branches, leathery, edges lightly rolled, lighter green underneath, midrib very prominent, pinnate veins closely spaced and almost perpendicular to the midrib, milky sap exudes from leaves when broken. Flowers are yellow, fragrant, double or single, in small terminal clusters, 5-parted. The petals are conspicuous for their spiraled arrangement

1.   2.

like the blades of a toy paper propeller, more tightly spiralled than those of *Plumeria* and other members of the family. Fruits thinly covered, hard, often twins, borne on the ends of stems up to 1' (31.5cm) long. Fruits are 1" (2.5cm) long, yellow or orange and beaked. Twigs long and slender, new growth dark brownish-green, aging to light brown and smooth except for leaf scars. Bark smooth, grey mottled.

Wood dark yellowish-brown, texture fine, figure strong flame, grain fine and close, density medium and wood hard. Vessels very fine, numerous, arranged strongly in annular bands, rays very fine and numerous, stability good and workability good. Hawaiians made a yellow dye for coloring TAPA from the bark and roots.

HOLEI is a tree of the dry to moderately wet forest and is on the verge of extinction unless current work to reestablish it is pushed vigorously.[1]

[1] See:
Hillebrand, p. 296.
Rock, p. 413.
Neal, p. 684.
St. John, p. 280.

3.

4.

1. Closeup of creamy white flower of Holei showing spiraled petals. HVNP.
2. Bark detail of Holei.
3. Leaves and fruits of Holei. Rock photo.
4. Leaf and flowering habit. Holei, *O. compta*, HVNP.

[2] See:
Rock, p. 407.
Carlquist, p. 294.
St. John, p. 281.

[3] See:
Hillebrand, p. 295.
Rock, p. 411.
Neal, p. 691.
Carlquist, p. 278.
St. John, p. 281.
Degener, FH, p. 305, with a key to the species.

1.

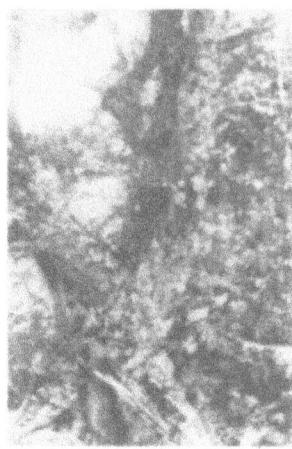

2.

3.

KAULA   **Pteralyxia** K. Schum.

Pteralyxia is represented by three species, all endemic; one, *P. caumiana* Deg., is listed as extinct, and another one, *P. Kauaiensis* Caum, listed as endangered. The more common one is *P. macrocarpa* (Hbd.) K. Schum., limited to Oahu. It is a tree 15 to 25' (4.7 to 7.8m) tall, found at one time in Nuuanu valley back of Honolulu and in Makaleha valley in the Waianae range.

Leaves long, edges rolled somewhat, prominent midrib with veins perpendicular to it. Small, yellowish flowers in small axillary clusters, with elongated corolla tube similar to *Rauvolfia*. Fruit large, bright red, about 1" (2.5cm) in diameter and 2.5" (6cm) long, with winged seed nearly as long as the pod, pointed at both ends. Wood not seen.[2]

HAO   **Rauvolfia** (Plum) L.

List of taxa of *Rauvolfia* from St. John:
Rauvolfia (Plum) L., 1753. (*Rauvolfia*)
  Degeneri Sherff, 1947. D:fam, 305, 12/1/49. Hao, Degener Rauvolfia,
    Devilpepper   end. Oahu
  Forbesii Sherff, 1947. D:fam. 305, 2/15/57   end. Oahu
  **Helleri Sherff, 1947. D:fam. 305, 2/15/57   end. Kauai
  heterophylla R.& S., 1819. Hao   cult. Mexico
  **mauiensis Sherff, 1947. D:fam. 305, 2/15/57   end. e. Maui
  molokaiensis Sherff, 1947, var. **molokaiensis** D:fam. 305, 2/15/57
                                          end. Molokai, Lanai, w. Maui
*** var. **parvifolia** Deg. & Sherff in Sherff, 1947. D:fam. 305, 2/15/57
                                          end. Molokai, e. Maui
  **remotiflora Deg.& Sherff in Sherff, 1947. Wahaula heiau, kalapana end. Hawaii
  *sandwicensis A.DC., 1844, var. **sandwicensis**. H:295, R:409; D:fam. 305,
    2/15/57. Hao, Hawaiian Rauvolfia, devilpepper end. Kauai, Oahu, w. Maui
  * var. **subacuminata** Sherff, 1947. D:fam. 305, 2/15/57   end. Kauai

HVNP Wahaulu

HAO   **Rauvolfia remotiflora** Deg.& Sherff

St. John specifically lists *R. remotiflora* as the HAO that is found at Wahaulu heiau in HVNP. It is sometimes listed as *R. sandwicensis* A.DC., but that species is confined to Kauai, Oahu and w. Maui. The writer saw possibly the same trees at Wahaulu, 25' (7.7m) tall, 3'5" (1m) in circumference with 23' (7m) crown spread.

Leaves in whorles of five, light green, slender, to 4" (10cm) long, very similar to *Ochrosia* leaves, with sharply right-angled veins, yellow midrib and short petiole. Flowers in small, terminal or axillary cymes or clusters, small, yellowish-green, with tube as long as or longer than the diameter of the flower. Fruits small, fleshy black, flattened at the ends instead of beaked as in *Ochrosia*, yellow when ripe and split open to release seed.

Wood, as described from a small dead limb, is dark yellowish streaked with brown, texture fine, figure streaked, grain straight and close, medium dense and medium hard. Vessels numerous, fine, scattered; rays numerous and fine. It was said to be very durable. No Hawaiian uses are recorded. Smoke from burning wood was thought to be poisonous. HAO is often found at HEIAUs and is thought by some to have had a religious significance.[3]

---

1. *Hao, R. remotiflora, leaves and flowering habit.*
2. *Bark detail, Hao, HVNP.*
3. *Mature Hao tree, R. remotiflora. One of two known trees, HVNP, Hawaii.*

HVNP General

MAILE **Alyxia olivaeformis** Gaud

MAILE is another member of the *Apocanaceae* family. It is a vine of the forest; leaves and bark aromatic. The vine is prized still today by Hawaiians for use in making a type of LEI that conveys a feeling of respect by the maker for the recipient. It is never a tree.[4]

[4] See:
Degener, PH NP p. 249.
Neal, p. 690.
Both Degener & Neal are good accounts.

BORAGE FAMILY **Boraginaceae**

The Borage family is represented by only one tree species indigenous to the islands, *Cordia subcordata* Lam. The family is well represented in Mexico and tropical countries. It is supposed to have been an early Hawaiian introduction and was planted near dwellings. It is now quite scarce. HVNP is helping to prevent its extinction with plantings at Kamoamoa on the Puna coast. It is said to have become a tree 30 to 50' (9.5 to 15.75m) tall and 3' (92cm) in diameter, with dense, wide spreading crown. William Ellis mentions it frequently as a village shade tree.

[1] See:
Hillebrand, p. 321.
Rock, p. 415.
Neal, p. 714; a good account with a legend.
St. John, p. 288.

2. Fruits of Kou, HVNP, Hawaii.

1. Kou tree in house yard, Lahina, Maui.

KOU **Cordia subcordata** Lam.

Large, alternate, ovate leaves up to 4" by 8" (10 by 20cm) or smaller on mature trees, on 3 to 4" (7.5 to 10cm) long petioles, wavy edged with very prominent midrib and heavy pinnate veins, bright green and shiny above, lighter beneath, long pointed apex. Flowers in terminal and lateral clusters, short stalked, orange, scentless, 1.5 to 2" (1.7 to 5cm) in diameter. Petals united and attached to .75" (1.8cm) long tube. Fruit a beaked drupe, ovate to nearly globose, 1" (2.5cm) long, growing in small clusters, dry, hard, and green to yellow, containing four seeds. Twigs bright green and smooth, aging to light brown and slightly roughened. Bark pale grey, grooved and flaky.

3. Closeup of flowers and leaves of Kou, HVNP, Hawaii.

Heart wood quite beautiful, reddish-brown with some purplish tint or even dark brown. Sapwood pinkish straw color. Texture medium fine, figure flame, grain straight or wavy in some pieces, medium density and medium soft. Vessels few and large, rays large and medium number. Good stability with low shrinkage, excellent workability made it good for Hawaiian uses, such as for POI bowls, calabashes, dishes and platters and for back scratchers.

KOU was a favorite shade tree in old Hawaii but never became a forest tree. It was attached by a moth and nearly exterminated. The flowers remind one of the garden four-o-clock.[1]

4. Kou, C. subcordata, bark detail.

[1] See:
Hillebrand, p. 308.
Rock, p. 419.
St. John, p. 300.

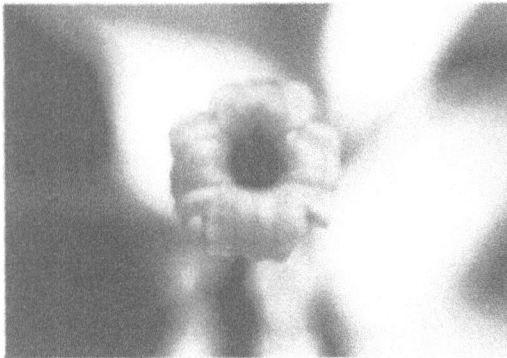

1. Very closeup of flower of Aiea, N. longifolium.

2. Leaf and flowering habit detail, Aiea.

3. Decadent Aiea tree, N. longifolium, under Ohia forest canopy, HVNP, Hawaii.

NIGHTSHADE FAMILY Solanaceae

Hawaii has only one native tree genus in the Nightshade family, *Nothocestrum* Gray with five species and three varities, all endemic to the islands. Of these, four taxa are endangered.

List of taxa of *Nothocestrum*:

Nothocestrum Gay, 1862. 'Aiea
****breviflorum** Gray, 1862, var. **breviflorum**. H:308. 'Aiea   end. Hawaii
***   var. **longipes** Hbd., 1888. H:308   end. H.I. locality?
****latifolium** Gray, 1862. H:308, R:421   end. H.I.
  longifolium Gray, 1862, var. **longifolium**. H:308, R:419
                                                                  end. Oahu, Molokai, Lanai, Maui

Platydesma Fauriei Lévl., 1911
   var. **brevifloium** Hbd., 1888. H:308   end. Kauai
** var. **rufipilosum** B.C. Stone, 1967   end. Hawaii
****peltatum** Skottsb., 1944   end. Kauai
*****subcordatum** Mann, 1867. N:309, R:423   end. Oahu

Key to the species of *Nothocestrum* from Rock:

Flowers single, rarely 2 or 3; berry longate . . . . **N. longifolium** Gray
Flowers several on short axillary spurs; berry globose
   Tube of corolla enclosed in the calyx
      Leaves elliptical-oblong; fruit enclosed in the calyx . . . . **N. breviflorum** Gray
   Tube of corolla longer than the calyx
      Leaves ovate or ovate-oblong, often sinuate;
         calyx remains with fruit . . . . **N. latifolium** Gray
      Leaves ovate-cordate;
         fruit not closed over by calyx . . . . **N. subcordatum** Mann
      Leaves peltate . . . . **N. peltatum** Skottsb
      (Flower characteristics not seen)

HVNP Manua Loa Strip
HNP species unspecified

AIEA **Nothocestrum longifolium** Gray

Since variety *rufipilosum* is the only one endemic to the island of Hawaii this must be the one seen near the Mauna Loa Strip road in HVNP. It was an old, decadent tree 30' (9m) tall, 2'2" (66cm) in circumference and with a 27'6" (8.5m) crown spread, in a badly suppressed condition under a canopy of MANELE trees.

Leaves elliptical-oblong, 2 by 4.5" (5 by 11.5cm), in whorls near ends of branches. Light green, pointed at each end, growing on a short petiole, midrib very prominent, few pinnate veins not distinct. Flowers borne usually singly or in small axillary clusters. Peduncle about 1" (2.5cm) long, petals four, united, attached to a tube about .5" (1.2cm) long. Petals light yellow with two parallel greenish lines, pistil not protruding beyond petals, calyx persistant. Fruit small, elongated, yellow berry that grows close to stem. Twigs smooth, tan to light brown, often very long and slender, bark smooth, dark grey on 8" (20cm) trunk. Wood not available for study.

Hawaiians used some part of the plant medicinally. Wood was used for WAI, a stick to brace canoe sides. This tree is also said to be found in one area of the Hamakua District of Hawaii. HVNP has plans to propagate this tree, along with others to save it from extinction.[1]

AIEA **Nothocestrum breviflorum** Gray

Since the variety *longipes* is listed as extinct it is presumed that the trees seen in the Puuwaawaa area of Hawaii were variety *breviflorum*. Several trees were seen in the Kaupulehu Reserve of the Pacific Tropical Botanical Garden. These were small trees but L.W. Bryan's big tree in the same general area measures 8'4" (2.5m) in circumference, 31' (10m) tall, with crown spread of 21' (6.6m). This would appear to be about the same size tree that Rock shows on page 419, Plate 171.

Leaves usually clustered near ends of branches, 1.25 to 2" (3 to 4cm) wide, 3 to 5" (7.7 to 12.5cm) long, dark green upper surface, light green under, petiole .75 to 2" (1.8 to 5cm) long, midrib pale green but very prominent on underside as are the few pinnate veins. Flowers with greenish-calyx, creamy white corolla, in small axillary clusters, 4-parted. Fruit globose or oblong, orange-red, about .5" (1.2cm) long, partly enclosed in bract. Twigs quite long, stout, rough and light brown, bark smooth, brown to greyish.

Wood reddish-brown to light tan, texture medium, figure streaked, grain not straight, density low and wood soft. Vessels and rays not visible at 10x. Stability good and workability good. Rock states that the trees are so full of sap that cattle chew off the bark to get moisture.

[2] See:
Hillebrand, p. 308.
Rock, p. 419.
St. John, p. 312.

[3] See:
Rock, p. 421.
St. John, p. 312.

1. Leaves of Aiea.

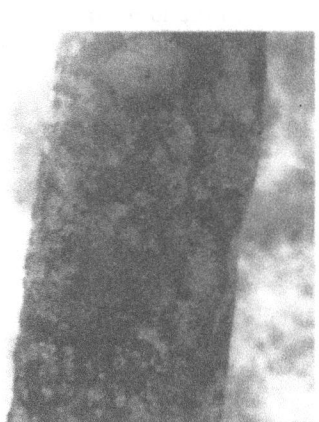

2. Bark detail, Aiea tree.

5. Flowering habit, Aiea, N. breviflorum.

No Hawaiian uses are recorded for the tree.

These are trees of the dry forest where they are a minor component of this surprisingly complex plant community. L.W. Bryan has listed 20 species of trees found on the one small area known as the Kaupulehu Reserve.[2]

AIEA   Nothocestrum latifolium Gray

Rock found this species to be common on the driest parts of Lanai and Molokai and also in the very dry area of Auahi beyond Ulupalakua, Maui where I saw one specimen. Leaves are lightly notched or serrate, flowers are tubular, yellow and fragrant. Trees are small, gnarled, with stiff branches. The dry, rough, rocky habitat is very severe. Trees are few and far between.[3]

6. Decadent Aiea tree, Kapulehu, Hawaii.

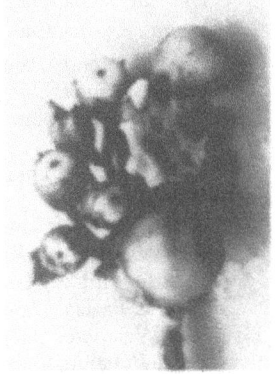

3. Aiea flower and fruit very closeup. Auahi, Maui.

4. Aiea leaves.

7. Aiea tree, N. latifolium, in very dry site, Auahi, Maui.

GESNERIA FAMILY   **Gesneriaceae**

There is only one native genus of the Gesneria family in Hawaii, *Cyrtandra* J.R. and G. Forst, but it is so variable that botanists have named 167 species plus 45 varieties and forms of this one genus, all endemic to one or many of the Hawaiian Islands. Many of them are now considered threatened, endangered or extinct. One of these can become a tree, *C. gayana*, endemic to Kauai. It is a woody shrub or tree as is *C. lysiosepala* (Gray) C.B. Clark, endemic to Maui and Hawaii.

List of taxa of *Cyrtandra* from St. John:

Cyrtandra J.R.& G.Forst., 1775
   adpressipilosa St. John, 1966   end. s. half of Koolau Range, Oahu
   adpressipilosa x **stupantha**. Natural hybrid.   end. Kahana, Oahu
 **alata St. John & Storey, 1950   end. Punaluu, Oahu
 **alnea St. John, 1966   end. Mt. Kaala, Oahu
      paludosa Gaud., var. *alnifolia* Hbd., 1888. H:336, non *alnifolia* Kraenzlin, 1913
 **ambigua (Hbd.) St. John & Storey, 1950   end. Niu, Oahu
      polyantha C.B. Clarke, var. *ambigua* (Hbd.) Rock, 1919
      triflora Gaud., var. *ambigua* Hbd. 1888. H:332
   arcuata St. John, 1966   end. Kahana, Oahu
   arguta (Gray) C.B. Clarke, 1883   end. Hawaii
      triflora Gaud, var. *arguta* Gray, 1862
   atomigyna St. John & Storey, 1950   end. Kipapa and Kahana, Oahu
 **axilliflora St. John & Storey, 1950   end. Punaluu to Kahana, Oahu
   baccifera C.B. Clarke, 1883   end. Hawaii
 **basipartita St. John, 1966   end. n. Koolau Range, Oahu
***begoniaefolia Hbd., 1888. H:328. 'Ilihia   end. e. Maui
  *biserrata Hbd., 1888. H:329   end. Molokai
   brevicalyx (Hbd.) St. John, 1966   end. n. half of Koolau Range, Oahu
      paludosa Gaud, var. *brevicalyx* Hbd., 1888. H:336
      paludosa Gaud, var. *brevicalyx* Hbd., f. *filipes* Hbd., ex Rock, 1919, and
         f. *linearis* Rock, 1919
 **brevicornuta St. John, 1966   end. Kailua, Oahu
 **Bryanii St. John & Storey, 1950   end. Kawailoa, Oahu
   calpidicarpa (Rock) St. John & Storey, 1950   end. Laie to Kipapa, Oahu
      longifolia (Wawra) Hbd. in C.B. Clarke, var. *calpidicarpa* Rock, 1917
   calycoschiza (St. John & Storey) St. John, 1966
                               end. Hauulu, and Wahiawa to Waimano, Oahu
      degenerans (Wawra) Heller, var. *calycoschiza* St. John & Storey, 1950
 **campaniformis St. John, 1966   end. Kawainui, Oahu
***carinata St. John & Storey, 1950   end. Niu, Oahu
 **caudatisepala St. John, 1966   end. Laie, Oahu
   caulescens Rock, 1918   end. e. Maui
   charadraia St. John, 1966   end. Mt. Kaala, Oahu
 **chartacea St. John & Storey, 1950   end. Kipapa, Oahu
  *Christopherseni St. John & Storey, 1950   end. Oahu
***collarifera St. John & Storey, 1950   end. Palolo, Manoa, Oahu
   confertiflora (Wawra) C.B. Clarke, 1883   end. Kauai
      paludosa Gaud., var. *confertiflora* Wawra, 1872
 **Conradtii Rock, 1919   end. Molokia
   cordifolia Gaud., 1829, var. **cordifolia**. H:327 (Fafara) = Hahala
                                                   end. Koolau Range, Oahu
***   var. **brevipilita** St. John, 1966   end. Waimano, Oahu
***   var. **gynoglabra** Rock, 1918   end. e. Maui
   cordifolia x **propinqua** Natural hybrid   end. Paalaa, Oahu
   cornuta St. John, 1966   end. Hauula to Waiahole, Oahu
 **crassior St. John & Storey, 1950   end. Punaluu, Oahu
 **crenata St. John & Storey, 1966   end. Waikane, and Kahana, Oahu
 **cupuliformis St. John & Storey, 1950   end. Mr. Kaala, Oahu
   cyaneoides Rock, 1913. Mapele   end. Kauai

  degenerans (Wawra) Heller, 1897   end. Kaluanui to Halawa, Oahu
   paludosa Gaud., var. *degenerans* Wawra, 1872.
   longifolia (Wawra) Hbd., in C.B. Clarke, var. *degenerans* (Wawra) C.B.
    Clarke, 1883
   punaluuensis St. John & Storey, 1950
   degenerans, forma *auriculaefolia* Rock, 1917
****dentata** St. John & Storey, 1950   end. Kawailoa, Oahu
****ellipticifolia** St. John, 1966   end. Pupukea, Oahu
****elliptisepala** St. John, 1966   end. Hauula, Oahu
  Elstonii Hochr., 1934   end. Kauai
****ferricolorata** St. John, 1966 (as *ferrocolorata*)   end. Kaluanui, Oahu
*****ferruginosa** St. John & Storey, 1950   end. Tantalus, Oahu
 ***filipes** Hbd., 1888. H:336   end. w. Maui
****Forbesii** St. John & Storey, 1950   end. Punaluu, Oahu
****Fosbergii** St. John & Storey, 1950   end. Kahana, Oahu
****Frederickii** St. John & Storey, 1950   end. Mokuleia, Makaha, Oahu
****fusiformis** St. John & Storey, 1950   end. Puu Kalena, Oahu
*****Garberi** St. John, 1966   end. Manoa, Oahu
  Garnotiana Gaud., 1829 (Fafara) = Hahala. H:332   end. Oahu
   var. *fulva* C.B. Clarke, 1883
  Gayana Heller, 1897, var. **Gayana**. Ha'i wale   end. Kauai
   var. *paludosa* Gaud. var. *Gayana* (Heller) Rock, 1917
   Cyrtandropsis kaululuensis Hochr., 1934
   var. **macrocarpa** Skottsb., 1944   end. Kauai
    Lectotype, Selling 2,869 (Bishop Mus.)
 ***Georgiana** Forbes, 1920   end. Lanai
 ***Giffardii** Rock, 1919   end. Hawaii
****glauca** Drake, 1892   end. Kauai
*****gracilis** Hbd., in C.B. Clarke, 1883. H:333   end. Palolo, Oahu
  grandiflora Gaud., 1829, forma **grandiflora**. H:35
            end. s. half of Koolau Range, Oahu
   forma **verticillata** St. John, 1966   end. Kipapa, Oahu
  Grayana Hbd., 1888, var. **Grayana**. H:330   end. Maui, Molokai
   kamoloensis Lévl., 1911
 * var. **lanaiensis** Rock, 1919   end. Lanai
   var. **latifolia** Hbd., 1888, f. **latifolia**   end. Molokai, Maui
    forma **grandis** Rock, 1919   end. Lanai
   var. **linearifolia** Rock, 1919   end. w. Maui
   var. **nervosa** Rock, 1919   end. w. Maui
*****grossecrenata** St. John & Storey, 1950   end. Oahu?
 ***halawensis** Rock, 1919   end. Molokai
  Hashimotoi Rock, 1919   end. e. Maui
****hawaiensis** C.B. Clarke, 1883   end. Hawaii
  hii Forbes, 1920   end. Kauai
****hirsutula** St. John & Storey, 1950   end. Mt. Kaala, Oahu
*****honolulensis** Wawra, 1872   end. Honolulu, and Niu, Oahu
   Pickeringii Gray, var. *honoluensis* (Wawra) Rock, 1918
   Pickeringii Gray, var. *crassifolia* Hbd., 1888. H:327
   crassifolia (Hbd.) Rock, 1918, as to basinym
 ***Hosakae** St. John & Storey, 1950   end. Kipapa, Oahu
  hyperdasa St. John, 1966   end. Kahana, and Kipapa, Oahu
****infrapallida** St. John, 1966   end. Kailua, Oahu
  infundibuliformis St. John, 1966   end. Waiahole, Oahu
****intonsa** St. John & Storey, 1950   end. Kipapa, and Kahana, Oahu
****intrapilosa** St. John, 1960   end. Pupukea, Oahu
   Lessoniana Gaud., var. *borealis* St. John & Storey, 1950
 ***intravillosa** St. John & Storey, 1950   end. Kipapa, Oahu
****kaalae** St. John & Storey, 1950   end. Mt. Kaala, Oahu
****kahanaensis** St. John & Storey, 1950   end. Kahana, Oahu
****kahukuensis** St. John & Storey, 1950   end. Pupukea, Oahu
  kailuaensis St., John 1966   end. Kailua, Oahu
  kalichii Wawra, 1872   end. Koolau Range, Oahu
   (as *kalihii*. H:334)
****kaluanuiensis** St. John, 1966   end. Kaluanui, Oahu
****kaneoheensis** St. John, 1966   end. Kaneohe, Oahu
*****kauaiensis** Wawra, 1872. H:332. Ulunahele   end. Kauai
 ***kaulantha** St. John & Storey, 1950   end. Waikane, Oahu
  kealiae Wawra, 1872. H:326   end. Kauai

	kipahuluensis St. John, 1971	end. e. Maui
	kipapaensis St. John & Storey, 1950	end. Kipapa and Palolo, Oahu
	Knudsenii Rock, 1918	end. Kauai
	kohalae Rock, 1919	end. Hawaii
**	**koolauensis** St. John & Storey, 1950	end. Laie, Oahu
**	**laevis** St. John, 1966	end. Moanalua, Oahu
	latebrosa Hbd., 1888, var. **latebrosa**. H:337	end. Koolau Range, Oahu
	var. **subglabra** Hbd., 1888, H:338	end. Molokai, Maui, Hawaii
	longifolia Hbd., var. *degenerans* C.B. Clarke, f. *subglabra* (Hbd.) Rock, 1917	
***	**laxiflora** Mann, 1867. N:333	end. Waialua Mts., Oahu
	Lessoniana Gaud. 1829, var. **Lessoniana**.H:331	end. Kipapa to Niu, Oahu
***	var. **angustifolia** Hbd., 1888. H:331	end. Wailupe, Oahu
**	var. **intrapubens** St. John, 1966	end. Puu Kanchoa, Oahu
	var. **koolauloaensis** St. John, 1966	end. n. half of Koolau Range, Oahu
	leucocalyx St. John, 1966	end. n. third of Koolau Range, Oahu
*	**limosiflora** Rock, 1919	end. Molokai
***	**linearis** St. John, 1966	end. Nuuanu, Oahu
**	**longicalyx** St. John, 1966	end. Kailua, Oahu
**	**longifolia** (Wawra) Hbd., in C.B. Clarke, 1883, var. **longifolia**	end. Kauai
	paludosa Gaud., var. *longifolia* Wawra, 1872	
	var. **arborescens** (Wawra) C.B. Clarke, 1883	end. Kauai
	paludosa Gaud., var. *arborescens* Wawra, 1872	
	var. **degenerans** (Wawra) C.B. Clarke, f. **auriculaefolia** Rock, 1917	end. Maui
	forma **cymosa** Rock, 1917	end. Molokai, Maui, Hawaii
	forma **oppositifolia** Rock, 1917	end. w. Maui
**	var. **parallela** C.B. Clarke, 1883	end. H.I.
	A dubious variety, without precise locality	
	var. **wahiawae** Rock, 1919	end. Wahiawa, Kauai
**	**longiloba** St. John, 1966	end. Mr. Kaala, Oahu
*	**Lydgatei** Hbd., 1888. H:335	end. Molokai, Maui
**	**lysiosepala** (Gray) C.B. Clarke, 1883, var. ***lysiosepala**	end. Maui, Hawaii
	triflora Gaud, var. *lysiosepala* Gray, 1862	
	var. **Fauriei** (Lévl.) Rock, 1919	end. Molokai
	Fauriei Lévl., 1911	
*	var. **Grayi** (C.B. Clarke) Rock, 1919	end. w. Maui
	Grayi C.B. Clarke, 1883	
*	var. **haleakalensis** Rock, 1919	end. e. Maui
	var. **hawaiiensis** Skottsb., 1936	end. Hawaii
	var. **latifolia** Rock, 1919	end. Molokai, Maui
	var. **pilosa** Hbd., 1888. H:330	end. Maui, Hawaii
	Macraei Gray, 1862. H:333	end. Koolau Range, Oahu
	var. *parvula* Rock, 1919	
**	**macrantha** C.B. Clarke, 1883	end. H.I.
	macrocalyx Hbd., 1888. H:329	end. Molokai
*	**malacophylla** C.B. Clarke, 1883, var. **malacophylla**	end. Kauai or w. Maui
	partifolia Hbd., 1888	
	var. **erosa** Rock, 1918	end. w. Maui
***	**Mannii** St. John & Storey, 1950	end. Waianaeuka, Oahu
	mauiensis Rock, 1918, var. **mauiensis**	end. e. Maui
	var. **truncata** Rock, 1918	end. e. Maui
**	**megastigmata** St. John, 1966	end. Halawa, Oahu
**	**Menziesii** H.& A., 1832, Haiwale	end. Hawaii
	Brighami C.B. Clarke, 1883	
	montis-loa Rock, 1919	end. Hawaii
*	**Munroi** Forbes, 1920	end. Lanai
***	**niuensis** St. John, 1966	end. Kalihi to Niu, Oahu
***	**nubincolens** St. John, 1966	end. Puu Konahuanui, Oahu
	nutans St. John, 1955. D:fam. 325. 3/15/59. Nodding cyrtandra	end. w. Maui
	oahuensis Lévl., 1911	end. Punaluu; Kiapapau, Oahu
	oblanceolata St. John & Storey, 1950	end. Waiahole and Kipapa, Oahu
**	**oenobarba** Mann, 1867, var. **oenobarba**. H:338	end. Kauai
*	var. **herbacea** (Wawra) Heller, 1897	end. Kauai
	paludosa Gaud, var. *herbacea* Wawra, 1872	
*	var. **petiolaris** Wawra, 1872. H:338	end. Kauai
	var. *obovata* Wawra, 1872 and of Hbd., 1888. H:338	
	var. *rotundifolia* Wawra, 1872	
**	**olivacea** St. John, 1966	end. Poamoho, Oahu
	Olona Forbes, 1920	end. Kauai

    opaeulae St. John & Storey, 1950   end. Paalaa, Oahu
    oulophylla St. John & Storey, 1950   end. Niu, Oahu
      Lessoniana Gaud. var. *pachyphylla* Hbd., 1888. H:331, in part
****paloloensis** St. John & Storey, 1950   end. Palolo, Kalihi, Oahu
    paludosa Gaud., 1829, var. **paludosa**. Kanawao-ke'oke'o, pi'ohi'a, moa
           end. s. half of Koolau Range, Oahu
*   var. **haupuensis** Rock, 1917   end. Kauai
      var. **integrifolia** Hbd., 1888. H:337   end. Hawaii
      var. **irrostrata** St. John, 1971   end. Maui, Hawaii
      var. **microcarpa** Wawra, 1872. H:336   end. Kauai
      var. **subherbacea** Wawra, 1872. H:337   end. Kauai
*****partita** St. John, 1966   end. Punaluu, Oahu
****Pearsallii** St. John, 1966   end. Kailua, Oahu
****perstaminodica** St. Joh, 1966   end. Kipapa, and Waikane, Oahu
*****Pickeringii** Gray, 1862, var. **Pickeringii**. H:327   end. Honolulu, Oahu
**   var. **waiheae** Rock, 1918   end. w. Maui
*****piligyna** St. John & Storey, 1950   end. Tantalus, Oahu
    platyphylla Gray, 1862, var. **platyphylla**. H:328   end. Hawaii
      var. **brevipes** Skottsb., 1942   end. Hawaii
*   var. **hiloensis** Rock, 1918   end. Hawaii
      var. **parviflora** Rock, 1918   end. Hawaii
      var. **robusta** Rock, 1918   end. Hawaii
        Clarkei Vatke ex Skottsb., 1936, non Stapf, 1894
        Hillebrandi C.B. Clarke, 1882, non Vatke, 1876. H:331
      var. **stylopubens** Rock, 1918, f. **stylopubens**   end. Hawaii
         forma**ovata** Rock, 1918   end. Hawaii
****plurifolia** St. John & Storey, 1950   end. Kahuku, Oahu
    poamohoensis St. John & Storey, 1950   end. Poamoho, Oahu
****polyantha** C.B. Clarke, 1883   end. Niu and Maunalua, Oahu
    procera Hbd., 1888. H:329   end. Molokai
    propinqua Forbes, 1920   end. n. half of Koolau Range, Oahu
****pruinosa** St. John & Storey, 1950   end. Kalauao, Oahu
****pubens** St. John, 1966   end. Kahana, and Kipapa, Oahu
    pupukeaensis St. John & Storey, 1950   end. Pupukea, and Malaekahana, Oahu
***ramosissima** Rock, 1919   end. Hawaii
    reflexa St. John & Storey, 1950   end. Kawailoa, and Paalaa, Oahu
    rivularis St. John & Storey, 1950   end. Kaluanui, Oahu
****Rockii** St. John & Storey, 1950   end. Hauula, Oahu
    rotata St. John, 1971   end. e. Maui
****sandwicensis** (Lévl.) St. John & Storey, 1950   end. Nuuanu to Palolo, Oahu
       Garnotiana Gaud., forma *uniflora* Skottsb., 1936
       Viola sandwicensis Lévl., 1917
*****scabrella** C.B. Clarke, 1883   end. Nuuanu, Oahu
       Oliveri Rock, 1919
       Hillebrandi Oliver in Hbd., 1888, non Vatke, 1876
    sessilis St. John & Storey, 1950   end. Kahana, Oahu
*****Skottsbergii** St. John & Storey, 1950   end. Kalihi, Oahu
       Pickeringii Gray, var. *latifolia* Skottsb., 1936
    spathulata St. John, 1971   end. e. Maui
    stupantha St. John & Storey, 1950   end. n. half of Koolau Range, Oahu
       triflora Gaud., var. *grandifolia* Hbd., 1888. H:332
       laxiflora Mann, var. *grandifolia* (Hbd.) Rock, 1919
       laxiflora Mann, var. *rhizantha* Rock, 1919
****subcordata** St. John, 1966   end. Moanalua, Oahu
*****subintegra** St. John, 1966   end. Tantalus, Oahu
****subrecta** St. John, 1966   end. Kipapa, Oahu
    subumbellata (Hbd.) St. John & Storey, 1950, var. **subumbellata**
           end. Kaluanui to Waiahole, Oahu
       gracilia Hbd., var. *subumbellata* Hbd., 1888. H:334
**   var. **intonsa** St. John, 1966   end. Kahana, Oahu
****ternata** St. John, 1966   end. Wahiawa, Oahu
    tintinnabula Rock, 1918   end. Hawaii
****triflora** Gaud., 1829, f. **triflora** Hahala   end. Honolulu, Oahu
      var. *Gaudichaudi* Gray, 1862
        forma **robusta** Wawra, 1872   end. Maui
    tristis Hbd., in C.B. Clarke, 1882   end. Kipapa to Wailupe, Oahu
       kalichii Wawra, var. *tristis* (Hbd.) Rock, 1919
****turbiniformis** St. John & Storey   end. Heeia, Oahu

[1] See:
St. John, p. 312.

umbracculiflora Rock, 1919	end. Kauai
Vanioti Lévl., 1911	end. Mt. Kaala, Oahu
villicalyx St. John & Storey, 1950, var. **villicalyx**	end. Waikane and Kahana, Oahu
var. **pubentigyna** St. John & Storey, 1950	end. Waikane and Kahana, Oahu
villosa St. John & Storey, 1950	end. Waikane, Oahu
villosiflora St. John, 1966	end. Moanalua, Oahu
viridiflora St. John & Storey, 1950	end. Punaluu to Lanihuili, Oahu
crassifolia (Hbd.) Rock, as to Punaluu specimen	
Pickeringee Gray, var. *crassifolia* Hbd., 1888. H:327	
waianaeensis St. John & Storey, 1950	end. Waianae Mts., Oahu
waianuensis Rock, 1917	end. Waianu, Oahu
wainihaensis Lévl, 1911	end. Kauai?
waiolani Wawra, 1872, var. **waiolani**. H:334	end. Halawa to Kalihi, Oahu
Hillebrandii Vatke, 1876	
var. **capitata** Hbd., 1888. H:334	end. Nuuanu, Oahu
waiomaoensis St. John, 1966	end. Palolo, Oahu
Wawrai C.B. Clarke, 1883. H:328	end. Kauai
peltata Wawra, 1872, non Jack, 1825	
Wilderi St. John & Storey, 1950	end. Mt. Kaala to Puu Kalena, Oahu

1. Haiwale, C. gayana, leaf detail and fruit, Kokee, Kauai.

HAIWALE or MAPELE — **Cyrtandra gayana** Heller

This species is described because it represents a type of *Cyrtandra* that is a woody shrub with long slender leaves in contrast to the broadly ovate to nearly round leaved, soft stemmed types so plentiful in the rain forest. The shrub may be as much as 10' (3.1m) tall or more in good environment such as Kokee, Kauai where the writer saw it.

Long slender opposite leaves acute at base but less acute at apex, 1 to 1.5" (2.5 to 3.7cm) wide by 3 to 4" (7.5 to 10cm) long, midrib and pinnate veins very deeply impressed on upper surface, clustered near the ends of slender branches, dark green. Flowers white, tubular, borne in the leaf axils, singly. Buds .75 (1.8cm) long and greenish-white. Fruit an egg-shaped white berry .5" (1.2cm) long. Twigs smooth between prominent leaf scars which are about .75" (1.8cm) apart, bark smooth, light grey on small trunks but grooved vertically.

Light brown sapwood, darker brown heartwood, soft pith. Texture fine, figure plain, grain close and straight, density low and wood soft. Vessels large and white against the darker background wood, arranged loosely in radial chains visible to the naked eye as are the few, large rays. Wood immediately turns deep brown in cross section when wetted. It warps badly, too small to be usable.[1]

NAIO FAMILY — **Myoporaceae**

The NAIO family has only one genus in Hawaii, *Myoporum* Soland ex Forst. It consists of one species, four varieties and one subspecies as follows:
Taxa of *Myophorum* from St. John:

M. sandwicense Gray, subsp **sandwicense**, var. **sandwicense**	end. Kauai, Niihau, Oahu, Molokai, Lanai, Maui
var. **degeneri** Webster	end. e. Maui
var. **fauriei** (Lévl.) Kraenzlin	end. Hawaii
var. **lanaiense** Webster	end. Lanai
var. **stellatum** Webster	end. Oahu
subsp.**st. johnii** Webster	end. Hawaii

None of the taxa are listed as threatened, endangered or extinct.

HVNP Kipuka Puaulu, Kilauea and Mauna Loa Strip

NAIO   **Myoporum sandwicense** Gray

[1] See:
Hillebrand, p. 339.
Rock, p. 427.
Neal, p. 791.
Degener, FH, p. 329.
Degener, PHNP, pp. 261-71.
St. John, p. 318.

Most references consider only the species without concern for the lesser taxa. Degener, *Flora Hawaiiensis*, gives a key and descriptions of these lesser taxa.

NAIO occurs as a shrub in some low lying parts of its range but is a large tree in best habitat. L.W. Bryan's big tree measures 17'2" (5.3m) in circumference, 70' (22m) tall with crown spread of 56' (17.5m) located at Keauhou, North Kona, Hawaii. NAIO is one of the most abundant of Hawaiian trees in certain localities. The large plateau in the center of the island of Hawaii is a fine example of mixed NAIO and MAMANE forest.

Leaves alternate, 2 to 6" (5 to 15cm) long, slender to broad, in variety *degeneri*, dark green, usually crowded towards the branch ends, often twisted. The resemblance to common peach tree leaves is strong. Midrib deeply impressed on upper surface, veins indistinct. Flower white or pink .5" (1.2cm) in diameter, 5 or 6-petaled, borne axillary, petals united so that when the flowers fall the petals form a ringlet. Fruits small, round, white, fleshy drupe, edible but with strong turpentine taste, large single seed thinly covered, crowned by the style. Twigs light brown, smooth; bark thick, dark grey, deeply and irregularly corrugated, nearly black. Older trunks often become badly distorted.

Wood golden yellowish-brown or greenish, texture fine, figure occasionally birdseye or curly, grain straight or curly, density medium and wood hard. Vessels few, fine and scattered, rays very fine. Wood durable, with low shrinkage, workability good. Wood has a waxy luster but its spicy-odored oil resembling sandalwood interferes with applied finishes. NAIO was sold as a substitute for sandalwood for a time. Logs were preferred for house construction and the long burning wood was used for torches for night fishing. Degener *PHNP* gives a long and interesting account of the Hawaiian uses.

NAIO is often only an occasional tree in the wet forest but forms almost pure stands in dryer areas, or stands of about half NAIO and half MAMANE in the driest habitat. It ranges all the way from sea level to 10,000 (3150m) on Mauna Kea giving it as wide a range as any plant in the islands.[1]

1. White flower and buds of Naio.

2. Naio trunk and leaves.

COFFEE FAMILY   **Rubiaceae**

The coffee family is well represented in Hawaii with seven genera of native plants that produce trees in addition to domestic coffee that is widely cultivated in Kona, Hawaii. Also there are two shrubby or creeping herbs, *Hedyotis* L. and *Nertera* Banks et Gaertn.

Key to the genera of *Rubiaceae* adapted from Rock:

Ovules many in each cell
    Ovary 2 – rarely 3-4 celled
        Fruit a bluish-black, indehiscent fleshy berry . . . . **Gouldia** Gray
    Ovary 1-celled
        Fruit larger globose or pyriform, succulent or dry,
            crowned with the calcine limb . . . . **Gardenia** Ellis
Ovules one in each cell
    Flowers hermaphrodite or polygamous
        Ovary 2 to 10 celled
            Flowers greenish, the corolla-lobes imbricate in bud . . . . **Bobea** Gaud
        Ovary 2-celled

3. Naio, *M. sandwicense*, tree, Central Hawaii.

[1] See:
Hillebrand, p. 173.
Rock, p. 439.
St. John, p. 319.

Flowers white, fragrant the corolla lobes valvate . . . . . **Canthium** Lam
Flowers white, small, rotate or larger, funnel shaped,
 drupe crowned by the long calcine limb, yellow . . . . . **Psychotria** L.
Ovary 4-celled
 Flowers in globose heads: drupes united into fleshy
  compound fruit . . . . **Morinda** (Vaill.) L.
Flowers dioecious, stigma bifid to the base, anthers 4 to 11
Coprosma Lam

HNP species ?

AHAKEA   Bobea Gaud.

There are five species and one added variety of *Bobea* In Hawaii.
List of taxa of *Bobea* from St. John:

Bobea elatior Gaud., var. **elatior**		end. Oahu, Molokai, Lanai, Maui
	var. **brevipes**	end. Oahu
hookeri Hbd.		end. Oahu, Moloaki
mannii Hbd.		end. Kauai
**	**sandwicensis** (Gray) Hbd.	end. Molokai, Lanai, Maui
**	**timonioides** (Hook. f.) Hbd.,	end. Hawaii

1. Ahakea, B. mannii, leaf detail, Kokee, Kauai.

AHAKEA or AHAKEA-LAU-NUI   **Bobea elatior** Gaud.
AHAKEA-LAU-LI'I   **B.e.** var. **brevipes** (Gaud.) Hbd.

AHAKEA-LAU-NUI means 'AHAKEA with big leaves.' A good specimen of the species can be seen in Manuka State Park, South Kona, Hawaii, where it has been planted. It is not endemic to this island. It is a tree about 30' (9.5m) tall and 1'6" (45cm) in diameter.

Opposite leaves pale green, veins reddish, long-tipped at apex, blunt at base. Midrib light green with several widely spaced lighter green pinnate veins. Flowers borne in cymes of three or more on short peduncles, white or greenish, .25" (.6cm) in diameter, 5-petaled, salver shaped, .5" (1.2cm) long corolla tube. Fruit a small, round, black berry .25" (.6cm) in diameter on short stalk, borne singly or in 2s or 3s. Twigs slender, light brown, smooth except for a few lenticles. Bark smooth on 6" (15cm) trunk, grey and patchy.

Wood yellow streaked with brown, texture medium, figure streaked, grain straight, density medium and hardness medium. Vessels numerous and scattered, rays very fine and fairly numerous. Stability good and workability good.

Hawaiians used the wood for the carved gunwales and end covers of canoes, for paddles and POI boards. [1]

AHAKEA   **Bobea manii** Hbd.

Hillebrand gives a very short description and Rock gives none of this species. One distinction between *B. elatior* and *B. mannii* is that the former has more or less upright peduncles while the latter has flowers on drooping peduncles. However, in the writer's specimens the leaves were very different. It is a small, upright tree about 30' (9.5m) tall growing in the wet forest of the Kokee area of Kauai.

Leaves are opposite, two or more pairs clustered near branch ends, light yellowish-green, with distinct red midrib and prominent veins pinnately arranged, hairy and rough on under side. Leaves much more rounded than those of *B. elatior*, nearly as broad as long, elliptic-oblong. Flowers borne in 3s on drooping peduncles, .25 to .5" (.6 to 1.2cm) long, calyx cylindrical, short, with truncate limb. Corolla two or three times as long, pubescent, as are calyx and peduncle. Fruit not seen. Twigs light brown, smooth and slender. Bark grey, rough, with small ridges formed on 3" (7.5cm) trunk.

2. Ahakea, B. elator, leaf and flower habit detail, Kokee, Kauai.

Wood yellowish or very light tan, texture medium fine, figure plain, grain straight and close, density low, wood soft. Vessels as wide as interray spaces, scattered, rays fine and very closely spaced. Wood warps and checks. Hawaiians used the wood the same as *B. elatior* and used the bark, mixed with other ingredients, as a cure for sores and as a tonic to purify the blood. The tree is not a conspicuous component of the mixed forest at Kokee.[2]

[2] See:
Hillebrand, p. 173.
St. John, p. 319.

[3] See:
Hillebrand, p. 174.
Rock, p. 445.
St. John, p. 319.

HVNP Naulu

AHAKEA   **Boboa timonioides** (Hook.f.) Hbd.

This AHAKEA has been found in HVNP in the Naulu forest. I was able to study a herbarium specimen and also saw trees growing in the forests of South Kona near Manuka State Park. The trees were 20' (6.3m) tall or more.

Opposite leaves .625 to .75" (1.4 to 2cm) wide by 2 to 2.25" (5 to 6cm) long or larger, sharp tipped apex, obtuse base, petiole, .5" (1.2cm) long, veins pinnate. Flowers very small, light green, borne in small clusters, axillary, near ends of branches. Fruit dark blue, size of small pea. Twigs slender, rough and dark grey, bark on 6" (15cm) trunk smooth.

3. Ahakea, B. timonioides, flower detail, white.

There are only a few of these trees known, in HVNP, in Hilo area and in Kau or South Kona. Stone listed this species at Kealakomo Pali.[3]

In addition Darrel Herbst is reported to have found *B. Hookeri* growing in Palikea Gulch, Waianae Mts., Oahu.

1. Alahee leaves and fruit.

2. Alahee bark detail.

4. Ahakea tree trunk, South Kona, Hawaii.

HVNP Wahaulu

ALAHE'E   **Canthium odoratum** Forst, f.) Seem
                    Syn. **Plectrona odorata** (Forst, f.) B&H ex Hbd.

There is only one species of ALAHE'E and it is indigenous to the Hawaiian Islands, Polynesia and Fiji. It is quite common on all the islands on the dry sides in the dry, mixed forest. It is plentiful in the forest back of Wahaulu Ranger Station, HVNP. It is generally a small tree to 20' (6.3m) tall and 1' (30.5cm) in diameter, but L.W. Bryan's big tree is 3'8" (1.1m) in circumference, 39' (12m) tall with 18' (5.6m) crown spread, located in the Puuwaawaa area of North Kona, Hawaii.

Very glossy leaves glistening in the sun make the shrub or small tree stand out among the LAMA, AKIA and guavas. Leaves opposite, duller green underneath, oblong, 2 by 3" (5 by 7.5cm), pointed both ends, very short petiole, prominent light green rib and veins. Flowers .25" (.6cm) across, fragrant, in clusters of 5 to 10, 5- or 6-parted, petals three times longer than broad, stamens as long as petals and stigma protruding beyond the petals.

5. Alahee, C. odoratum, small tree in Puna, Hawaii.

[4] See:
Hillebrand, p. 175.
Rock, p. 437.
Carlquist, p. 278.
St. John, p. 320.

Fruit, a small berry .33" (.8cm) in diameter, compressed, greenish-black and juicy, small circular indentation near apex. Fruit clustered along stem of new growth. New twig growth smooth and green, older growth light to dark grey. Bark light and dark grey, smooth on 6" (15cm) trunk.

Wood whitish with black streaks, texture fine, figure streaked, density high and wood very hard. Vessels extremely fine and scattered, rays very fine and very numerous. Wood durable and with good workability.

Used by Hawaiians for OO and other tools, also for adz blades to cut soft wood. Leaves furnished black dye. Trees are abundant in dry forest.[4]

PILO **Coprosma** J.R.& G. Forst.

Coprosma is represented by 18 species and nine varieties. They range from a prostrate form to shrubs and small trees.

List of species and varieties of *Coprosma* from St. John:

Coprosma J.R. & G. Forst., 1775. Pilo
  Baueri Endl., 1838. N:803. Angiangi   cult. New Zealand
  cymosa Hbd., 1888; H:186   end. Hawaii
  elliptica Oliver, 1935   end. Kauai
  ernodeoides Gray, 1858, var. **ernodeoides**. H:185, N:803. Kukae-nene
      leponene, 'ai-a-ka-nene, black-fruited coprosma   end. Hawaii
      var. **mauiensis** St. John, 1935   end. Maui
  Fauriei Lévl., 1911, var. **Fauriei**   end. Kauai
** var. **lanaiensis** Oliver, 1935   end. Lanai
      var. **oahuensis** Oliver, 1935   end. Oahu
  foliosa Gray, 1858. H:186   end. Oahu
  kauensis (Gray) Heller, 1897. R:463. Koi   end. Kauai
      pubens Gray, var. *kauensis* Gray, 1858
      stephanocarpa Hbd., var. *kauaiensis* (Gray) Hbd., 1888. H:187
  longifolia Gray, 1858, var. **longifolia**. H:188, R:465. Pilo   end. Oahu
      var. **oppositifolia** Fosb., 1943   end. Oahu
  Menziesii Gray, 1858. H:185. Kilo, kopa   end. Hawaii
  molokaiensis St. John, 1935   end. Molokai
  montana Hbd., 1888, var. **montana** H:185, R:459. Pilo   end. Maui, Hawaii
      var. **crassa** Oliver, 1935   end. Maui
** var. **orbicularis** Oliver, 1935   end. Hawaii
  ochracea Oliver, 1935, var. **ochracea**   end. Hawaii
** var. **kaalae** St. John, 1935   end. Oahu
      var. **Rockiana** Oliver, 1935. Pilo, Kopa   end. Molokai, Hawaii
  pubens Gray, 1858, var. **pubens**. H:188, R:463. Pilo   end. Maui, Hawaii
      Grayana Rock, 1913. R:461
** var. **sessiliflora** Oliver, 1935   end. Lanai
  rhynchocarpa Gray, 1860. H:187. Pilo   end. Hawaii
  robusta Raoul, 1844, Karamu   cult. New Zealand
****serrata** St. John, 1935   end. Hawaii
  Skottsbergiana Oliver, 1942   end. Molokai
  stephanocarpa Hbd., 1888. H:187. Pilo   end. Maui
      Vontemskyi Rock, 1913. R:461
      parvifolia Lévl., 1911
  ternata Oliver, 1935   end. Molokai
  waimeae Wawra, 1874. R:465. 'Olene   end. Kauai

Key to some species of *Coprosma* adapted from Rock and Hillebrand:
Prostrate shrub, leaves linear, 1-nerved, drupe black . . . . . . **C.ernodeoides** Gray
Upright shrubs or trees
  Leaves opposite
    Flowers sessile or on short axillary spurs . . . . **C.montana** Hbd.
      (Rock's two varieties of *C montana* have been raised to species
      C.ochraceae and *C.elliptica* and presumably fit in this section)
    Flowers raised on distinct peduncles
      Drupes beaked with long tubular limb of the calyx
        Flowers 3 to 5 or 6, subsessile at end of short peduncle,
          calyx limb long . . . . **C.rhynchocarpa** Gray

  Flowers single or in racemes, pedicellate, calyx limb
   shorter than above . . . . **C.stephanocarpa** Hbd.
                syn. **C.vontemski** Rock
 Drupes crowned by calcine teeth
  Flowers 2 on axillary peduncles of .5cm, drupes largest of
   all Hawaiian species . . . . **C.waimeae** Wawra
 Drupes shortly dentate, 3-sessile in head or single
  Leaves coriaceous, with nerves impressed above, obovate,
   drupes small, ovoid . . . . **C.menziesii** Gray
  Leaves thin, acute at both ends, drupes large, globose or
   obovoid . . . . **C.foliosa** Gray
 Drupes naked at apex
  Drupes ovoid or ellipsoidal . . . . **C.pubens** Gray
  Drupes globose, single in a cyme . . . . **C.cymosa** Hbd.
  Drupes small, obovate, very obtuse . . . . . . **C.kauaiensis** (Gray) Heller
Leaves ternate, 3 arising from one point
 Flowers many, crowded at the ends of very
  long peduncles . . . . **C.longifolia** Gray

[5] See:
Hillebrand, p. 185.
St. John, p. 320.
Degener, PHNP, p. 280.

1. Kukainene, C. erinoides, showing prostrate growth, HVNP.

HVNP Kilauea area
HNP var. *mauaiensis*

KUKAENENE, KUKAINENE
PUNENE or LEPONENE   **Coprosma ernodeiodes** Gray

 This *Coprosma* grows prostrate, sending its long branches out across the lava. It is conspicuous because of its large, round jet black fruits spaced all along the stem. By its creeping habit it invades new lava very quickly from the edge of the flow as can be seen at various places along the Chain of Craters Road, HVNP.

 The small, shiny dark green, linear nerved, leaves are crowded on short spur branches that stand out nearly at right angles from the main stem. Flowers solitary and sessile, hidden between the leaves, calyx tubular, 4-fid, .3cm long, the acute teeth shorter than the tube, corolla funnel shaped with lobes or teeth erect. Fruit a large, round or ovoid, jet black, fleshy drupe .5" (1.2cm) in diameter, crowned by short calcine teeth and containing two seeds.

 This is the only black fruited *Coprosma* in Hawaii. The fruits are said to be quickly and easily harvested by NENE, the Hawaiian goose that inhabits areas where the plants grow.[5]

[6] See:
Hillebrand, p. 135.
St. John, p. 320.

[7] See:
Hillebrand, p. 185.
Rock, p. 459.
St. John, p. 321.

1. Pilo, C. ochracea, leaves, HVNP.

2. Pilo leaf and stem, C. montana.

3. Pilo, C. ochracea, shrub, Hilo entrance, HVNP.

HVNP Chain of Craters

PILO   **Coprosma menziesii** Gray

    PILO and *Coprosma* both mean 'evil smelling', a characteristic of the leaves when crushed. This PILO is generally a sprawling shrub but not prostrate. It may be 4 to 8' (1.2 to 2.4m) tall with angular, ascending branches. It has been found near Pauahi Crater, and in the Ainahou area of HVNP.

    Leaves vary greatly from large, .75 by 2" (1.8 by 5cm) to small, .375 by .75" (1 by 2cm), opposite, pointed at both ends, with short petiole, thick and shiny, nerves impressed on upper surface. Flowers greenish, small, inconspicuous, male and female on separate plants. Fruit a small ovoid drupe, reddish orange, toothed at top. Twigs smooth and grey. No wood was gathered. Hillebrand reported the plant from many areas on Hawaii.[6]

4. Pilo, C. montana, whole plant showing upright growth, HVNP.

HVNP Mauna Loa
HNP Haleakala

PILO   **Coprosma montana** Hbd.

    As its species name suggests this PILO occurs on the mountains of Hawaii and Maui. It is a shrub, sometimes prostrate but generally a small tree to 18' (5.6m) and 6" (15cm) in diameter. L.W. Bryan's big tree is 3'8" (1.1m) in circumference, 35' (11m) tall with 29' (9.2) crown spread located in Mauna Kea Forest Reserve, Humulu, Hawaii.

    Opposite leaves thick, glabrous and succulent, small, nearly round to oblong, .5 by .75" (1.2 by 1.8cm), 4-ranked, clustered on spur branches that get progressively shorter toward the end of the main branch. This gives the whole branch a spear shaped appearance. Flowers green, small, about .188" (.5cm) across, 6-petaled, very numerous on the branches. Fruit a drupe, yellow or reddish, ovoid, about .25" (.6cm) in diameter. Twigs nearly black and very rough because of the many leaf scars. Bark dark grey and warty. No wood was gathered.

    This PILO can be seen readily along the upper reaches of the Mauna Loa Strip road in HVNP, off the saddle road on Puu Huluhulu on Hawaii, and high on Haleakala along the road to the summit on HNP.[7]

HVNP Thurston Lava Tube area

PILO   **Coprosma ochracea**
                                  var. **rockiana** Oliver

    This PILO is usually a shrub but I saw a small tree 20' (6.3m) tall and 5" (12.5cm) in diameter near the entrance to Thurston Lava Tube, HVNP, in the wet forest.

Opposite leaves about .75 by 1.5" (1.8 by 3.6cm) with .25" (.6cm) petiole, long pointed at base, shorted point at apex, point reflexed. Leaves dark green, dull upper surface, lighter below, midrib prominent and whitish underside, pinnately veined. Yellow to red fruits borne on short spurs close to twig. Twigs slender, brown, rough with leaf scars.

Heart wood greyish to light brown, sapwood very thin and white, texture fine, figure plain, grain straight and close, density high, wood hard. Vessels small, scattered, rays prominent and closely spaced. Wood warps and is too small to work.

This PILO is an inconspicuous component of the wet OHIA forest understory. No Hawaiian uses are recorded.[8]

[8] See:
St. John, p. 321.

[9] See:
Hillebrand, p. 187.
St. John, p. 321.

HVNP Kipuka Puaulu

PILO   **Coprosma rhynchocarpa** Gray

This PILO has become very plentiful in Kipuka Puaulu in recent years. It has filled in many openings and is the chief plant of the understory in many places. It is a slender, straight tree. L.W. Bryan's big tree measures 3'4" (1m) in circumference, 21' (6.6m) tall and has a crown spread of 16 (5m), located in HVNP.

Leaves are smooth, glossy, long and slender, with prominent midrib and closely spaced pinnate veins on petioles about 1" (2.5cm) long. Leaves pointed at both ends. Flowers small, greenish, 3 or rarely 5 or 6 subsessile at the end of a peduncle 4 to 6mm long. Fruit a drupe, red or yellowish-red, conspicuous with its long beak, borne singly or in small clusters along the branches, closely attached. Twigs slender, light grey. Bark smooth and grey.

Wood light brown with darker streaks. Texture medium fine, figure plain, grain straight, density medium and wood medium hard. Vessels few and very fine, rays not visible at 10x. Wood shrinks and warps badly, workability poor. This PILO occurs in many areas of Hawaii.[9]

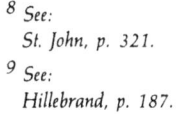
3. Slender Pilo trees, HVNP.

4. Olena leaves and fruit.

1. Pilo, C. rhynchocarpa, leaf detail.

2. Bright red long-beaked fruits of Pilo, HVNP.

OLENA   **Coprosma waimeae** Wawra

OLENA is so called because of the yellow color of the wood. It occurs in the wet forest in the Kokee region of Kauai and up to 4000' (1260m) at Kalalau lookout. It is a tall shrub to 10' (3.1m) with 2" (5cm) trunk.

Opposite leaves 1.5 by 3" (3.7 by 7.5cm) on .75" (1.8cm) petiole, acute at base and obtuse at apex, yellowish-green, smooth both sides, prominent midrib, yellowish veins quite widely spaced, prominent. Flowers small and greenish about .188" (.5cm) across, 6 sepals, borne in small clusters on crowded branches. Fruit a drupe, ovoid, red or yellowish-red, in clusters of 10 or more that surround the twig just below the leaves, or axillary. Twigs nearly black and very rough because of the many leaf scars. Bark grey and warty.

5. Olena, C. waimeae tree. Lillian Lamb at base. Kokee, Kauai.

[10] See:
  Hillebrand, p. 185.
  Rock, p. 459.
  St. John, p. 321.

[11] See:
  Hillebrand, p. 171.
  Rock, p. 433.
  St. John, p. 321.
  Carlquist, p. 310, including picture.
  Neal, p. 800.

[12] See:
  Carlquist, p. 310, including picture.
  Neal, p. 800.
  St. John, p. 321.

1. Nau shrub, Manuka State Park, Hawaii.

2. Nau, G. brighami, white flower and leaves. Manuka State Park, Hawaii.

3. Decadent Nanu, Gardenia remyi.

Wood light brown, texture fine, figure plain, grain straight and close, density medium and hardness medium. Vessels very small and scattered, rays very fine and closely spaced. Wood warps, too small to work.[10]

NANU or NA'U   **Gardenia** Ellis
Gardenia

There are three species of native *Gardenia* plus one variety, all endemic to Hawaii.

List of taxa of *Gardenia* from St. John:
Gardenia brighamii Mann	end. Oahu, Molokai, Lanai, Maui, Hawaii
G. manii var. **manii**	end. Oahu
var. **honoluluensis**	end. Oahu
G. remyi Mann	end. Kauai, Molokai, Maui, Hawaii

Key to the species of *Gardenia*:
Leaves short, shrub or small tree 6 to 18' (1.8 to 5.6m) tall
  4 calyx lobes, 6 corolla lobes . . . . **G. brighami**
Leaves long, trees 15 to 45' (4.7 to 14m) tall
  4 or 5 calyx lobes, 2 or 8 corolla lobes . . . . **G. remyi**
  4 to 6 calyx lobes, narrower than in G.remyi, 7 to 9 corolla lobes . . . . . . **G. manii**

NANU or NA'U   **Gardenia brighamii** Mann

This NANU or native Gardenia is a shrub or small tree to 18' (5.6m) tall and with trunk 6 to 8" (15 to 20cm) in diameter, found on all the islands on the dry side, except Kauai. It is considered to be endangered.

Glossy leaves ovate, about 4" (10cm) long, petiole short, prominent straight veins. Flowers terminal, white and very fragrant, about 1.5" (3.7cm) in diameter, 6 petals attached to long tube, somewhat spiralled. Fruit globose, black, 1" (2.5cm) in diameter with four faint lines, seeds many in yellowish pulp. Twigs slender, grey; bark smooth or slightly roughened. Wood whitish yellow. The pulp of fruit was used in preparing yellow dye for use in dying TAPA.

I saw specimens in Manuka State Park, one place where the plant is being saved from extinction. It has been seen in other places recently.[11]

NANU or NA'U   **Gardenia mannii** St. John & Kuykend

This NANU is endemic to Oahu along with the variety *honoluluensis*. Carlquist found it along the Waikane Trail.

Leaves are larger than those in *G. brighamii*, bright glossy green with distinct light colored midrib and few pinnate veins. Terminal flowers white with up to 9 petals, overlapping spirally, attached to tube, fragrant. Recently reported also from fork of Kaluaa Gulch, Waianae Mts., Oahu.[12]

HNP

NANU or NA'U   **Gardenia remyi** Mann

This NANU can still be seen in the wild in the wet forest outside Hilo but the trees are decadent or dead. A bark beetle had riddled the cambium layer of one tree so that the bark was falling off but it could not be determined whether this was a primary cause of death or whether the insect was one that works on dead trees. L.W. Bryan's big tree from this same area is 3'6" (1m) in circumference, 36' (11.4m) tall with 25' (7.8m) crown spread.

Leaves 4 to 9" (10 to 23cm) long, inverted ovate to oblong, light green, covered with varnish-like material from twigs, midrib and veins deeply impressed on upper surface. Flowers large, terminal, single, white and fragrant, 6 petals. Fruit 4-angled, 2" (5cm) diameter, crowned with 4 wings.

Heart wood dark and light brown streaked, sapwood light straw color, texture medium coarse, figure streaked, grain straight, density low and wood soft. Vessels large and scattered, rays very fine. Yellow fruit pulp used for dye, sticky buds for glue.[13]

[13] See:
Hillebrand, p. 122.
Rock, p. 435.
Neal, p. 800.
St. John, p. 321.

MANONO   **Gouldia** Gray

Gouldia is represented in Hawaiian Islands by three species according to St. John, but some botanists add a fourth, *G. axillaris* Wawra, which may be a hybrid. What this extremely variable genus lacks in species it makes up for in lesser taxa, of which there are 41 varieties and 47 forms. St. John lists the varieties of *G. axillaris* under *G. hillebrandii*.

List of taxa of *Gouldia* from St. John:

Gouldia Gray, 1859, Manono
(axillaris Wawra, 1874, is considered by Fosberg a hybrid, but Skottsberg, 1944, disagrees.)
  Hillebrandii Fosb., 1937, var. **Hillebrandii**. D:fam. 332, 11/2/38
    forma **Hillebrandii**   end. e. Maui
    forma **glabriflora** Fosb., 1937   end. w. Maui
      axillaris Wawra, var. *glabriflora* (Fosb.) Deg.& Deg., 1967.
      axillaris f.*glabrifolia* (Fosb.) Deg.& Deg., 1961
    forma **microphylla** Fosb., 1937   end. e. Maui
      axillaris Wawra, var. *microphylla* (Fosb.) Deg.& Deg., 1961
  var. **hawaiiensis** Fosb., 1937. D:fam. 332, 11/2/38   end. Hawaii
    axillaris Wawra, var. *hawaiiensis* (Fosb.) Deg.& Deg., 1961
  var. **nodosa** Fosb., 1937, f. **nodosa**   end. Molokai, Maui
    axillaris Wawra, var. *nodosa* (Fosb.) Deg.& Deg., 1961
    forma **lancifolia** Fosb., 1937   end. Molokai
      axillaris Wawra, var. *nodosa*, f. *nodosa*, f. *lancifolia* (Fosb.) Deg.& Deg., 1961
(hirtella (Gray) Hbd., 1888. H:169.)
  Fosberg considers this a confusion, non-identifiable.
  G. hirtella (Wawra p.p.) Hbd., adopted by Skottsberg is invalid
St. Johnii Fosb., 1937, var. **St. Johnii**. D:fam. 332, 11/2/38   end. Oahu
* var. **Munroi** Fosb., 1937. D:fam. 332, 11/2/38   end. Lanai
    Munroi (Fosb.) Deg.& Deg., 1967
terminalis (H.& A.) Hbd. 1888, var. **terminalis** f. **terminalis**. H:168   end. Oahu
Petesia? terminalis H. & A., 1832
G. affinis (DC.) Wilbur, 1963, is based upon *Kadua affinia* DC., 1830. It is a valid combination based upon the earliest epithet, but the holotype lacked flowers. Until the holotype is reexamined, there seems no way to use this binomial in the systematics of the genus.
    forma **gracilis** Fosb., 1937   end. Oahu
      affinis (DC.) Wilbur, var. *gracilis* (Fosb.) Deg.& Deg., 1967
    forma **robusta** Fosb., 1937   end. Oahu
      affinis, var. *robusta* (Fosb.) Deg.& Deg. 1967. D:fam. 332, 11/2/38
  var. **angustifolia** Fosb., 1937, D:fam. 332, 11/2/38   end. Molokai
    angustifolia (Fosb.) Deg.& Deg., 1967. D:fam. 332, 11/2/38
  var. **antiqua** Fosb., 1937, f. **antiqua** D:fam. 332, 11/2/38   end. Hawaii
    antiqua (Fosb.) Skottsb., 1944
    forma **acuta** Fosb., 1937   end. Hawaii
      antiqua var. *acuta* (Fosb.) Deg.& Deg., 1967
    forma **hirtellifolia** Fosb., 1937   end. Hawaii
      antiqua, var. *hirtellifolia* (Fosb.) Deg.& Deg., 1967
    forma **kauensis** Fosb., 1937   end. Hawaii
      antiqua, var. *kauensis* (Fosb.) Deg.& Deg., 1967
    forma **kehena** Fosb., 1937   end. Hawaii
      antiqua, var. *kehenaensis* (Fosb.) Deg.& Deg., emend., 1967.
      The Drs. Degener alter the epithet from *kehena* to *kehenaensis* citing the 1961 International Code of Botanical Nomenclature, Art. 73, Note 3, which does not apply, and Rec. 73D, which is only advisory, not mandatory. Art. 23, second paragraph, validates Fosberg's epithet.
    forma **oblonga** Fosb., 1956   end. Hawaii
      antiqua, var. *oblonga* (Fosb.) Deg.& Deg., 1967
  var. **arborescens** (Wawra) Fosb., 1937., f. **arborescens**. D:fam. 332, 11/2/38
                                                                      end. Kauai

1. *Nanu* leaf detail. Bryan photo.

Fosbergii Deg.& Deg., 1967
sandwicensis Gray, var. *arborescens* Wawra, 1874
arborescens (Wawra) Heller, 1897
 forma **albicaulis** Fosb., 1937   end. Kauai
  Fosbergii Deg.& Deg., var. *albicaulis* (Fosb.) Deg.& Deg., 1967
 forma **macrophylla** Fosb., 1937   end. Kauai
  Fosbergii, var. *macrophylla* (Fosb.) Deg.& Deg., 1967
 var. **aspera** Fosb., 1956   end. Hawaii
  aspera (Fosb.) Deg.& Deg., 1967
** var. **bobeoides** Fosb., 1937. D:fam. 332, 11/2/38   end. Lanai
  bobeoides (Fosb.) Deg.& Deg., 1967
** var. **congesta** Fosb., 1937. D:fam. 332, 11/2/38   end. Hawaii
  congesta (Fosb.) Deg.& Deg., 1967
 var. **cordata** (Wawra) Fosb., 1937, f. **cordata**. D:fam. 332, 11/2/38   end. Maui
  cordata (Wawra) Skottsb., 1944
  sandwicensis Gray, var. *cordata* Wawra, 1874
  forma **acuminata** Fosb., 1937   end. Maui
   cordata, var. *acuminata* (Fosb.) Deg.& Deg., 1961
  forma **Nealae** Fosb., 1937   end. Maui
   cordata, var. *Nealae* (Fosb.) Deg.& Deg., 1961, emend. in 1967 to *Nealiae*
  forma **molokaiensis** Fosb., 1937   end. Molokai
   cordata, var. *molokaiensis* (Fosb.) Deg.& Deg., 1961
 var. **coriacea** H.& A.) Fosb., 1937. D:fam. 332, 11/2/38   end. Oahu
  sandwicensis Gray, var. *lanceolata* Wawra, 1874
  sandwicensis Gray, var. *coriacea* Gray, 1861
  Petesia coriacea H.& A., 1832
** var. **crassicaulis** Fosb., 1937. D:fam. 332, 11/2/38   end. e. Maui
  crassicaulis (Fosb.) Deg.& Deg., 1967
** var. **Degeneri** Fosb., 1937. D:fam. 332, 11/2/38   end. Oahu
  Degeneri (Fosb.) Deg.& Deg., 1967
 var. **elongata** (Heller) Fosb., 1937, f. **elongata**. D:fam. 332, 11/2/38 end. Kauai
  elongata Heller, 1897
  forma **hirtellicostata** Fosb., 1937   end. Kauai
   elongata, var. *hirtellicostata* (Fosb.) Deg.& Deg., 1967
  forma **kahili** Fosb., 1937   end. Kauai
   elongata, var. *kahiliensis* (Fosb.) Deg.& Deg., emend, 1967, an invalid name
 var. **Forbesii** Fosb., 1937. D:fam. 332, 11/2/38   end. Hawaii
  Forbesi (Fosb.) Deg.& Deg., 1967
 var. **glabra** Fosb., 1937, f. **glabra**. D:fam. 332, 11/2/38   end. Hawaii
  glabra (Fosb.) Deg.& Deg., 1967
  forma **parvithyrsa** Fosb., 1937   end. Hawaii
   glabra, var. *parvithyrsa* (Fosb.) Deg.& Deg., 1967
  forma **waipioensis** Fosb., 1937   end. Hawaii
   glabra var. *waipioensis* (Fosb.) Deg.& Deg., 1967
 var. **Hathewayi** Fosb., 1937   end. Hawaii
  Hathewayi (Fosb.) Deg.& Deg., 1967
 var. **Hosakae** Fosb., 1937. D:fam. 332, 11/2/38   end. Hawaii
  Hosakae (Fosb.) Deg.& Deg., 1967
 var. **kaala** Fosb., 1937   end. Oahu
  kaala (Fosb.) Skottsb., 1944
  kaalana (Fosb.) Skottsb., emend Deg.& Deg., 1967, an illegal alteration
 var. **kapuaensis** Fosb., 1937, f. **kapuaensis** D:fam, 332, 11/2/38 end. Hawaii
  kapuaensis (Fosb.) Deg.& Deg., 1967
  forma **pittosporoides** Fosb., 1937   end. Hawaii
   kapuaensis var. *pittosporoides* (Fosb.) Deg.& Deg., 1967
  f. **rigidifolia** Fosb., 1937   end. Hawaii
   kapuaensis var. *rigidifolia* Fosb.) Deg. & Deg., 1967
  f. **rigidifolioides** Fosb., 1956   end. Hawaii
   kapuaensis, var. *rigidifolioides* (Fosb.) Deg.& Deg., 1967
  f. **Violetae** Fosb., 1943   end. Hawaii
   kapuaensis, var. *Violetae* (Fosb.) Deg.& Deg., 1967
 var. **konaensis** Fosb., f. **donaensis**. D:fam. 332, 11/2/38   end. Hawaii
  konaensis (Fosb.) Deg.& Deg., 1967
  f. **latifolia** Fosb., 1937   end. Hawaii
   konaensis, var. *latifolia* (Fosb.) Deg.& Deg., 1967
** var. **lanai** Fosb., 1937. D:fam. 332, 11/2/38   end. Lanai
  lanaiensis (Fosb.) Deg.& Deg., 1967, an illegal alteration of the epithet

var. **macrocarpa** (Hbd.) Fosb., 1937, f. **macrocarpa**. D:fam. 332, 11/2/38
    end. Kauai
  macrocarpa Hbd., 1888. H:170
  f. **cuneata** Fosb., 1937   end. Kauai
    macrocarpa, var. *cuneata* (Fosb.) Deg.& Deg., 1967
  f. **sambucina** (Heller) Fosb., 1937   end. Kauai
    sambucina Heller, 1897
    macrocarpa, var. *sambucina* (Heller) Deg.& Deg., 1967
  f. **teres** Fosb., 1937   end. Kauai
    macrocarpa, var. *teres* (Fosb.) Deg.& Deg., 1967
var. **macrothyrsa** Fosb., 1937. D:fam. 332, 11/2/38   end. Oahu
  macrothyrsa (Fosb.) Skottsb., 1944
var. **myrsinoidea** Fosb., 1956   end. Hawaii
  myrsinoidea (Fosb.) Deg.& Deg., 1967
var. **osteocarpa** Fosb., 1937. D:fam. 332, 11/2/38   end. Kauai
  osteocarpa (Fosb.) Deg.& Deg., 1967
var. **ovata** (Wawra) Fosb., 1937, f. **ovata** D:fam. 332, 11/2/38   end. Maui
  ovata (Wawra) Skottsb., 1944
  sandwicensis Gray, var. *ovata* Wawra, 1874
  f. **heterophylla** Fosb., 1937   end. Molokai
    ovata, var. *heterophylla* (Fosb.) Deg.& Deg., 1961
  f. **kalaupapa** Fosb., 1937   end. Molokai
    ovata, var. *kalaupapana* (Fosb.) Deg.& Deg., 1967, an illegal alteration of
      the epithet
    ovata, var. *kalaupana* (Fosb.) Deg.& Deg., 1961
  f. **Lydgatei** Fosb., 1937   end. e. Maui
    ovata, var. *Lydgatei* (Fosb.) Deg.& Deg., 1961
  f. **makawaoensis** Fosb., 1937   end. e. Maui
    ovata, var. *makawaoensis* (Fosb.) Deg.& Deg., 1961
  f. **maunahui** Fosb., 1937   end. Molokai
    ovata, var. *maunahui* (Fosb.) Deg.& Deg., 1961
    ovata, var. *maunahuiensis* (Fosb.) Deg.& Deg., emend, 1967, an illegal
      alteration of the epithet
  f. **membranacea** Fosb., 1937   end. e. Maui
    ovata, var. *membranacea* (Fosb.) Deg.& Deg. 1961
  f. **oahuensis** Fosb., 1956   end. Oahu
    ovata, var. *oahuensis* (Fosb.) Deg.& Deg., 1961
  f. **obovata** Fosb., 1943   end. Lanai
    ovata, var. *obovata* (Fosb.) Deg.& Deg., 1961
  f. **petiolata** Fosb, 1937   end. Molokai
    ovata, var. *petiolata* (Fosb.) Deg.& Deg., 1961
  f. **punaula** Fosb., 1937   end. Molokai
    ovata, var. *punaula* (Fosb.) Deg.& Deg., 1961
    ovata var. *punaulana* (Fosb.) Deg.& Deg., emend, 1967, an illegal
      alteration of the epithet
  f. **Russii** (Fosb.) Fosb., 1956   end. Oahu
    var. *kaala* Fosb., f. *Russii* Fosb., 1937
    ovata, f. *Russii* (Fosb.) Deg.& Deg., 1961
    ovata, var. *Russii* (Fosb.) Deg.& Deg., 1967
  f. **santalifolia** Fosb., 1937   end. Molokai, w. Maui
    ovata, var. *santalifolia* (Fosb.) Deg.& Deg., 1961
  f. **Storeyi** Fosb., 1937   end. Molokai
    ovata, var. *Storeyi* (Fosb.) Deg.& Deg., 1961
  f. **Surehiroae** Fosb., 1937   end. Molokai
    ovata, var. *Surehiroae* (Fosb.) Deg.& Deg., 1961
  f. **wailauensis** Fosb., 1937   end. Molokai
var. **parvifolia** (Wawra) Fosb., 1937, f. **parvifolia**. D:fam. 332, 11/2/38
    end. e. Maui
  sandwicensis Gray, var. *parvifolia* Wawra, 1874
  parvifolia (Wawra) Deg.& Deg., 1967
  f. **subpilosa** Fosb., 1937   end. e. Maui
    parvifolia , var.*subpilosa* (Fosb.) Deg.& Deg., 1967
  f. **impressa** Fosb., 1943   end. e. Maui
    This was published under the nonexistent var. *parvula*, by error. It is
    obvious that the author meant to place it under var. *parvifolia*
    parvula, var. *impressa* (Fosb.) Deg.& Deg., 1967
var. **pedunculata** Fosb., 1937   end. Hawaii
  pedunculata (Fosb.) Deg.& Deg., 1967

** var. **pseudodichotoma** Fosb., 1937. D:fam. 332, 11/2/38	end. Lanai
pseudodichotoma (Fosb.) Deg.& Deg., 1967	
** var. **pubescens** Fosb., 1937	end. e. Maui
pubescens (Fosb.) Deg.& Deg., 1967	
var. **pubistipula** Fosb., 1968	end. e. Maui
var. **purpurea** Fosb., 1937. D:fam. 332, 11/2/38	end. Hawaii
purpurea (Fosb.) Skottsb., 1944	
** var. **quadrangularis** Fosb., 1937. D:fam. 332, 11/2/38	end. Hawaii
quadrangularis (Fosb.) Deg.& Deg., 1967	
** var. **rotundifolia** Fosb., 1937. D:fam. 332, 11/2/38	end. Molokai
rotundifolia (Fosb.) Deg.& Deg., 1967	
var. **sclerotica** Fosb., 1956	end. Hawaii
sclerotica (Fosb.) Deg.& Deg., 1967	
var. **Skottsbergii** Fosb., 1937. D:fam. 332, 11/2/38	end. Hawaii
Skottsbergii (Fosb.) Deg.& Deg., 1967	
var. **stipulacea** (Wawra) Fosb., 1937, f. **stipulacea** D:fam. 332, 11/2/38	
	end. Kauai
stipulacea (Wawra) Deg.& Deg., 1967	
sandwicensis Gray , var.*stipulacea* Wawra, 1874	
f. **Rockii** Fosb., 1937	end. Kauai
stipulacea, var. *Rockii* (Fosb.) Deg.& Deg., 1967	
** var. **subcordata** Fosb., 1937. D:fam. 332, 11/2/38	end. Lanai
subcordata (Fosb.) Deg.& Deg., 1967	
var **tenuicaulis** Fosb., 1937. D:fam. 332, 11/2/38	end. Kauai
tenuicaulis (Fosb.) Deg.& Deg., 1967	
var. **Wawrana** Fosb., 1937. D:fam. 332, 11/2/38	end. Oahu

Wawrae (Fosb.) Deg.é Deg., emend, 1967, an illegal alteration of the epithet Fosberg has also described some 65 interspecific or varietal or informal hybrids in the genus *Gouldia*. These are omitted in the present list.

Key to the species of *Gouldia* adapted from Degener, *FH*:
Panicles axillary only . . . . **G. hillebrandii** Fosb.
Panicles mainly terminal
    Leaf veins very prominent below and impressed above; calyx lobes
       in fruit fleshy, at right angles to its axis . . . . **G. St.-Johnii** Fosb.
    Leaves, etc., otherwise . . . . **G. terminalis** (H&A) Hbd.
                                                  and varieties

HVNP Many varieties, some in Kipuka Puaulu
HNP 2 var., several forms and hybrid; unspecified one at Paliku

MANONO   **Gouldia terminalis** Hbd.

1. Manono leaf and cluster of dark bluish fruit.

2. Manono, G. terminalis, leaf and terminal flower clusters. Stainback Highway, Hawaii.

To describe all of the 82 taxa of *G. terminalis* would require a volume in itself. For the person interested in identifying a plant to variety or form, Degener's *Flora Hawaiiensis*, p. 332 presents a key that should be of assistance It requires attention to a large number of details such as length of nodes, petioles, panicles, etc. In general MANONO is a shrub or small tree rarely over 20' (6.3m) in height with trunk 1' (31.5cm) in diameter. L.W. Bryan's big tree is 3' (91.5cm) in circumference, 29' (6.3m) tall and with crown spread of 12' (3.8m), located in HVNP. There are varieties on all the islands. The description that follows was taken largely from trees growing in HVNP from where many varieties have been collected.

Leaves thick, leathery, opposite, 3 to 7" (7.5 to 18cm) long, midrib prominent, impressed above, dark green, shiny with smooth margin, petiole short, stout and brown. Flowers terminal or occasionally axillary, panicles pyramidal in form, large and loose, each tiny flower .25" (.6cm) across, lavender, with short tube. Fruit small, purple, in clusters, apex roughened, each fruit with two cells surrounded by purple pulp. Each cell contains many small seeds. Twigs often drooping, slender to fairly stout, glabrous, tending to be 4-angled in new growth. Bark smooth, grey.

Heart wood medium to dark brown, sapwood very light pinkish brown, texture fine, figure plain, grain straight, density medium, hardness medium. Vessels numerous, very fine, scattered, rays numerous and very fine. This is a poor wood that warps and checks badly. Hawaiian use seems to have been limited to canoe trim and rigging.

MANONOs and their near relatives KOPIKOs, occupy a conspicuous place in the wet forest where they are strong invaders of the OHIA forest and form an understory between the low fern layer nearest the ground and the tall OHIAs. They resemble each other except that while the fruits of MANONO are deep purple, those of KOPIKO are orange.[14]

MANONO   **Gouldia hillebrandii** Fosb.
syn. **G. axillatis** Wawra

One variety, *hawaiiensis*, is endemic to Hawaii but all the others are confined to Molokai and Maui.

The chief distinction between *G. hillebrandii* and *G. terminalis* is whether the flowers are borne in axils of the leaves as in the former or mostly terminal as in the latter. Otherwise the general descriptions are much the same.

Wood is tan, streaked with brown, texture medium, figure plain with a few lines, grain straight, density low and wood soft. Vessels in moderate numbers, small, scattered and open rays barely visible at 10x. This is a poor wood with poor stability and workability. It is also a tree of the wet forest.[15]

NONI or NONI-KUAHIWI   **Morinda** (Vaill) L.

Morinda is represented in Hawaii by three species and one added variety, listed by St. John as follows:

Morinda citrifolia L.	introduced Polynesia
M. sandwicensis f. sandwicensis	end. Oahu
f. **glabrata** Deg.	end. Oahu
M. trimera	end. Maui

Key to the species of *Morinda*:

Leaves oblong, 10 to 18cm long, 3.5 to 6cm wide
    fruit 2.5cm diameter .... **M. trimera**
Leaves ovate, 15 to 20cm long, 10 to 15cm wide
    fruit 5 to 10cm in diameter .... **M. citrifolia**
Leaves obovate-oblong to broadly elliptic,
    13 to 18cm by 6cm wide............................ **M. sandwicensis**

Degener, *FH*, states that *M. sandwicensis* was known from only one tree in deteriorating habitat, thus it had very minimal impact on the forest and may well be extinct unless preserved in gardens. He describes the species and variety in *FH*, page 332.

HVNP

NONI   **Morinda citrifolia** L.

NONI is presumed to have been an early Hawaiian introduction. Since its introduction predates the arrival of Europeans and North Americans, it is classed as indigenous. It is found in Asia, Australia and the Pacific islands. It is really a large shrub rather than a tree but may become treelike and 20′ (6.3m) tall. It occurs in the lowland zone and does not invade the forest. It is found mostly around homes and fields where it may have been planted.

Leaves large and shiny dark green, about 6″ (15cm) wide by 8″ (20cm) long or larger in fast growing plants with strongly impressed midrib and widely spaced veins, margins smooth, petiole 1 to 1.5″ (2.5 to 3.7cm) long. Flowers borne on a small ball-like organ that grows in the axils of leaves. Each flower is small, .5″ (1.2cm) in diameter, with white corolla, 5 petals attached to .5″ (1.2cm) tube, pistil green. There may be several flowers on any one ball. The

[14] See:
Hillebrand, p. 169.
Rock, p. 431.
Carlquist, p. 309.
St. John, p. 322.
Degener, FH, p. 332, including keys.

[15] See:
Hillebrand, p. 170.
Rock, p. 431.
St. John, p. 322.
Degener, FH, p. 332, including key.

1. Noni, leaf and fruit detail.

2. Noni, *M. citrifolia*, shrub, HVNP.

[16] See:
Hillebrand, p. 177.
Rock, p. 467.
Neal, p. 804.
Carlquist, p. 268.

[17] See:
Hillebrand, p. 177.
Rock, p. 467.
St. John, p. 331.

balls continue to enlarge to produce the ovoid fruit. Surface of fruit is divided into angular divisions, each of which originally had a flower. Fruits are 2 to 3" (5 to 7.5cm) in diameter, yellow, fleshy and somewhat evil smelling but edible. They resemble small breadfruit in appearance. Twigs are hollow, green turning to brown, flattened on one side; bark smooth, light brown.

Wood very light yellow streaked with brown or black, texture medium fine, figure plain, cross grained, density low and wood soft. Vessels large, open and scattered, rays fine and closely spaced. Wood is of no value.

Hawaiians used the fruit as a food in times of famine and also in poultices. Roots furnished a yellow dye and the bark a yellowish-red dye.[16]

NONI-KUAHIWI   **Morinda trimeria** Hbd.

NONI-KUAHIWI is endemic to Maui, where Rock found it along a ditch trail on Haleakala. It is very rare and is listed as endangered. It, and also *M. sandwicensis*, can be distinguished from the common NONI by the much smaller fruits.[17]

KOPIKO   **Psychotria** L.
                                                              Syn. **Straussia** Gray

Psychotria is another variable genus of 13 species, 1 subspecies, 13 varieties and three forms listed as follows by St. John:

Psychotria L., 1759
    Fauriei (Lévl.) Fosb., 1962   end. Oahu
        Straussia Fauriei Lévl., 1911. R:449
    Greenwelliae Fosb., 1964   end. Kauai
    **grandiflora Mann, 1867. H:181, R:457   end. Kauai
        The *Straussia kaduana* Gray, var. *grandifolia* Wawra, 1874, may well belong in this affinity.
    Hathewayi Fosb., 1964, var. **Hathewayi**   end. Oahu
        Straussis sessilis Deg.& Hosaka, 1940, non *Psychotria sessilis* Vell., 1825
        var. **brevipetiolata** Fosb., 1964   end. Oahu
    hawaiiensis (Gray) Fosb., 1962, var. **hawaiiensis**   end. Hawaii
        Straussia hawaiiensis Gray, 1858. H:180, R:451
        var. **glabrithyrsa** Fosb., 1964   end. w. Maui
        var. **glomerata** (Rock) Fosb., 1964   end. Hawaii
            Straussia glomerata Rock, 1918
        var. **Hillebrandii** (Rock) Fosb., 1962. Kopiko, opiko, Hillebrand straussia
                                                                          end. Hawaii
            Straussia Hillebrandii Rock, 1913. R:453, D:fam. 332, 12/1/49
        var. **molokaiensis** (Rock) Fosb., 1964   end. Molokai
            Straussia Hillebrandii Rock, var. *molokaiensis* Rock, 1913. R:455, D:fam. 332
            12/1/49
        var. **scoriacea** (Rock) Fosb., 1964   end. Hawaii
            oncocarpa Hbd., var. *scoriacea* Rock, 1913, R:449
    hexandra Mann, 1867. subsp. **hexandra**, var. **hexandra**, f. **hexandra**.
        H:181, R:455   end. Kauai
        f. **waialuana** Fosb., 1964   end. Kauai
        var. **hirta** Wawra, 1874. H:181, R:457   end. Kauai
            hirta (Wawra) Heller, 1897
            hirtula Skottsb., 1944
        var. **dealiae** Fosb., 1964   end. Kauai
        subsp. **oahuensis** Deg.& Fosb., 1964 , var.**oahuensis**   end. Oahu
            var. **Hosakana** Fosb., 1964, f. **Hosakana**   end. Oahu
                f. **Forbesii** Fosb., 1964   end. Oahu
            var. **Rockii** Fosb., 1964   end. Oahu
            var. **St.-Johnii** Fosb., 1964   end. Oahu
    ***insularum Gray, var. **paradisii** Fosb., 1964   end. (indefinite locality) H.I.
    kaduana (C.& S.) Fosb., 1962, var. **kaduana**   end. Kauai, Oahu, Molokai, Lanai
        Coffea kaduana C.& S., 1829
        Straussia kaduana (C.& S.) Gray, 1858. H:179, R:447

    var. **longissima** (Rock) Fosb., 1964   end. Oahu
        Straussia longissima Rock, 1913. R:447
        var. *coriacea* Hbd., 1888. H:179. The holotype in Berlin was redetermined
            by Skottsberg as *S. longissima* Rock
    var. **pubiflora** (Heller) Fosb., 1964   end. Oahu
        Straussia pubiflora Heller, 1897
leptocarpa (Hbd.) Fosb., 1964   end. e. Maui
    Straussia leptocarpa Hbd., 1888. H:180
Mariniana (C.& S.) Fosb., 1962   end. Kauai, Oahu, Molokai, Maui
    Coffea Mariniana C.& S., 1829
    Straussia Mariniana (C.& S.) Gray, 1858. H:179, R:451
mauiensis Fosb., 1964   end. e. Maui, Lanai
    Straussia oncocarpa Hbd., 1888, non *P. oncocarpa* Schum., 1898. H:180, R:448
    Of this affinity but not yet reclassified is *Straussia oncocarpa* Hbd.,
        var. *subcordata* Rock, 1913
psychotrioides (Heller) Fosb., 1964   end. Kauai
    Straussia psychotrioides Heller, 1897
waianensis Fosb., 1964   end. Oahu

[18] See:
Hillebrand, p. 178.
Rock, p. 453.
St. John, p. 332.

HVNP Kipuka Puaulu
HNP species not determined

KOPIKO   **Psychotria hawaiiensis** Gray

Two specimens of KOPIKO, one labeled *P. hawaiiensis* var. *hillebrandii* and the other labeled P. hawaiiensis var. *hawaiiensis* were studied in HVNP herbarium but there was not enough difference between them to develop a clear set of distinctions recognizable in the field. The following description is specific for the common KOPIKO of Kipuka Puaulu in HVNP and labeled *P. hawaiiensis* var. *hillebrandii*. The other specimen was collected from a wetter forest area near Napau Crater beyond the end of the Chain of Craters road.

KOPIKO is a small upright tree wth sharply ascending branches. It reaches a height of about 20' (6.3m) but is seen mostly as a sapling about 10' (3.1m) tall in the forest understory. L.W. Bryan's big tree is 4'9"(1.45m) in circumference, 45' (14m) high, and with crown spread of 30' (9.5m), located on Hoomau Ranch, Honomolino, Hawaii.

Leaves opposite, large, leathery, glossy, pointed both ends, the base long tapering to the 1" (2.5cm) petiole. Midrib light green and prominent but pinnate veins light and fine. Flowers largely 4-petaled, borne in large, loose terminal panicles, 4" (10cm) long or more, whose branches protrude at right angles to the main axis. petals creamy white and slender. Fruits yellow or orange berries, borne in loose terminal clusters. Twigs slender, light brown and smooth; bark medium grey on 6" (15cm) trunks, smooth except for small, light grey warts. Wood reddish brown, texture medium fine, figure plain, grain straight, density medium and wood medium soft. Vessels few and scattered, rays very fine. Wood was used for TAPA anvils.

When Kipuka Puaulu was fenced to exclude livestock in the 1930s the forest consisted of large, old, mature trees of about 40 species. Reproduction and other undergrowth was nearly absent as is shown in many of Rock's pictures, taken around 1910. A few years after fencing seedling trees began to appear so that when I visited the area again in 1960 there were stands of KOPIKO, MANONO and other species forming a dense understory. Now, after another 20 years, the KOPIKOs seem less evident. They have, in turn, given way to OLOPUA, PILO and other species. This makes an interesting study of ecological succession in a disturbed area of Hawaiian forest.

KOPIKO is locally quite common in many of the wetter areas of Hawaiian forest.[18]

1. Kopiko, P. hawaiiensis v. hillebrandi, leaf and fruit. Red when ripe.

2. Kopiko bark detail, Saddle Road, Hawaii.

[19] See:
Hillebrand, p. 179.
Rock, p. 451.
St. John, p. 332.

1. Kopiko, P. mariniana, leaf and fruit detail. Kokee, Kauai.

KOPIKO **Psychotria mariniana** (C&S) Fosb.
syn. **Straussia mariniana** C&S

This KOPIKO occurs on Kauai, Oahu, Molokai and Maui in wet forest. It is also a small tree. I saw specimens in the Kokee area and at Kalalau overlook on Kauai.

Leave opposite, dark green and leathery, with domita, small brown spots at junction of midrib and pinnate veins. Edges slightly rolled, midrib very light green and prominent, veins indistinct. Fruits yellow when ripe, born in crowded terminal clusters, each berry about .375" (1cm) in diameter and with calyx scar at apex. Twigs purplish and smooth but with prominent leaf scars.

Wood hard, light pinkish color, texture very fine, figure plain, grain straight and close, density high. Vessels very tiny in radial chains, rays numerous and very fine. Wood warps and checks badly, too small to work.[19]

HVNP Kipuka Puaulu

KOPIKO **Psychotria hawaiiensis** var.**hawaiiensis**

This KOPIKO, from the Kona side of Hawaii as well as in HVNP has so nearly the same description as *P. hawaiiensis* var. *hillebrandii* that it is not repeated. It is interesting that Rock found many of the trees he described and photographed near the Hoomau Ranch, Honomolino, Hawaii at a place he called Kapua. He found this same species there at about 3000' (950m). So much of the Hawaiian terrain is so rough that access is severely limited unless roads are built. This has happened around ranches and now happens in subdivisions. As more of the forest is closely studied many species may be shown to be more abundant than previously supposed.

LOBELIA FAMILY
Lobeliaceae
Campanulaceae in part

According to St. John there are seven genera of this family represented in Hawaiian Islands. These plants are so variable that dozens of species, subspecies, varieties and forms have been named. Rock considered only *Clermontia* and *Cyanea* to include tree species. All the genera are included in this key for sake of comparison. Carlquist gives a long account of the members of this family, complete with many good pictures.

Key to the genera of *Lobeliaceae* adapted from Degener, FH:
Fruit dehiscent, a capsule at times first fleshy; corolla curved or
   straight, evenly or unevenly 5-lobed:
  Corolla salverform, straight, not dorsally slit, lobed
    evenly or nearly so . . . . **Brighamia** Gray in Mann
  Corolla tubular, more or less curved, dorsally slit, unevenly 5-lobed
   Capsule dehiscent by 2 apical valves; inflorescence racemose,
    more or less erect; flower color various . . . . **Lobelia** (Plum) L.
   Capsule dehiscent by numerous irregular lateral pores after decay
    of non-woody elements; inflorescence racemose,
    candelabra-like . . . . **Trematolobelia** Zahlbr.
Fruit indehiscent, a berry; corolla curved, unevenly 5-lobed;
  Corolla slit dorsally
   Stamens free from corolla tube, flower color various;
    seeds smooth or rugose
    Seeds shiny, smooth, yellow or dark;
     Shrubs or small trees with candelabra-like branching;
      inflorescence 2-flowered to rarely subumbelate 10-flowered;
      dorsal slit deep; flower green or white or yellowish to
      pinkish purple or purplish black . . . . **Clermontia** Gaud
     Coarse herbs or shrubs with more or less erect branches or
      small palm-like raceme, flower white through blue, violet,
      purplish-red and almost black . . . . **Cyanea** Gaud

Seeds dull, transversely undulate-rugose, flowers
white to greenish .... **Delissia** Gaud
Stamens adnate to base of laterally compressed corolla tube;
dorsal slit shallow; seeds not white, smooth; flower
claret to rarely purplish or white .... **Rollandia** Gaud

OHA WAI or OHA KEPAU   **Clermontia** Gaud

Clermontia is represented by 40 species plus several varieties and forms. Only *C. hawaiiensis* is tree-like. The other taxa are listed as given by St. John to show the number of extinct and endangered taxa.

Taxa of *Clermontia* as listed by St. John:

Clermontia Gaud., 1826. 'Oha-wai, 'oha, haha
  arborescens (Mann) Hbd., 1888. H:242, R:483; D:fam. 339, 11/11/60
    'Aha-wai, 'oha, haha   end. Molokai, Lanai, Maui
    Cyanea arborescens Mann, 1867
    Delissea waihiae Mann, 1867
  aspera E. Wimm., 1968   end. Oahu
  calophylla E. Wimm., 1956   end. Hawaii
  clermontioides (Gaud.) Heller, 1897, var. **clermontioides**   end. Kauai
    Gaudichaudii Hbd., 1888. H:243, R:479
    Fauriei Lévl., 1911
    Delissea clermontioides Gaud., 1842
    var. **barbata** (Rock) St. John, comb. nov.   end. e. Maui
      Gaudichaudii Hbd., var. *barbara* Rock, Bishop Mus., Mem.7(2), 293, 1919
      clermontioides, var. *mauiensis* Hochr., 1934
    var. **epiphytica** Hochr., 1934   end. Kauai
    var. **hirsutiflora** Rock, 1957   · end. Kauai
  coerulea Hbd., 1888. subsp. **coerulea**, var. **coerulea**. H:243, R:485; D:fam.
    339, 8/1/34. Kona clermontia   end. Hawaii
    (Corolla bluish or purplish)
    var. **Degeneri** Skottsb., 1944   end. Hawaii
    var. **Greenwelliana** E.Wimm., 1953   end. s.w. Hawaii
    var. **parvifolia** Rock, 1957   end. s.w. Hawaii
    subsp. **brevidens** (Skottsb.) St. John, subsp. nov.
      Dentibus calycis 3-4mm longis. Typus: var. *brevidens* Skottsb., Hort.Gotob.,
        Acta 2:268, 1926
    var. **brevidens** Skottsb., 1926, f. **brevidens**   end. s.e. Hawaii
      f. **flavescens** (E.Wimm.) St. John, comb.nov.   end. Hawaii
        coerulea, var. *coerulea*, f. *flavescens* E.Wimm., Engler, Pflanzenreich IV,
          276b:762, 1953. Wimmer's typification of *C.coerulea* as with tooth-like
          3-5mm. calyx lobes was incorrect, as Skottsberg (1944) had removed
          this kind as var. *brevidens*, leaving as the species those plants with
          the calyx lobes broad deltoid and 18-25mm. long.
  convallis E. Wimm., 1968   end. Hawaii
drepanomorpha Rock, 1913. R:473; D:fam. 339, 7/31/58. Kohala clermontia
                                                                       end. Hawaii
Forbesii St. John, 1939   end. Molokai
fulva Lévl., 1913   end. Kauai
furcata E.Wimm in Deg.& Deg., 1956. D:fam. 339, 8/20/56   end. w. Maui
grandiflora Gaud., 1826, var. **grandiflora**, f. **grandiflora**. H:240, R:473
                                                   end. Molokai, Lanai, Maui
    f. **hamata** E. Wimm., 1956   end. w. Maui
    f. **nitida** E. Wimm., 1968   end. Lanai
***haleakalensis** Rock, 1913. R:489; D:fam. 339, 5/1/66. Haleakala clermontia
                                                                       end. e. Maui
hanaensis St. John, 1939. D:fam. 339, 11/11/60. Hana clermontia, 'oha-wai
                                                                     end. e. Maui
***hawaiiensis** (Hbd.) Rock, 1913, var. **hawaiiensis**. R:477; D:fam. 339, 7/31/58
    N:816. 'oha-kepau, Hawaii clermontia   end. Hawaii
    macrocarpa Gaud., var. *hawaiiensis* Hbd., 1888. H:241
    var. **grandis** Rock, 1957   end. Hawaii
  hirsutinervis St. John, 1939   end. e. Maui
  kakeana Walp, 1835, var. **kakeana**, f. **kakeana**. D:fam. 339, 7/31/58.
    Oha-wai, haha, kakea clermontia   end. Oahu, Molokai, Maui
    macrocarpa Gaud., 1842. H:240
    macrocarpa, f. *rosea* Hbd., 1888. H:241

f. **gracilis** E. Wimm., 1968	end. e. Maui
var. **orientalis** St. John, 1971	end. e. Maui

kohalae Rock, 1913, var. **kohalae**. R:476; D:fam. 339, 11/11/60.
   Blackflowered clermontia   end. Hawaii
  var. **hiloensis** E.Wimm., 1943. D:fam. 339, 8/8/60   end. Hawaii
  var. **robusta** Rock, 1913. D:fam. 339, 8/8/60   end. Hawaii
leptoclada Rock, 1913, var. **leptoclada**. R:477; D:fam. 339, 11/11/60 end. Hawaii
  var. **holopsila** E.Wimm., 1943. D:fam. 339, 11/11/60   end. Hawaii
  var. **urceolata** Rock, 1957   end. Hawaii
****Loyana** Rock, 1957   end. s.w. Hawaii
micrantha (Hbd.) Rock, 1919. D:fam. 339, 8/8/60. w. Maui clermontia
      end. w. Maui
  multiflora Hbd., var. *micrantha* Hbd., 1888. H:242
  multiflora, var. *micrantha*,f. *montana* Rock, 1913
molokaiensis St. John, 1939   end. Molokai
  grandiflora Gaud., var. *vulgata* E.Wimm., 1956, in part
montis-loa Rock, 1913, var. **montis-loa**, f. **montis-loa**. R:511   end. hawaii
  f. **globosa** Rock, 1919   end. Hawaii
  f. **molokaiensis** E.Wimm., 1968   end. Molokai
  var. **tenuifolia** Skottsb., 1926   end. Hawaii
multiflora Hbd., 1888, H:242   end. Oahu, w. Maui
****Munroi** St. John, 1939   end. Lanai
  grandiflora Gaud., var. *vulgata* E.Wimm., 1956, in part
oblongifolia Gaud., 1829, f. **oblongifolia**. H:241, R:476; D:fam. 339, 9/27/37
  'Oha-wai, haha, Oahu clermontia   end. Oahu
  f. **brevipes** E.Wimm., 1956   end. Molokai
  f. **kaalae** Deg., 1937. D:fam. 339, 9/27/37   end. Oahu
  f. **mauiensis** (Rock) Deg., 1937. D:fam. 339, 9/27/37   end. e. Maui, Lanai
  var. *mauiensis* Rock, 1913. R:476
pallida Hbd., 1888, var. **pallida**. H:241, D:fam. 339, 11/11/60. Pale clermontia
      end. Molokai
  var. **ramosissima** Rock, 1919. R:319; D:fam. 339, 11/11/60   end. Molokai
paradisia E.Wimm., 1953. D:fam. 339, 3/15/56. Paradise clermontia   end. Hawaii
parviflora Gaud. ex Gray, 1862, var. **parviflora**. H:242; D:fam. 339, 8/20/56
      end. Hawaii
  var. *pleiantha* Hbd., 1888. H:242
  var. **calycina** Rock, 1913. R:512; D:fam. 339, 8/20/56   end. Hawaii
  var. **grandis** Rock, 1919. D:fam. 339, 8/20/56   end. Hawaii
  var. **intermedia** Skottsb., 1944. D:fam. 339, 8/20/56   end. Hawaii
  var. **umbraticola** Skottsb., 1926. D:fam. 339, 8/20/56   end. Hawaii
****Peleana** Rock, 1913. R:483; D:fam. 339, 11/11/60. Pele clermontia   end. Hawaii
persicifolia Gaud., 1826. H:241, R:475; D:fam. 338, 10/20/56   end. Oahu
  epiphytica St. John, 1939
*****pyrularia** Hbd., 1888. H:243; D:fam. 339, 8/8/60. Pear clermontia   end. Hawaii
reticulata St. John, 1939, f. **reticulata**   end. e. Maui
  grandiflora Gaud, var. *vulgata* E.Wimm., 1956, in part
  f. **pilifera** St. John, 1939   end. w. Maui
Rockiana E. Wimm., 1956   end. Hawaii
rosacea St. John, 1971   end. e. Maui
Samuelii Forbes, 1920. D:fam. 339, 7/31/58. Baldwin clermontia   end. e. Maui
singuliflora Rock) Rock, 1919   end. e. Maui
  Gaudichaudii Hbd., var. *singuliflora* Rock 1913
  clermontioides (Gaud.) Heller, var. *singuliflora* (Rock) Hochr., 1934
subpetiolata St. John, 1939   end. Molokai
  grandiflora Gaud, var. *subpetiolata* (St. John) E.Wimm., 1956
tuberculata Forbers, 1912. R:485; D:fam. 339, 11/28/60. Warty clermontia
      end. Maui
wailauensis St. John, 1939   end. Molokai
waimeae Rock, 1913, var. **waimeae**   end. Hawaii
  var. **longisepala** Rock, 1957, f. **longisepala**   end. Hawaii
    f. **lanceolata** E.Wimm., 1968   end. Hawaii
  var. **obovata** Rock, 1957   end. Hawaii
(**carinifera** Lévl., 1913), doubtful species   end. Kauai

1. *Ohawai, C. hawaiiensis*, leaves, flower and fruit. Stainback Highway, Hawaii.

2. *Ohawai, C. hawaiiensis*, small, candelabra-shaped.

HVNP Wet forest
HNP *C. arborescens; C. kakeana; C. reticulata;* unspecified at Paliku

[1] See:
Hillebrand, p. 239.
Rock, p. 277.
St. John, p. 337.
Degener, FH, p. 239, describes several species.

OHA WAI or ANA KEPAU   **Clermontia hawaiiensis** (Hbd.) Rock

This OHA WAI is chosen for description because is is accessible in the Hilo-HVNP area of Hawaii. It grows in the wet rain forest, usually as a large, candelabra-shaped shrub but also as a tree up to 20' (6.3m) tall. It often grows on the side of a tree fern or OHIA tree but also on the ground.

Leaves are long and slender, bunched near the ends of the branches; stem and midrib greenish to purplish; milky sap exudes from broken leaves. Flowers white, green or purple with tubular corollas 1" (2.5cm) long, 10-petals .25 by 1" (.6 by 2.5cm) or more, curved sharply out. Fruit globular, yellow, 1" (2.5cm) in diameter, prominent calyx scar at apex, thin shell breaks open to reveal bright orange pulp of dough-like consistency. Twigs are very rough from leaf scars, light tan and quite stout. They branch from main trunk in candelabra fashion. Bark on 3" (7.5cm) trunk, smooth.

Wood white, texture fine, figure plain, grain straight and close, density medium, hardness medium. Vessels not visible at 10x, rays broad, light colored and very closely spaced. Wood checks badly, too small to work.

The thick milky sap was used as bird lime to spread on branches to catch small birds.[1]

2. *Cyanea* sp., flower detail.

3. *Cyanea* sp. found off Stainback Highway, small tree with very large leaves.

1. Bryan Cyanea, *C. bryanii,* small tree in Honaunau Forest Reserve, Hawaii.

HNP *Cyanea aculeatifolia; C. angustifolia; C grimesiana; C. hamatiflora;*
  C. holophyla, var. *obovata; C. horrida; C. macrostegia;*
  C. multispicata; C. scrabra, var. *varibilis* f. *sinuata;*
  C. scabra, var. *varabilis,* f. *varabilis; C. sp.*

HAHALUA or HAHANUI   **Cyanea** Gaud.

Cyanea is another genus that has attracted the attention of botanists as it is very variable. St. John lists 81 species, 39 varieties and 4 forms for 124 taxa. To show the problem when so many taxa are named, Carlquist makes a pretty good case when he illustrates that *C. bryani, C. noli-me-tangere, C. platyphylla* and *C. rollandioides* can all be shown to be growth phases of *C. tritomantha.* If this proves to be a fact, it affirms that the genus needs further study toward simplification of the nomenclature.

Rock found that only *C. arborea* (Gray) Hbd., and *C. leptostegia* A. Gray, become tree-like. *C. arborea* has been extinct since 1919 according to the list of

4. *Hahalua, C. leptostegia,* small tree, Kokee, Kauai.

[2] See:
Hillebrand, p. 261.
Rock, p. 483.
St. John, p. 338.
Degener, FH, p. 339, describes several species.

[3] See:
Hillebrand, p. 248.
Degener, FH, p. 339, describes one species.

endangered, threatened and extinct plants in Hawaii. *Cyneas* have been known to reach heights of 12 to 24' (3.8 to 7.5m) with stems of 4" (10cm). *C. carlsonii* Rock, which is listed as extinct since 1966 was shown to the writer in 1974 in Honaunau Forest Reserve, Hawaii, by Mr. Carlson, the man for whom the plant was named. These plants were 15 to 20' (4.7 to 6.3m) tall with single stems 2 to 3" (5 to 7.5cm) in diameter. The leaves, clustered at the top of the stem, were about 2" (5cm) broad by 12")31cm) long, or more, dark green and quite sharply upright. Leaf scars are spirally arranged on the trunk giving it a rough appearance. No flowers or fruit were seen.

Another nearby plant was identified as *C. marksii* Rock. It differed from *C. carlsonii* in that the leaf petioles and midribs were rough with spur-like growths. The trunk was 6' (1.8m) tall and 2" (5cm) in diameter and also very rough. Leaves were clustered at the top and there were numerous flower buds borne axillary and along the trunk below the leaves. Some were singular and some were in clusters of two to several, all peduncles longer than the bud.

Another Hawaiian *Cyanea* is *C. bryanii* Rock, named for State Forester L.W. Bryan. Bryan's photo of this plant shows it to have leaves 4 to 6" (15 to 20cm) wide and 18 to 20" (45 to 50cm) long on a stem of about 2" (5cm), whole plant about 8' (2.4m) tall. The leaves are smooth.

A *Cyanea* on Kauai was determined to be *C. leptostegia* Gray. It reared its crown of leaves well above the brush of the forest understory on a 2" (5cm) stem. The leaves, 18 to 24" (45 to 60cm) long by 3 to 4" (7.5 to 10cm) wide, were lobed and yielded a yellow milky sap when broken. The whole plant was 10' (3.1m) tall. Several were seen in the Kokee area.

Another beautiful specimen was seen along the Stainback highway behind Hilo. It resembled *C. marksii* with the thorn-like growth on the leaf petioles but the leaves were longer. The flowers were light blue or greenish with long pistils extending beyond the length of the petals. The leaves stood out at right angles to the trunk and the whole tree was 6' (1.8m) tall.[2]

1. Carlson Cyanea, *C. carlsonii*, Hanaunau Forest Reserve, small trees.

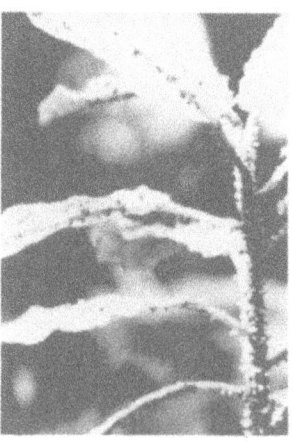

2. Carlson Cyanea showing spiny-ribbed leaves and trunk. Seekins photo.

3. Marks Cyanea, *C. marksii*, trunk and flowering habit, Honaunau Forest Reserve.

OTHER GENERA OF **LOBELIACEAE**

Neither Rock nor Bryan and Walker considered any species of *Rollandia* Gaud., *Lobelia* (Plum) L., *Delissea* Gaud of *Trematolobelia* Zahlbr. to become tree-like.

Hillebrand lists *Delissea* as shrubs generally but possibly small trees to 10' (3.1m) tall in the case of *D. rhytidosperma* Mann, endemic to Kauai.[3]

Rollandia is another genus that sends up a single trunk with a crown of spreading leaves. Most of them are 6' (1.8m) or under but *R. humboldtiana* Gadu., is listed by Hillebrand as having a trunk 10 to 15' (3.1 to 4.7m) tall, endemic to Oahu.[4]

Brighamia Gray, is described as having a tall tapering trunk several inches in diameter at the base and 5 to 12' (1.5 to 3.8m) tall with a clump of leaves resembling a cabbage head at the top of a naked pole. There are only four species and one variety endemic to Niihau, Kauai, Maui and Molokai, where Hillebrand found what he called *B. insignis* in great numbers. St. John says it is found only on Niihau.[5]

Hawaiian *Lobelias* are woody shrubs, upright or trailing, mostly in the range of 4 to 6' (1.2 to 1.8m) tall.[6]

Degener, *FH*, describes one variety of *Trematolobelia* but does not mention the type or size of the plant. Carlquist's picture on page 247 shows them to be short woody stems with a large clump of drooping leaves at the top. There are three species and one variety with one or more endemic to each of the islands.[7]

[4] See:
Hillebrand, p. 248.
Degener, FH, p. 339.

[5] See:
Hillebrand, p. 235.
Degener, FH, p. 339.

[6] See:
Hillebrand, p. 235.
Degener, FH, p. 339, *describes two species.*

[7] See:
Degener, FH, p. 339.
St. John, p. 347.

NAUPAKA FAMILY — **Goodenaceae**

This family is represented by only one genus, *Scaevola* L., in Hawaii. St. John lists 11 species, 10 varieties and six forms, or 28 taxa as follows:

Scaevola L., 1771. Naupaka
  ×**cerasifolia** Skottsb., 1927. Naupaka. A natural hybrid   end. Oahu
    (*Gaudichaudiana* × *mollis*)
   × *kahanae* Deg., 1933. D:fam. 340, 6/14/33
   × *cerasifolia*, f. *tomentosa* Skottsb., 1944
  Chamissoniana Gaud., 1829, var. **Chamissoniana**. H:267, R:495; D:fam, 340,
    12/1/68, N:819. Naupaka, naupaka-kuahiwi   end. Molokai, Maui
    var. **bracteosa** Hbd., 1888. H:268, D:fam. 340, 12/1/68
                                 end. Molokai, Lanai, Maui, Hawaii
      var. **caerulescens** Lévl., 1911   end. Kauai
      var. **cylindrocarpa** (Hbd.) Krause, 1912. D:fam. 340, 12/1/68   end. Lanai
        cylindrocarpa Hbd., 1888. H:268
      var. **Hitchcockii** Skottsb., 1927. D:fam. 340, 12/1/68   end. w. Maui
      var. **Piccoi** Deg.& Deg., 1968. D:fam. 340, 12/1/68   end. Hawaii
  coriacea Nutt., 1843. H:266; D:fam. 340, 8/15/50. Naupaka, false jadetree   end.HI
  Gaudichaudiana Cham, 1833, var. **Gaudichaudiana**, f. **Gaudichaudiana**
    H:266; D:fam. 340, 12/27/57; N:819. Naupaka-kuahiwi,
    mountain naupaka   end. Oahu
    For hybrids with *S. mollis*, see. *S.* × *cerasifolia*
        f. **kauaiensis** Skottsb., 1927. D:fam. 340, 12/27/57   end. Kauai
        f. **leucocarpa** Skottsb., 1927. D:fam. 340, 12/27/57   end. Oahu
      var. **dentata** Krause, 1912   end. Kauai
      var. **stenolithos** Skottsb., 1927. D:fam. 340. 12/27/57   end. Oahu
  glabra H.& A., 1832. H:269. 'Ohenaupaka. Camphusia   end. Oahu
    Camphusia glabra (H.& A.) DeVriese, 1851. D:fam. 340, 10/14/38
  kauaiensis (Deg.) St. John, 1952   end. Kauai
    Camphusia glabra (H.& A.) DeVriese, var. *kauaiensis* Deg., 1938. D:fam. 340,
      10/14/38
  kilaueae Deg., 1930, var. **kilaueae** D:fam. 340, 6/14/33; N:819. Huahekiliuka,
    papa'ahekili, Kilauea scaevola   end. Hawaii
    var. **Powersii** Deg. & Deg., 1971   end. Hawaii
  Gaudichaudi H.& A., 1832   end. H.I.
    montana Gaud., 1829, non Labill., 1825
    Menziesiana Cham., 1833
  mollis H.& A., 1832, f. **mollis**, D:fam. 340, 6/30/32. Naupaka,
    purple-flowered scaevola   end. Oahu
    f. **albiflora** (Deg.& Greenw.) St. John, 1952   end. Oahu
      var. *albiflora* Deg.& Greenw., 1932. D:fam. 340, 6/30/32
    f. **trilobata** St. John, 1940.D:fam. 340, 6/30/32   end. Oahu

[1] See:
Hillebrand, p. 268.
St. John, p. 346.
Degener, FH, p. 340.
Degener, PHNP, p. 292.

1. *Naupaka, S. kauaiensis, leaf and fruit detail, Kokee, Kauai.*

2. *Naupaka, S. chamissoniana, leaf and flower detail.*

3. *Naupaka, S. chamissoniana, small tree near Hilo entrance, HVNP.*

    procera Hbd., 1888, var. **procera**, f. **procera**. H:268. Naupaka-kuahiwi
                                                               end. Kauai, Molokai
        f. **dolichocarpa** Skottsb., 1944   end. Molokai
        var. **pseudomollia** Skottsb., 1927, f. **pseudomollis**   end. Kauai
        f. **macrocalyx** Skottsb., 1927   end. Kauai
****Skottsbergii** St. John, 1933   end. Oahu
    Taccada (Gaertn.) Roxb., var. **Taccada**. Naupaka-kahakai
        indig. Leeward Is., Kauai, tropical Pacific and Indian Oceans
        Koenigii Vahl, 1794
            var. *glabra* Matsumura, 1900
        frutescens Krause, 1912, non *Lobelia frutescens* Mill., 1768. D:fam. 340, 12/1/49
        Lobelia sensu Hbd., non Murr., 1774. H:265
        Lobelia Taccada Gaertn., 1788.
        var. **sericea** (Vahl) St. John, 1960. Naupaka-kahakai, huahekili, Beach scaevola,
            half-flower   indig. H.I., tropical Pacific and Indian Oceans
    sericea Vahl, 1791: N:820
    plumerioides Nutt., 1843
    Fauriei Lévl., 1912
    frutescens Krause, var. *moomomiana* Deg.& Greenw., 1949. D:fam. 340, 12/1/49
    sericea Vahl, var. *Fauriei* (Lévl.) Deg., f. *moomomiana* (Deg.& Greenw.)
        Deg.& Deg., 1958

HVNP Kilauea region
HNP var. *bracteosa*

NAUPAKA or NAUPAKA KUA HIWI   Scaevola chamissoniana Gaud
probably var. **bracteosa** Hbd.

    St. John confines the species to Maui and Molokai and lists the above variety as well as variety *piccoi* Deg.& Deg., as endemic to Hawaii. Plants are numerous in the area in, and just below, the HVNP boundary along the road to Hilo. A new section of road has just recently been opened and NAUPAKA have invaded the cleared shoulders in great numbers. Generally a shrub but may be said to be tree-like at 8 to 10' (2.4 to 3.1m) tall with 2" (5cm) trunk.
    Leaves bright green, up to 4" (10cm) long, edges toothed, base of leaf blade tapering narrowly to the attachment of petiole to twig. Midrib deeply impressed on leaf surface and very distinct below. Veins pinnate but indistinct. Leaves alternate, 4-ranked, clustered toward twig ends.
    Characteristic split or half flowers are white, .75" (1.8cm) across, in small loose pinacles with individual flowers on long, branched stems 3" (7.5cm) long or more, axillary. Corolla tube 1")2.5cm) long. Fruit black, .25" (6cm) in diameter with remains of tube showing at apex. Twigs green, aging to light brown, smooth except for numerous leaf scars, slender. Bark warty and light brown splotched with light grey on 2" (5cm) stems.
    Wood light tan, texture fine, figure plain, grain close, density light, wood soft. Vessels few, medium sized and scattered, rays not visible at 10x. Stability good but too small to work.
    No Hawaiian uses are listed. Hawaiian legend says that the half flower came about when a scorned maiden grabbed a flower and tore it in half. She told her lover she would not see him again until he brought her a full flower. From that day on NAUPAKAs have had only half flowers and the lover died of a broken heart.[1]

OHE NAUPAKA   Scaevola kauaiensis (Deg.) St. John

    OHE NAUPAKA is endemic to Kauai where it occurs in the Kokee area along with the black-seeded *S. procera*. It is a scraggly shrub up to 8' (2.4m) tall with 1" (2.5cm) trunk. Carlquist states this plant becomes a tree with a trunk 12" (31.5cm) in diameter in favorable habitat.
    Leaves large, 1.5 by 4" (3.7 by 10cm), bright green, leathery, very fine dentations on leaf margins and yellow colored midrib deeply impressed on

upper surface and very prominent below, veins indistinct. Fruits large for the genus, .75" (1.8cm) long, egg shaped with .25" (.6cm) long 5-pointed beak, purple. Fruits borne in pairs or 3s in axils of leaves on short peduncles. Flowers characteristic half flower, yellow petals with long protruding pistil. Twigs stout and green, aging to light brown. Older stems rough with leaf scars. Bark smooth and thin. Wood not studied.

On Oahu a very similar plant is called *S. glabra*. Both the Kauai and Oahu plants were called *Camphusia glabra* (H&A) DeVriese, at one time.[2]

PAPA AHE KILI   **Scaveola kilaueae** Deg.
Kilauea Naupaka   also var. **powersii** Deg.& Deg.

This species was found and described by Degener early in his career in the Kau desert southwest of Kilauea Crater. He and Mrs. Degener later found and described a variety that he named in honor of Dr. Powers, long-time volcanologist at HVNP. It is a low growing, spreading shrub 2 to 2.5' (63 to 76cm) tall. It can be seen along the Hilina Pali road before Kipuka nene is reached.

Leaves are small, blunt at apex except for a fine tip, midrib lighter than the yellowish-green blade but not prominent, veins indistinct. Flowers much more numerous than in some other species, in clusters with long peduncles in the axils of many of the leaves. Flowers white, seeds small and black.[3]

NAUPAKA KUAHIWI   **Scaevola procera** Hbd.

Carlquist suggests this NAUPAKA is more properly a hybrid between *S. gaudichaudiana* Cham., and *S. mollis* H&A. He lists them as trees with trunks up to 9" (23cm) in diameter. The ones seen by the writer near Kalalau lookout on Kauai were 12 to 18' (3.8 to 5.6m) tall and 3" (7.5cm) in diameter.

Leaves bright green, thin, sharply pointed at both ends, veins faint, midrib prominent and light yellowish-green. Flowers white with purple veins, suggesting the *S. mollis* affinity as that is the purple-flowered NAUPAKA. Black fruits borne axillary in profusion along the stems. Twigs whitish grey, trunk grey with lighter patches; bark smooth or broken in rough squares.

Soft wood very light creamy white, medium texture, plain figure, straight and open grain, density low. Vessels small, few and scattered, rays unevenly spaced, some large and distinct, some very fine. Stability good, wood too small to work.

Scaevola procera and *S. kauaiensis* form a conspicuous part of the moderately wet forest of the Kokee area of Kauai. There was no evidence here that it was such an invader of recent openings as seen at Kilauea in the case of *S. Chamissoniana*.[4]

NAUPAKA KAHAKAI   **Scaevola taccada** var. **serica** (Vahl) St. John
Beach scaevola   syn. **S. frutescens** Kraus.

NAUPAKA-KAHAKAI is the beach scaevola so common to the shore areas of all the islands. According to St. John the species is indigenous to Kauai, the Leeward Islands, tropical Pacific and Indian Oceans while the variety is indigenous to all the Hawaiian Islands as well as tropical Pacific and Indian Ocean areas. It grows 3 to 10' (.91 to 3.1m) tall, in large tangled clumps along the shores of the islands just above high tide. The variety is more downy than the much rarer species.

Leaves 3-ranked, not in true whorls, crowded toward the ends of branches, toothed very slightly with black dots along the perimeter. Midrib a little lighter green and very prominent on underside, veins not prominent, some silkiness along midrib on underside. Flowers small, white streaked with violet, typically 'half flower' with 5 petals attached to a .5" (1.2cm) long tube

[2] See:
Carlquist, p. 155.
St. John, p. 347.
[3] See:
Degener, PHNP, p. 293.
[4] See:
St. John, p. 347.

1. *Kilauea scaevola, S. kilaueae*, flowers and leaves, HVNP.

2. *Naupaka-kuahiwi, S. procera*, leaves, flower and fruit. Kalalau Lookout, Kauai.

3. Lillian Lamb under tall *Naupaka-Kuahiwi, S. procera*, tree, Kalahau, Kauai.

[5] See:
St. John, p. 347.
Neal, p. 820.

1. *Naupaka Kahakai, S. taccada*, leaves, white flowers and fruits.

2. *Naupaka Kahakai, S. taccada*, clump in seaside habitat, Hawaii.

3. *Kokolau, B. skottsbergii*, small foreground tree, HVNP.

split open showing the pistil. Fruit globose, white, .5 to .75" (1.2 to 1.8cm) diameter on short axillary pedicles. Twigs stout and green, soon aging to brown, very numerous leaf scars give rough appearance. Bark smooth and light brown. Soft tough wood white to very light tan, with large soft, white pith, texture fine, figure plain to streaked with strong ray pattern on radial cut, grain straight and close, density low. Vessels medium large, open, scattered, rays wide, closely spaced and quite uniform. Good stability and workability considering small size.

Wood is durable and was used for pegs in shipbuilding. Leaves were used for poultices, as a treatment for beriberi and indigestion and cooked at times for greens. The white fruit were called HUA HEKILI, meaning hail stones. The soft pith found uses in pith helmets, floats, pressed for 'rice' paper and colored for artificial flowers.

Beach scaevola is a very prominent component of the strand vegetation, where it shares space with coconut palms, Pandanus, and other plants of the typical shore scene. The plant can also be grown inland under some conditions.[5]

SUNFLOWER FAMILY   Compositae

The sunflower family includes five genera of plants native to Hawaii that are shrubs or may become trees.

Key to the genera of *Compositae* adapted from Neal:

Flower heads few together, each head 2 or more inches long;
  Leaves alternate, 4 to 9 inches long, entire or toothed;
    flowers yellow . . . . **Hesperomannia** Gray
Flower heads in panicles (loose compound clusters),
  each head much less than 2" (5cm) long
  Leaves whorled, narrow, 6 to 16" (15 to 40cm) long;
    flower heads globose, .5" (1.2cm) in diameter,
    100 or more florets . . . . **Wilkesia** Gray
  Leaves opposite or alternate, narrow, .5 to 8" (1.2 to 20cm) long;
    flower heads with comparatively few florets.
    Florets deep orange or purple . . . . **Dubautia** Gaud.
    Florets yellow . . . . **Railliardia** Gaud.
  Leaves opposite, broad, 1.5 by 4" (3.7 by 10cm)
    flowers few, showy yellow, 2 to 2.5" (5 to 6.7cm)
    in diameter . . . . **Bidens skottsbergii** Sherff.

HVNP Ainahou area
HNP species not given

KOKOOLAU   **Bidens skottsbergii** Sherff

This is the only KOKOOLAU that I found that is woody or even approaching tree-like stature, but L.W. Bryan collected a wood sample from a tree of *Bidens menziesii*, var. *f.l. formis* Sherff.

This KOKOOLAU is found in the Ainahou area and at one point along the Hilina Pali Road in HVNP, growing in a moderately dry environment in rather open, scrubby OHIA forest. It may become as much as 15 to 18' (4.7 to 5.6m) tall with a trunk up to 2" (5cm) in diameter but is more likely to be only about half as large, with a single, slender, or branched trunk.

Leaves opposite, 1.5 by 3" (3.7 by 7.5cm), edge serrated and reddish, petiole and midrib reddish, midrib and pinnte veins prominent. Flowers 2 to 2.5" (5 to 6.7cm) in diameter with numerous florets in the head and six or more large yellow petals. The best flowers are in axils of terminal leaves. Seed head 1" (2.5cm) long, two points on the tip of each seed but not barbed, thus the seeds do not cling to clothing as in other *Bidens* or 'stick-tights'. Twigs slender, smooth and red. Bark on 1" (2.5cm) trunk smooth except for rings, about 1" (2.5cm) apart, remains of leaf scars.

Wood description derived from a dead branch on the ground, severely weathered. Soft wood, white to light tan, texture coarse, figure streaked, grain open and wavy, density low. Vessels open, scattered and numerous, rays numerous, very fine and much more durable than the wood between them so that the ray ends show prominently on the perimeter of the weathered stem, as the wood between the rays has rotted away. Wood brittle.

This plant is an interesting but very minor component of the OHIA forest of this area. It is subject to extinction by lava flows if intense activity continues in this general area.[1]

[1] See:
Neal, p. 825.
St. John, p. 353.

[2] See:
St. John, p. 355.

1. Kokolau, bright yellow flowers and leaf detail, HVNP.

NAENAE   Dubautia Gaud.

St. John lists 35 taxa of Dubautia, of which many are listed as endangered, threatened or extinct. However, only two species, *D. knudsenii* Hbd., and *D. plantagenia* Gaud., both listed as endangered, can be considered as shrubs or small trees.

NAENAE   Dubautia knudsenii Hbd.

Most of the species of *Dubautia* are endemic to Kauai, with a few on Oahu, Molokai, Lanai and Maui but only one variety, *D. plantagenia* var. *strigosa* reported for Hawaii. There are at least two species of *Dubautia* in the Kokee area of Kauai, one of which, *D. knudsenii* is a small to medium sized shrub to about 9' (2.8m) tall, with slender branches and trunk.

Leaves crowded toward ends of branches, opposite in pairs rather than in threes as in *Railliardia*, oblong, pale green, 1.25 by 6" (3 by 15cm), broad in center but slender pointed at each end with sheath clasping the twig, veins parallel to indistinct midrib, dark green upper surface, lighter under. Flowers in loose terminal panicles, 6 to 8" (15 to 20cm) long, dark purple or brown when dry. Florets in small heads, many to each branch of the inflorescence, seeds small and light. Twigs slender, glabrous, brownish, smooth between leaf scars. Bark smooth and grey. Wood not studied.

This is a very minor component of the moderately wet forest.[2]

2. Na'ena'e, D. knudsenii, leaf and flower cluster, Kokee, Kauai.

[3] See:
Rock, p. 499.

[4] See:
Rock, p. 503.
St. John, p. 363.

[5] See:
Rock, p. 507.
St. John, p. 359.

1. Naenae, R. scabra, leaf, fruit and stem, HVNP.

2. Naenae, R. menziesii, clump. Bryan photo.

3. Naenae, R. menziesii, growing on slopes of Mt. Haleakala, Mauai, near Puuniamiau crater; elevation 6,000 ft. Rock photo.

HNP plus 3 other species and one unspecified at Paliku

NAENAE   **Dubautia plantaginea** var. **platyphylla** Hbd.

This NAENAE, endemic to e. Maui, has been known to reach heights of 10 to 16' (3.1 to 5m) and with trunk a few inches in diameter. The leaves are long, lanceolate, bright green, opposite, strongly 7 to 13 nerved. Flowers are small, yellow or purplish, borne on long pyrimidal panicle extending beyond the leaves, drooping or erect. It occurs in the wet forest.[3]

NAENAE   **Railliardia menziesii** Gray
                 syn. **Dubautia menziesii** (Gray) Keck
                     also **Railliardia arborea** Gray
                 and **Railliardia struthioloides** Gray'
                  syn. **Dubautia struthioloides** Gray

All of the *Railliardias* have been renamed *Dubautia* by some writers but the above synonymy follows St. John. These three species are lumped together for the purpose of this publication as they appear in similar habitat. *R. menziesii* is confined to the upper slopes of Haleakala on Maui from 6000 to 10,000' (1829 to 3050m) the other two to Mauna Kea on Hawaii at 10,000 to 11,500' (3050 to 3505m). These are all small trees with heights of about 20' (6.3m) and trunk diameter of 9" to 1' (23 to 31cm).

Leaves ternate or 3-ranked, around the twigs, crowded toward the ends, long, slender and sharp pointed, parallel nerved. Yellow flowers in loose, terminal panicles with many florets. Seeds winged. Twigs black and very rough.

Heart wood medium brown with darker streaks, sapwood straw colored, texture medium, figure plain or somewhat streaked, grain straight, density low, rays numerous and fine.

These trees are said by Rock to emit an odor that gives a clue to their presence from a distance. They are one of the very few species of trees that occur at these elevations on the mountains.[4]

HESPEROMANNIA   **Hesperomannia** Gray

St. John lists three species and three subspecies of *Hesperomannia* endemic to Kauai, Oahu and w. Maui. Since all are listed as endangered or extinct the list is given as follows:

Hesperomannia
*****arborescens** subsp. **arborescens**   end. Lanai
 **   subsp. **bushiana**   end. Oahu
 **   subsp. **Swezeyi**   end. Oahu
*****arbuscula** subsp. **arbuscula**   end. w. Maui
 **   subsp. **oahuensis**   end. Oahu
 ****Lydgatei**   end. Kauai

Rock and other botanists have found a few individuals of this genus of small trees on the various islands but they are not common.

H. arborescens Gray, has thin or somewhat fleshy leaves, obovate-oblong 5 to 13" (12 to 35cm) long by 1.5 to 8" (4 to 20cm) wide, with reddish midrib and petiole .75 to 1.5" (2 to 4cm) long. Flowers in heads 2" (5cm) high, 5 to 7 in terminal cluster on thick pedicle, about 4 to 5.5" (10 to 14cm) long. Twigs quite stout.[5]

ILIAU   **Wilkesia** Gray

Wilkesia is represented only on Kauai and by only two species, *W. gymnoxiphium* Gray and *W. hobdyi* St. John, the latter listed as endangered.

ILIAU **Wilkesia gymnoxyphium** Gray

ILIAU occurs on dryer sites on the rim of Waimea Canyon and on the dry ridges below Kokee on Kauai. One special site has been dedicated to its preservation on the rim of the canyon near the road to Kokee. Here it is protected from encroachment from the introduced guava, silk oak and other species that threaten to crowd it out.

ILIAU sends up a straight, slender, hollow, woody stem about 8' (2.4m) tall with a tuft of long, slender leaves at the top. When it is mature it sends out a long flower stalk up to 4' (1.25m) long. This grows out of the top of the stem from the center of the leaf cluster. This flower stem then sends out hundreds of short branches at the ends of which are flowers. The result is an inflorescence resembling a silversword *Argyroxiphium* Sp., in full bloom. The plant blooms once and dies.

It is an interesting small plant of the moderately dry forest complex but it is not known to have had any Hawaiian uses.

1. Iliau, W. gymnoxyphium, flower stalk left and young plant right, Kauai.

GLOSSARY OF BOTANICAL TERMS

ANNULAR RING – Any distinct ring-like formation visible in cross section. This is not necessarily an annual ring. Annual rings are seldom seen in Hawaiian wood due to the continuous growing season.

APICALLY – Toward the apex, generally of a leaf.

APOCARPUS – Carpels or ovaries all free and distinct.

ARIL – An appendage growing at or about the hilum of a seed.

AXIL – Point of joining of leaf stem to twig.

AXILLARY – Growing out of the point of joining of leaf to stem.

BAST – Fibers from bark used in making cordage.

BIPINNATE – Twice pinnate, each leaflet of a compound leaf again divided into secondary leaflets.

CALCINE CUP – A powdery cup.

CALYX – The outer series of segments of a flower, the sepals.

CARPEL – A simple pistil, or one of the members of a compound pistil

CORDATE – Heart shaped with point upward, usually referring to the base of leaf blades.

COROLLA – The inner perianth consisting of the distinct or connate petals.

CRENATE – Shallowly dentate with the teeth much rounded.

CUNATE – Wedge-shaped with the narrow part below; triangular with the acute end at the point of attachment.

DEHISCENT – Splitting open, as a capsule to release seeds.

DISCUS – A circular plate.

DOMITA – Dark spots on the underside of leaves at the junction of midrib and veins.

DRUPE – A fleshy or pulpy fruit with hard or stony seed.

ELLIPTICAL – Oval and narrowed at both ends.

FLAME FIGURE – Figure seen in wood in tangential section that resembles, in shape, the outline of a candle flame.

FOLLICLE – A dry fruit opening along the single suture, the product of a simple pistil.

GLAUCOUS – Covered with a bluish or whitish bloom that rubs off.

SCIENTIFIC FAMILY NAMES
ALPHABETICAL INDEX

Amaranthaceae, 38
Anacardiaceae, 74
Apocanaceae, 117
Aquifoliaceae, 75
Araliaceae, 96
Boraginaceae, 119
Celastraceae, 75
Chenopodiaceae, 36
Compositae, 150
Dicksoniaceae, 19
Ebenaceae, 111
Epacridaceae, 104
Ericaceae, 103
Euphorbiaceae, 64
Flacourtiaceae, 89
Gesneraceae, 122
Goodenaceae, 147
Guttiferae, 88
Lauraceae, 40
Leguminosae, 46
Liliaceae, 25
Lobeliaceae, 142
Loganaceae, 114
Malvaceae, 82
Moraceae, 28
Musaceae, 27
Myoporaceae, 126
Myrsinaceae, 105
Myrtaceae, 92
Nyctaginaceae, 40
Oleaceae, 113
Palmae, 21
Pandanaceae, 51
Pittosporaceae, 42
Rhamnaceae, 80
Rosaceae, 45
Rubiaceae, 127
Rutaceae, 53
Santalaceae, 33
Sapindaceae, 76
Sapotaceae, 109
Saxifragaceae, 41
Solanaceae, 120
Theaceae, 88
Thymeliaceae, 90
Tiliaceae, 82
Ulmaceae, 28
Urticaceae, 30

COMMON FAMILY NAMES
ALPHABETICAL INDEX

Akia, 90
Amaranth, 38
Banana, 27
Bittersweet, 75
Borage, 119
Buckthorn, 80
Cashew, 74
Citrus, 53
Coffee, 127
Ebony, 111
Elm, 28
Epacris, 104
Fern, 19
Flacourtia, 89
Four-o-clock, 40
Gesneria, 122
Ginseng, 96
Goosefoot, 36
Heath, 103
Holly, 75
Laurel, 40
Legume, 46
Lily, 25
Linden, 82
Lobelia, 142
Logania, 114
Mallow, 82
Mango, 74
Mangosteen, 88
Mulberry, 28
Myrsine, 105
Myrtle, 92
Naio, 126
Naupaka, 147
Nettle, 30
Nightshade, 120
Olive, 113
Palm, 21
Periwinkle, 117
Pittosporum, 42
Rose, 45
Rue, 53
Sandalwood, 33
Sapodilla, 109
Saxifrage, 41
Screwpine, 51
Soapberry, 76
Spurge, 64
Strichnine, 114
Sunflower, 150
Tea, 88

HISPID – Pubescent with rigid or bristly hair or with bristles.

IMBRICATE – Overlapping somewhat like the shingles of a roof.

INDEHISCENT – Not splitting open by valves or other method, but remaining persistently closed like an achene.

LANCEOLATE – Shaped like a lance head, several times longer than wide, broadest above the base and tapering to both ends.

OBLANCEOLATE – Lanceolate but with the broadest part toward the apex.

OBOVATE – Inversely ovate.

OBOVOID – Appearing as an inverted egg.

OVATE – Egg-shaped with the broad end toward the base.

OVOID – A solid object with ovate or oval outline.

PALMATE – Said of a leaf radiately lobed like the fingers of a hand.

PALMATELY BRANCHED – Branches radiating out from a central point like the fingers of a hand.

PALMATELY VEINED – Said of a leaf when the veins all branch out from the base.

PANICLE – A loosely branched flower head.

PANICULATE – Borne in or resembling a panicle

PEDICLE – The supporting stem of a single flower in a head.

PEDUNCLE – Primary flower stalk supporting a cluster or a single flower.

PERIANTH – The floral envelope consisting of sepals and petals.

PERIGONE – Rim of tube or cup surrounding pistil or pistols.

PETIOLE – Leaf stalk at base of blade, attaching the blade to the stem.

PHYLLODIA – A flattened leaf stalk with no blade.

PINNAE – Plural of pinna, a main division of a compound leaf.

PINNATELY BRANCHED – Parallel branchlets arranged on opposite sides of a common branch.

PINNATELY VEINED – Veins of a leaf arranged in parallel ranks on opposite sides of the midrib.

PISTIL – Seed bearing organ of a flower consisting of ovary, stigma and style.

PISTILLATE – Provided with pistils, but lacking functional stamens.

PUBESCENT – Term denoting hairiness but generally soft, short hair.

PUBESCENCE – A covering of short hair.

RACEME – A simple indeterminate inflorescence of pedicled flowers upon a common more or less elongated axis.

RACEMOSE – In racemes.

RAY – The marginal florets of a compound flower when these differ from the florets of the disk or center.

RAY : WOOD – As seen in cross section the rays are lines radiating out from the center like spokes of a wheel. These may be prominent and readily seen with the naked eye as in oak, or may be very fine, visible only with magnification. In radially cut wood the rays appear as plates on the surface of the wood, if the rays are prominent. In tangential section rays may appear as lines or dots on the surface of the wood depending on the size, length and color of the rays.

RECEPTACLE – The expanded portion of the axis that bears the floral organs.

REVOLUTE – Rolled or turned under or downward toward the under surface

RING POROUS – Said of wood when the pores as seen in cross section are arranged in rings rather than scattered throughout the wood.

SALVERFORM – Referring to a corolla with slender tube abruptly expanded into a flat limb.

STAMEN – One of the male or anther-bearing organs of a flower.

STAMINATE – Bearing stamens but usually lacking pistils.

STAMINODIA – Sterile stamens or other organs in the position of a stamen often modified to function as a nectary.

STIGMA – The part of the pistil that is modified for the reception and germination of the pollen.

STIPE – Stalk-like support of pistil or carpel.

STIPULE – An appendage at the base of petiole or on each side of its insertion

STRIATE – With fine grooves, ridges or lines.

TERNATE – Divided into three parts.

TOMENTUM – Wooly or cottony hair.

TOMENTOSE – Covered with densely matted and entangled wooly or cottony hair.

TRIFOLIATE – Leaflets arranged in threes.

UMBEL – An inflorescence with numerous pedicles springing from the end of the peduncle, as with the ribs of an umbrella.

VESSEL – The tubes in wood, also called pores, that conduct water vertically in the tree trunk. These appear as small circles in the cross section of wood and may be open as in red oak or closed as in white oak.

GENERIC NAMES ALPHABETICAL INDEX

Acacia, 46
Alectron, 76
Aleurites, 64
Alphitonia, 80
Alyxia, 119
Antidesma, 65
Artocarpus, 28

Bidens, 150,
Bobea, 128
Brighamia, 147
Broussaisia, 41
Broussonetia, 29

Calophyllum, 89
Canthium, 129
Cassia, 49
Charpentiera, 38
Cheirodendron, 96
Chenopodium, 36
Chrysophyllum, 109
Cibotium, 19
Claoxylon, 67
Clermontia, 143
Cocos, 21
Colubrina, 81
Coprosma, 130
Cordia, 119
Cordyline, 25
Cryptocarya, 40
Cyanea, 145
Cyathoides, 104
Cyrtandra, 126

Delissia, 146
Diospyros, 111
Dodonea, 76
Drypetes, 73
Dubautia, 151

Eleaocarpus, 82
Erythrina, 49
Eugenia, 92
Euphorbia, 67
Eurya, 88
Exocarpus, 33

Freycinetia, 51

Gardenia, 134
Gouldia, 135

Hesperomanii, 152
Hibiscadelphus, 83
Hibiscus, 85

Ilex, 75

Kokia, 87

Labordia, 116
Lobelia, 146

Mesoneuron, 48
Metrosideros, 94
Morinda, 139

Musa, 27
Myoporum, 127
Myrsine, 107

Neowawraea, 73
Nesoluma, 109
Nothocestrum, 120
Nototrichum, 39

Ochrosia, 117
Osmanthus, 113
Ostomeles, 45

Pandanus, 52
Pelea, 53
Perrottetia, 75
Pipturus, 31
Pisonia, 40
Pittosporum 43
Planchonella, 109
Platydesma, 60
Pleomele, 26
Pouteria, 110
Pritchardia, 21
Pseudomorus, 30
Psychotria, 140
Pteralyxia, 118
Pterotropia, 100

Railliardia, 152
Rapanea, 107
Rauvolfia, 118
Reynoldsia, 99
Rhus, 74
Rollandia, 147

Santalum, 33
Sapindus, 79
Scaevola, 148
Sida, 83
Sideroxylon, 109
Sophora, 50
Straussia, 140
Styphelia, 104
Suttonia, 107

Tetraplasandra, 100
Thespesia, 86
Touchardia, 31
Trema, 28
Trematolobelia, 146
Triplasandra, 102

Urera, 32

Vaccinium, 104

Wikstroemia, 91
Wilkesia, 152

Xylosma, 89

Zanthoxylum, 61

157

HAWAIIAN NAMES ALPHABETICAL INDEX

Aalii, 76
Aalii kumakani, 77
Ae, 61,
Ahakea-laulii, 128
Ahakea-lau-nui, 128
Aheahea, 37
Aiaa, 30
Alaa, 109
Aiea, 120
Akia, 90
Akoko, 67
Alahee, 129
Alani, 53
Ana Kepau, 145
Anapanapa, 82
Anini, 88
Aulu, 79
Aulu or Alaa, 109

Haa, 65
Hahalua or hahanui, 145
Haiwale, 126
Hala, 52
Halapepe, 26
Hame, 65
Hao, 118
Hap'u, 20
Hapu i'i'i, 20
Hau, 85
Hau-hele ula, 87
Hau kuahiwi, 83
Heae, 63
Heau, 33
Heuhiuhi, 49
Hoawa, 43
Holei, 117
Holia or holio, 40

Ieie, 51
Iliahi, 34
Iliau, 152
Ilima, 83

Kalia, 82
Kamakahala, 116
Kamani or Kamane, 89
Kanawao, 41
Kaula, 118
Kaulu, 79
Kauila, 80
Kawau, 75
Kea, 48
Keahi, 109
Keulu, 80
Ki or Ti, 25
Koa, 46
Koaia or Koa oha, 47
Kokia or kokio, 84
Kokoolau, 150
Kolea, 107
Kolea laulii, 107
Kolomona, 49
Kopiko, 140
Kou, 119
Kukaenene or Kukainene, 131
Kukui, 64

Kului, 39
Kumakani, 76

Lama, 112
Lapalapa, 96
Lauhala, 52
Leponene, 131
Lonomea, 80
Loulu, 21

Mahoe, 76
Maia, 27
Maile, 119
Mamake or mamaki, 31
Mamane or mamani, 50
Manele, 79
Manena, 53
Manono, 135
Mapele, 126
Maua, 89
Mehame, 66
Mehamehame, 73
Milo, 86
Mokihana, 53

Naenae, 151
Naio, 126
Nanu or nau, 134
Naupaka or naupaka kuahiwi, 148
Naupaka kahakai, 149
Neneleau, 74
Nioi, 92
Niu, 21
Noni or Noni-kuahiwi, 139

Oa, 80
Oha wai or Oha kepau, 143
Ohe ohe, 100
Ohe and Ohe Makai, 99
Ohelo kaulaau, 104
Ohe Naupaka, 148
Ohia-ai, 92
Ohia-ha, 92
Ohia and Ohia lehua, 95
Olapa, 96
Olena, 133
Oliko, 109
Olomea, 75
Olona, 31
Olopua, 113
Opuhe, 32

Papa ahe kili, 149
Papala, 38
Papala kepau, 40
Pilo, 130
Pilo kea, 60
Poola, 67
Puahanui, 41
Pukiawe, 104
Punene, 131

Ti or Ki, 25
Trema, 28

Uahe a Pele, 59

Uhiuhi, 48
Ulei, 45
Ulu, 28
Uulei, 45

Wauke, 29
Wiliwili, 49

BIBLIOGRAPHY & SUGGESTED READING

AMERICAN FORESTS MAGAZINE. *AFA's Social Register of Big Trees: New Champions on the Continent and Hawaiian Islands.* American Forestry Association, 919 17th Street, N.W., Washington, D.C., 20006: February 1969.

_____. *Champion Trees of Hawaii.* American Forestry Association, 919 17th Street, N.W., Washington, D.C., 20006: May 1974.

BISHOP MUSEUM, Honolulu, Hawaii. Numerous scientific monographs of the plant genera of Hawaii.

BRYAN, L.W., and CLYDE M. WALKER. *A Provisional Check List of Some Common Native and Introduced Forest Plants of Hawaii.* Pacific Southwest Forest and Range Experiment Station, Berkeley, California: U.S. Forest Service, Department Agriculture Miscellaneous Paper No. 69: 1962, revised 1966, 34pp.

CARLQUIST, SHERWIN. *Hawaii: A Natural History.* The American Museum of Natural History, New York. 463 pp., illustrated.

CARLSON, NORMAN K. and L.W. BRYAN. *Hawaiian Timber for the Coming Generations.* Trustees of the Estate of Bernice P. Bishop: 1959. 112 pp., illustrated.

DEGENER, OTTO. *Plants of Hawaii National Park.* Edward Brothers, Inc., Ann Arbor, Michigan: 1945. 314 pp., illustrated. (Reprinted from 1930 edition.) (Illustrative of plants and customs of the South Seas.)

_____. *Flora Hawaiiensis.* Vols I-VI. Published under patronage, Honolulu, Hawaii: 1946 to present. Illustrated, looseleaf.

ELLIS, WILLIAM. *Polynesian Researches: Hawaii.* Charles E. Tuttle Company, Rutland, Vermont: 1977, 3rd printing. 471 pp. Originally written in 1823.

HILLEBRAND, WILLIAM F. *Flora of the Hawaiian Islands.* Westermann, New York: 1888; Hafner Publishing Company, New York: 1965, reprint. 673 pp.

LAMB, SAMUEL H. "The Trees of the Kilauea-Mauna Loa Section, Hawaii National Park." *Natural History Bulletin, No. 2.* Hawaii National Park: 1936. 32 pp., mimeographed.

_____. "Wood Collecting in Hawaii." *The Bulletin,* International Wood Collectors Society: November 1974, pp. 6 - 8.

LAMOUREUX, CHARLES H. *"The Vascular Plants of Kipahulu Valley, Maui."Kipahulu Valley Expedition of Nature Conservancy, 1967.* Chapter 3 of unpublished but processed report, file copy.

LITTLE, ELBERT L., JR. "Common Forest Trees of Hawaii." Unpublished manuscript under preparation.

NEAL, MARIE C. *In Gardens of Hawaii,* Rev. Ed. Bernice P. Bishop Museum Special Publication No. 50, Honolulu, Hawaii: 1965. 924 pp., illustrated.

PACIFIC SOUTHWEST FOREST & RANGE EXPERIMENT STATION. Numerous Technical Bulletins on Hawaiian Forestry. Forest Service, United States Department of Agriculture, Post Office Box 245, Berkeley, California.

ROBYNS, W. and SAMUEL H. LAMB. "Preliminary Ecological Survey of the Island of Hawaii." *Bulletin of the Belgian Botanical Garden,* Vol. XV, Fascicule 3 Extract, Brussels, Belgium: July 1939. 52 pp., illustrated.

ROCK, JOSEPH F. *The Indigenous Trees of Hawaii* First Edition published under patronage, Honolulu, 1913. Pacific Tropical Botanical Garden, Lawai, Kauai, Hawaii & Charles E. Tuttle Company, Rutland, Vermont: 1974 reprint. 548 pp., 215 photographic plates.

ST. JOHN, HAROLD. *List and Summary of the Flowering Plants in the Hawaiian Islands.* Memoir No. 1, Pacific Tropical Botanical Garden, Lawai, Kauai, Hawaii: August 30, 1973. 519 pp.

UNITED STATES DEPARTMENT OF THE INTERIOR. "List B: List of Endangered, Threatened and Recently Extinct Species of Hawaii." Part V of Fish and Wildlife Service publication "Threatened or Endangered Fauna and Flora." *Federal Register,* Washington, D.C.: Tuesday, July 1, 1975.

MAINLAND EQUIIVALENT, COMMON FAMILY NAMES, ALPHABETICAL INDEX

Akia	*NMQ	90
Amaranth	Cockscomb	38
Banana	Same	27
Bittersweet	Same	75
Borage	Heliotrope	119
Buckthorn	Same	80
Cashew	Same	74
Citrus	Orange	53
Coffee	Gardinia	127
Ebony	Persimmon	111
Elm	Same	28
Epacris	NMQ	104
Fern, Tree Fern	Same	19
Flacourtia	NMQ	89
Four O'Clock	Same	40
Gesneria	African Violet, Gloxinia	122
Ginseng	English Ivy	96
Goosefoot	Ragweed, Lambs Quarter	36
Heath	Cranberry	103
Holly	Holly	75
Laurel	Avocado	40
Legume	Sweet Pea	46
Lily	Yucca	25
Linden	Hibiscus	82
Lobelia	Same	142
Logania	Logan, Buddleja	114
Mallow	Basswood	82
Mango	Cashew	74
Mangosteen	St. Johnswort	88
Mulberry	Same	28
Myrsine	NMQ	105
Myrtle	Eucalyptus	92
Naio	NMQ	126
Naupaka	NMQ	147
Nettle	Stinging Nettle	30
Nightshade	Angel's Trumpet	120
Olive	Olive, Privet Hedge	113
Palm	Coconut	21
Periwinkle	Periwinkle, Plumeria	117
Pittosporum	NMQ	42
Rose	Wild Rose	45
Rue	Orange	53
Sandalwood	NMQ	33
Sapodilla	Bromelia	109
Saxifrage	Hydrangea	41
Screwpine	Same	51
Soapberry	Soapberry, Hopseed	76
Spurge	Castorbean	64
Strichnine	Loganberry	114
Sunflower	Sunflower, Aster	150
Tea	Same	88

*No Mainland Equivalent

ABOUT THE AUTHOR

SAMUEL H. LAMB, is the author of *Woody Plants of New Mexico*, *Trees of Hawaii National Park* and the popular *Woody Plants of the Southwest* published by Sunstone Press. *Woody Plants of the Southwest* is the winner of the Border Regional Library Association Award for literary excellence and enrichment of the cultural heritage of the Southwest. Mr. Lamb now offers us *Native Trees and Shrubs of the Hawaiian Islands*.

Mr. Lamb spent four and a half years as ranger and naturalist of Hawaii National Park where he wrote the *Preliminary Ecological Survey of the Island of Hawaii*, published by the Belgian Botanical Garden. Since that time, he has spent several winters in Hawaii photographing trees and other native flora and gathering material for this, his newest book.

A former President (now a Trustee) of the International Wood Collectors Society, Mr. Lamb has an extensive, worldwide collection of woods, including nearly 100 specimens from native and introduced trees and shrubs growing in Hawaii. He obtained his Bachelor's degree in forestry from Colorado State University and his Master's degree in wildlife management from the University of Michigan.

Sam Lamb is currently undertaking another book project with Howard A. Miller about the Oaks of North America. The book will detail particularly those Oaks which are virtually extinct.

www.ingramcontent.com/pod-product-compliance
Lightning Source LLC
Chambersburg PA
CBHW081848170426
43199CB00018B/2851